Theory and Practice in British Politics

Series editors: Desmond S. King and Jeremy Waldron

The Law

he Law brings issues of legal theory to life by relating them to :al problems in British politics. Questions about human rights, the ıle of law, the unwritten constitution, the role of judges, law and olitics, and civil disobedience are often discussed as purely bstract issues. Jeremy Waldron, however, considers them in the ontext of events like the GLC's 'Fares Fair' case, the Clay Cross ıcident, the choice of Prime Minister, interrogation techniques in 'orthern Ireland, the 1984-5 Miners' Strike, and so on. He shows tıat the role of law is not a dry conceptual study but instead raises ˙ˀsues that lie at the very heart of British politics, and he points out ı ıat many political controversies in turn cannot be understood without looking at the issues of legal philosophy at stake.

This lively text is intended primarily for students of politics as v˙ell as law, but it will also be of interest to anyone who is concerned about the rule of law in Britain.

D1079719

Theory and Practice in British Politics

This new series bridges the gap between political institutions and political theory as taught in introductory British politics courses. While teachers and students agree that there are important connections between theory and practice in British politics, few textbooks systematically explore these connections. Each book in this series takes a major area or institution and looks at the theoretical issues which it raises. Topics covered include the police, Northern Ireland, Parliament, electoral systems, the law, cities, central government, and many more. No other textbook series offers both a lively and clear introduction to key institutions and an understanding of how theoretical issues arise in the concrete and practical context of politics in Britain. These innovative texts will be essential reading for teachers and beginning students alike.

The Law

Jeremy Waldron

London and New York

First published 1990 by Routledge
11 New Fetter Lane, London EC4P 4EE

Simultaneously published in the USA and Canada by Routledge
a division of Routledge, Chapman & Hall, Inc.
29 West 35th Street, New York, NY 10001

Reprinted 1997

© 1990 Jeremy Waldron

Typeset by Ponting–Green Publishing Services, London
Printed in Great Britain by Clays Ltd, St Ives plc

British Library Cataloguing in Publication Data
Waldron, Jeremy
    The law (Theory and practice in British
    Politics)
    1. Law
    I. Title   II. Series
    340

    ISBN 0–415–01426–3
    ISBN 0–415–01427–1 pbk

Library of Congress Cataloguing in Publication Data
Waldron, Jeremy
    The law / Jeremy Waldron.
        p. cm. – (Theory and practice in British politics)
    Bibliography: p.
    Includes index.
    ISBN 0–415–01426–3. – ISBN 0–415–01427–1 (pbk.)
    1. Great Britain–Constitutional Law.   2. Rule of law–Great
    Britain.   I. Title.   II. Series.
    KD3989.W35   1989
    349.41–dc19
    [344.1]
                                                    89–5972
                                                       CIP

Contents

Acknowledgements

I would like to thank Henry Drucker, Desmond King, Kim Scheppele, Philip Selznick, and especially Michael Moore and Susan Sterett for their comments and criticisms on earlier drafts of some of these chapters; they are not responsible for the errors that remain. I am grateful also to Margo Martinez for help with word processing, to my research assistants Sean Gallagher and Barbara Liebhardt for their hard work, and to the University of California at Berkeley for its support. As always, Nancy Marten has been a generous and patient editor at Routledge.

Series editors' preface

Students of British politics are often given the impression that there are two quite distinct enterprises going on in political science departments. There is the empirical and historical study of political life and political institutions – voting systems, electoral dealignment, the committee structure of the House of Commons and so on. And there is the theoretical and philosophical study of concepts and values – democracy, justice, rights, representation and authority. They are studied by different people, taught by different lecturers, in different parts of the curriculum; indeed they are more or less different disciplines. Theory is theory, and institutions are institutions, and never the twain shall meet.

We are basing this series of books on the assumption that that is a sterile and uninteresting way to teach political science. Of course there has got to be some sort of academic division of labour. But the issues that theorists teach are called *political* theory because they arise out of politics and they concern politics. You simply do not understand debates about justice or democracy or authority unless you see their relevance to contemporary political conflict – indeed, unless you see that they are exactly the sort of things that are at stake in political conflict. If you see those debates as simply the anatomy of concepts, you will, quite understandably, find it difficult to see why anyone should be interested. And the same is true if you see them as simply an excuse for reading old books! The theory of democracy is not studied simply because John Stuart Mill wrote about it in *Considerations on Representative Government*; rather, Mill's book is read because it contains a fund of insight that may help us to address real issues in political life more consistently, more clear-headedly and with a more sensitive awareness of the variety of interests and principles at stake.

The books in this series each take a major area or institution of British politics and explore the political theoretical issues which it raises. The objective of each volume is to introduce the institution

vii

under study but to do so in relation to a set of theoretical problems and political values. The books, therefore, do not supplant existing institutional analyses in their respective areas. Rather, they offer a distinct and unprecedented examination of the interaction of political institutions with political values in British politics from which the reader should learn a good deal about both. The reader should come away with a grasp of each institution and an appreciation of how dominant issues in political theory occur in all areas of politics. And their understanding of political theory should be the richer for this appreciation.

Desmond S. King
Jeremy Waldron

Chapter one

Introduction

The law in Britain is not just of interest to lawyers. The legal system affects us all because it purports to regulate a lot of our behaviour and to provide a framework for much of our interaction in personal, social, and economic life. More than that, the law is also the deliberate and articulate expression of our political decision-making; the legal system is part of the political system. So we are interested in law, not only in a passive capacity as people affected by it, but also in our active capacity – as citizens, voters, agitators, and politicians – because it represents what has been done or resolved in our name and in the name of our community. It is not merely a law *for* us; if we are a democracy, it is also supposed to be *our law*.

Legal theory

My aim in this book is to introduce students of British politics to some of the main issues of legal theory. Hard-headed cynics should not be put off by the word 'theory'. I mean our general and rigorous thinking about the law, the sort of thinking we do when we are determined to work something out at a general level, and pay attention to all the complications, without being seduced by any of the easy conventional solutions. I hope to show in this book that that sort of general thinking can maintain its philosophical rigour while still being rooted in the concrete reality of the British political system.

We have stressed in our Introduction to the *Theory and Practice in British Politics* series that topics in political theory are best presented and most usefully thought about as issues that arise out of concrete problems generating concrete implications. We don't study political theory purely in order to do conceptual analysis, to distinguish 'power' from 'authority' or to catalogue the nineteen different meanings of 'democracy'. Nor do we do it purely to resuscitate 'great books' like John Stuart Mill's *On Liberty* or Hobbes's *Leviathan*. We study it because the conceptual questions represent in abstract terms things that have actually mattered so much that real people have fought and died over them, and because the 'great books' represent some of the best efforts that have been made down the ages to address those issues honestly in the face of the conflict and the danger with which they were always fraught.

The same is true for the philosophy of law. We don't study jurisprudence because the definition of the word 'law' matters to us; what matters is that we have a clear sense of everything that is at stake when disputes break out about obedience and disobedience or about the proper framework within which to pursue some social policy. And we certainly don't study the philosophy of law just because we want to know what John Austin wrote in *The Province of Jurisprudence Determined* or what Ronald Dworkin said in *Law's Empire*. Rather we read and study those books because, again, we have reason to believe they contain a fund of insight that will help us to address and understand real issues about courts, constitutions, and social conflicts.

What I shall do in the chapters that follow is to give an indication of the way theoretical issues about the law arise out of the part law plays in the political life of the United Kingdom. The legal system is part and parcel of the political system, and questions about legality, judicial decision-making, and the respect and obedience that the law commands (if it does) are integral to the political life of this country. Certainly, it would be over-ambitious in a small book to try to explain the political importance of every single topic in jurisprudence. But I have taken seven of the main issues in the philosophy of law, and I will try to show that they are not just issues of abstraction and conceptual analysis, but that they concern us all in our understanding of what is actually going on.

Besides students of British politics, the other audience I want to address are those who teach and study jurisprudence in law schools. Here again, there is a traditional distinction between practice and theory: between 'black-letter' law – the study of the law as it is – and legal philosophy, which is put out as a different set of issues entirely. The one studies the validity of contracts, the formation of companies, and the defences to homicide; the other studies the concept of law and its relation to the concept of morality or the hundred and one different meanings that the word 'right' can have. As they are traditionally taught, the main debates in jurisprudence must seem completely mysterious to law students. How do you decide whether to be a legal positivist or a defender of natural law? Is it like registering in America as a Democrat or a Republican –

something you do as a matter of course when you come of age? Or – worse still – is it like picking sides for a friendly game of football – you join one team because you want to play the game, rather than playing the game because you care about one of the sides? Once again, what has to be done is to put some flesh on the theoretical bones of legal philosophy. We need to show why the issues matter, and to show that they matter is to show the difference they might make in the practical arenas where laws are crafted, judgements given, and obedience or disobedience counselled or procured.

The legal system

Before proceeding, it may be worth giving those who are unfamiliar with it a brief sketch of the main institutions of the legal system in Britain and of the sources of legal materials. (Law students can proceed directly now to Chapter two.)

Technically, there is not one legal system in the United Kingdom but two or (depending how you count) several. The Acts of Union, bringing England and Scotland together under one Parliament in 1707, guaranteed the independence of the Scottish courts and the preservation of Scots law, particularly in areas like tort, contracts or delict: areas in which people sue one another for damages. At the time, the legal system in Scotland differed from its English counterpart not only in substance but in ethos and tradition (it was much more heavily influenced by the tradition of Roman law), and many of these differences remain. There has also been a separate system for the administration of justice in Northern Ireland; indeed from 1921 till the introduction of 'direct rule' from Westminster in 1972, the Northern Ireland Parliament made laws for the Province under the auspices of its own constitution. From a political point of view, however, the legal system in the United Kingdom is unitary and the Parliament at Westminster remains the most powerful source of law, with authority to legislate for the whole realm or for Scotland and Northern Ireland separately if that is thought desirable. Britain as a whole is now subject also to European Community law, and that takes precedence over all British legislation.

Almost every aspect of law in Britain is governed both by statute and by judge-made law. Statutes are Acts of Parliament, passed by the House of Commons and the House of Lords and assented to by the Queen.[1] Unlike their counterparts in the United States, the courts in Britain have no authority to hold a statute 'unconstitutional'. Acts of Parliament prevail over all other sources of law, and (subject to the force of European Community law) where they conflict, the earlier statute gives way to the later. This is what

3

people mean (among other things) when they say Parliament is 'sovereign'.[2] Readers should not need to be told that for the most part Parliament is controlled in effect by the Cabinet, and most legislative proposals originate there. A collection of *Statutes in Force* can be found in any good library, usually ordered by subject matter. Statutes are organized into sections and sub-sections which lay down particular rules and definitions, and they are usually cited by what is called their short title and date, for example the Tumultuous Petitioning Act 1661, followed by the number of the section in question.

Specific statutes may authorize the making of regulations – sometimes referred to as subordinate legislation – by Ministers of the Crown, local councils, or other public bodies. These have the force of law, but they are governed strictly by the requirement that they must fall within the terms of reference which Parliament has laid down. If they go beyond this, they are *ultra vires* and have no legal validity. The Crown (in effect the Cabinet) also has authority to issue orders which have the force of law in areas governed by the royal prerogative (examples include the dissolution of a parliament or the declaration of war).

It is customary to say that the law is applied and interpreted in the courts. For the most part that is false. Law is interpreted and applied to particular situations by ordinary people and ordinary officials doing roughly what they think it says and ordering their relations in some kind of accordance with its provisions. The courts are involved only in the comparatively rare case where an official or a private individual wants to make an issue of someone else's behaviour so far as the law is concerned.

When someone raises such an issue, the courts will attempt to interpret and apply not only statute law but also earlier reported decisions of other courts in similar cases. The practice of following decisions in earlier cases is known as 'the doctrine of precedent' and is discussed in more detail in Chapter six. There is a hierarchy of courts; those lower in the hierarchy are expected slavishly to follow the decisions of those above them, and in most cases they are also expected to follow the decisions of other courts at the same level. Obviously, though, a certain amount of flexibility derives from the fact that no two cases are ever *exactly* alike and, even when they are, no two people will give exactly the same account of *how* they are alike.

In the judicial hierarchy the courts above hear appeals from the courts immediately beneath them. There is not always an automatic right of appeal: sometimes the aggrieved party has to have the approval of the court she is appealing from or the one she is appealing to before she can proceed. Though occasionally serious issues of law are raised in Magistrates' Courts, and though serious criminal cases always originate in the Crown Courts, most of the *influential* cases in our law begin life in one of the divisions (Family, Chancery, or Queen's Bench) of what is called 'the High Court'. From a political point of view, the Queen's Bench Division of the High Court is the most interesting, for it has responsibility for reviewing the legality of governmental and administrative action. Appeals from the High Court are taken to the Court of Appeal. Above the Court of Appeal, the highest court in the land is Parliament, in the guise of the House of Lords. Appeals there are heard not by the whole House (earls, bishops, and all), but by a committee of senior judges called Lords of Appeal or Law Lords. They sit usually five at a time on each case and they decide by a majority.

Court decisions that are thought noteworthy are published in the *Law Reports*. A reported decision will begin with a summary of the facts and of what was decided, and it will then set out the full text of the judge's decision (often running to many pages) saying why this particular finding was given in this particular case. If there is more than one judge, then all the decisions will be printed. If they disagree, the side with the greater support wins (though the majority decision may still comprise several distinct speeches). Cases are referred to by the (often abbreviated) names of the parties – for example, *Swallow and Pearson v. Middlesex C.C.* – and the year and abbreviated title of the volume in which they appear.

The official Law Reports are published every month or so, and bound into one or more volumes corresponding to each year. When they first come out, they are called *The Weekly Law Reports* (WLR), but they are eventually organized into separate volumes corresponding to the different levels and areas of judicial decision-making. Thus, for example, '*Christie v. Leachinsky* [1947] AC 573' refers to the report of a decision of the House of Lords taken in the case of Christie against Leachinsky (or, as we say in the trade, 'Christie and Leachinsky'), published in the 1947 volume of the official Law Reports devoted to 'Appeal Cases', beginning on page 573. And '*R. v. Kulynycz* [1971] 1 QB 367' refers to a report of a criminal case – the Queen ('R.' or 'Regina') against Kulynycz – decided by a court a little lower down in the hierarchy and reported in the first volume of the 'Queen's Bench' reports for 1971, beginning at page 367. You get the idea. In a law library, you will find the volumes organized chronologically for each series: all the ACs are together from the earliest reported cases till the present, all the QBs (or, before 1953, KBs) are together in order, and so on. (As well as these official reports, most law libraries also stock an excellent series of semi-official reports known as the *All England Reports* (All ER). These are published quite quickly, and they accumulate into two or three volumes for each year. Unlike the official reports, they do not divide the cases up by level of court or subject-matter.)

It is important to realize that, when they decide the cases and the appeals that come before them, judges are not only interpreting Acts of Parliament (saying what the various sections and subsections mean), nor are they merely following other judges' interpretations. They are also often following and developing principles of law which have no statutory basis at all, and which have grown up entirely in the courts. Thus, for example, the principle that if you are injured in a road accident you can sue the careless driver for negligence, and the various elaborations and qualifications to that, have been developed entirely in the courts, though it interlaces with and is modified by statute law in various respects. Much of our law is judge-made and not made by Parliament. Judge-made law, to the extent that it can be separated from the rest is referred to as 'common law', and a system like the English one in which this sort of law plays a significant role is called a 'common law' system.[3]

For the most part, the common law systems of the world represent a residue of English influence: apart from the United States of America, they are mainly the legal systems of the British Commonwealth (some of which still preserve a right of appeal to the House of Lords, known for that purpose as 'the Judicial Committee of the Privy Council'). Common law systems may be contrasted with 'civil law' systems. The difference is one of ethos and tradition: in civil law systems, such as France or Germany, the law tends to have been developed in a more systematic and abstract way. Nothing like the same emphasis is put on the role of the judge; the emphasis is on the logical structure of a code of laws developed from first principles. (As a matter of fact, judges do have to decide hard questions of interpretation just as their common law counterparts do, but in a civil law system this is not *advertised* as the primary vehicle for the development of the law, in the way that it is in England or America.)[4] The inspiration for the civil law systems was, of course, the great Roman Law code of Justinian and more recently the Code Napoleon. The differences between English and Scots law are to be explained in part by the much greater influence of civil law in Scotland.

So much for preliminaries and technicalities. Let's begin at the beginning, in Chapter two, with the relation between law and politics.

Notes

1 But the House of Commons is dominant: see note 6 to Chapter two p.27.
2 The sovereignty of Parliament is discussed in Chapter four.
3 We discuss common law and judicial decision-making in much more detail in Chapter six.
4 There is an excellent discussion in J.H. Merryman, *The Civil Law Tradition* (Stanford, Calif.: Stanford University Press, 1969).

Chapter two

Law and politics

Clay Cross

I shall start each chapter of this book with a story, because I want
to show how theoretical issues about law crop up naturally when
we reflect on the practice and experience of British politics.

The incidents with which I begin happened between 1972 and
1975 and involved a clash between central government – first a
Conservative administration, then a Labour one – and the local
councillors of a Derbyshire town called Clay Cross.

Clay Cross was a Labour town. It had been a mining area, but as
pits closed in the 1960s it became a centre of unemployment and
deprivation in the region. When Labour gained control of the local
council in 1963, it embarked on a programme of slum clearance
and public housing. This, combined with a deliberate decision to
keep council house rents low, placed considerable pressure on the
local authority's finances. Their deficit grew to twice the Derbyshire
average, and a number of residents argued that services like road
maintenance were suffering so that local rates could be devoted to
the subsidization of council rents. In 1970 complaints by ratepayers
to the district auditor produced a slight increase in rents and some
disquieting revelations about housing practices. But as the 1970s
went on, Clay Cross, with 1,600 council houses in an electorate of
7,000, remained 'a government of the council house tenants, for the
council house tenants, and, since all but one of the councillors live
there, by the council house tenants'.[1]

In 1972 the Conservative government of Edward Heath passed a
Housing (Finance) Act through Parliament to bring the activities of
local councils like Clay Cross under control. Section 49 of the new
law said the following:

49 (1) . . .it shall be the duty of every local authority and of every
new town corporation to charge for each of their Housing

Revenue Account dwellings a fair rent determined on the principles set out in sections 50 and 57 below.

Section 50 required the council to determine a fair rent for each house on the basis of, among other things, 'the return that it would be reasonable to expect on it as an investment'. The council was required to charge an amount approaching the rents that would emerge in a free market. Each authority had to determine fair rents for its area and submit them to a Rent Scrutiny Board for approval. If the Board decided the proposed rents did not meet the statutory criteria, it could substitute proposals of its own. Once fair rents were determined, local councils were required to make increases over the following few years to bring what they actually charged into line with the figures that were specified.

Needless to say, the eleven Labour councillors of Clay Cross were not enthusiastic about the new legislation. In September 1972, in common with a number of other Labour authorities, they resolved not to implement the Act. When the Rent Scrutiny Board determined that rents in the area should be raised by slightly more than £1 a week, the councillors refused to comply. The stage was set for a confrontation with the government.

By defying the law, the councillors were embarking on a perilous course. Section 228 of the Local Government Act 1933 provides that 'it shall be the duty of the district auditor at every audit held by him . . . to surcharge the amount of any loss or deficiency upon any person by whose negligence or misconduct the loss or deficiency has been incurred'. In other words, the councillors might be obliged to make up the difference between the old rents and the new 'fair' rents out of their own pockets. At the beginning of 1973, the auditor held each of the Clay Cross councillors personally liable to pay £635 – his share of the extra revenue that would have been collected if they had implemented the new law. That was enough to bankrupt most of them. The councillors challenged the auditor's decision in the courts, all the way up to the Court of Appeal, but all they got for their trouble was a legal bill for £2,000 to divide among them. In addition, they were barred from holding public office for five years, under legislation (passed after similar crises in the 1920s) providing automatic disqualification for anyone surcharged £500 or more. As the dispute continued through 1973 and 1974, the deficit from uncollected rents continued to grow, and the councillors faced the threat that a fresh audit might bring an additional surcharge of £100,000 or more.

The Labour party had always opposed the 1972 Act. When it was passed, the Shadow Secretary of State for the Environment,

9

Anthony Crosland, had warned that to legislate in this way – without consent, without consultation and with no willingness to compromise – would invite councillors to defy the law. Now, with the Clay Cross eleven facing huge financial penalties, the Labour Party came under pressure to do something. Quite apart from the unpopularity of the Act, many felt that the government had deliberately allowed the rent deficit to accumulate in order to ensure penalties high enough to make the councillors an example to others.[2] In October 1973, the Labour Party Conference, with the support of Ted Short, the Deputy Leader, pledged that if elected it would retrospectively remove all penalties from the Clay Cross councillors 'who have courageously refused to implement the Housing Finance Act'.

The resolution sparked a public controversy about the politics of law-breaking. The *New Law Journal* commented in an editorial that Mr Short should resign since he had 'publicly and with bravura encouraged a nationwide attack on the rule of law'. Within the party the controversy was even more fierce. Many on the right were appalled at what amounted to a proposal to pass a retrospective act of indemnity for the councillors and by the party's commitment to use taxpayers' money to exonerate partisan law-breakers. Sam Silkin, the shadow Attorney-General, advised that the proposal would 'contravene all constitutional practice and would set a dangerous precedent'.

But a Labour government was elected in 1974 and the problem had to be faced. Embarrassed by the conference commitment, the new government announced its intention to repeal the Housing Finance Act, to remove the disqualifications from the Clay Cross eleven, to prevent any further surcharges on councillors resulting from rent deficits, but to see that their existing penalties were settled privately rather than out of public funds. The announcement was widely regarded as an unsatisfactory compromise. The Clay Cross councillors thought it illogical that the disqualification should be removed but not the surcharges that had led to it. And the government's critics inside and outside the party charged that the removal of the disqualification amounted to the very act of indemnity that had been condemned as 'unconstitutional' in 1973.

Nevertheless, what *The Times* referred to as 'a grubby little Bill' – the Housing Finance (Special Provisions) Bill – was introduced into the Commons in March 1975. The debate was fierce. Anthony Crosland, who sponsored the Bill (admittedly in some discomfort – 'I have not,' he said, 'in my political life faced a problem as difficult as this'), called it an act of 'clemency' and 'magnanimity' to heal 'the sores opened up by the Housing (Finance) Act'.[3] Other supporters argued that 'the sovereignty of Parliament surely meant that Parliament could change its mind about any law'. That, they claimed, was the whole point of regular elections to the legislature – so that the representatives of the people could get rid of every last vestige of a policy they now detested.

But other members on both sides of the House opposed the measure vehemently. Some asked, 'Why should Mr Skinner of Clay Cross be let off while the motorist who overparks suffers the full penalty of the law?' The Conservative spokesman on legal issues said that Crosland's Bill 'undermined the rule of law for selective political reasons'. The next step, he said, would be for Parliament to 'decide that an action was innocent when committed but in retrospect was an offence for which people could be punished'. To 'condone, encourage and finally indemnify' law-breaking, he said, was the beginning of the end of law and Parliamentary government.

The affair finally fizzled out messily, as these things do. The Labour government was defeated on the issue in the Commons in August, 1975 and forced to accept an amendment which prevented the removal of the councillors' disqualifications. But by then it was largely an academic question. In the meantime, the eleven councillors had been surcharged once again, for financial irregularities unrelated to the Housing (Finance) Act. The Clay Cross council was abolished and swallowed up in a new regional authority for north-west Derbyshire. The 1972 Act was swept away by a new Labour housing law, and the other councillors around the country who had resisted the Tory measure did not face any further penalties.[4]

Two models of law

The story of Clay Cross raises many issues about law and disobedience, and we shall discuss some of them in the chapters that follow.

But I want to begin by looking at a phrase that people bandied around throughout this controversy – the phrase 'the rule of law'. As the councillors continued their defiance, as they were surcharged and disqualified, as the Labour party pledged its support, and as Anthony Crosland introduced his Bill partially indemnifying the Clay Cross eleven, the criticism was made over and over again that 'the rule of law' was being sacrificed for party political advantage. So what is this thing called 'the rule of law', and why do people say that in a democracy the ruling party is not entitled to manipulate it to its advantage? If we start with these questions, we may find a useful route in to the way law figures in the theory and practice of British politics.

There are two different ways we can think about law and law-making. To put it crudely: we can think of law as *partisan*, as nothing more than the expression in legislative terms of the particular ideology or policies of a political party; or we can think of law as *neutral*, as something that stands above party politics, at least in the ·sense that once passed it ought to command the obedience and respect of everyone. The contrast is of course exaggerated; still it is worth exploring the extreme positions for a moment because they cast some light on the controversies about law-making and law-breaking that erupted in the Clay Cross affair.

(1) The partisan model of law

Representative democracy involves a struggle between political parties to win the support of the public. At regular intervals, that struggle takes the form of a General Election in which parties compete for the popular vote to gain control of the House of Commons. It is accepted that control of the Commons gives the leadership of the party control of government: it can then make foreign policy, implement domestic policy, make official appointments, raise taxes, and pass laws.

The last of these is the one that interests us. Parties compete for control of Parliament because they want their values, their ideology, and their programme to be reflected in the law of the land.[5] Of course, legislation has several stages: it involves the Queen and the House of Lords, as well as the elected MPs.[6] But no-one doubts that the Commons stage is the most important, and the reason surely is that the House of Commons is the institution most subject to popular control. If laws passed by one Parliament turn out to be unpopular, the electorate can install a majority that is sworn to repeal them. That is what elections and representative politics are all about.

On this model, it is simply fatuous to pretend that law is somehow 'above' politics. Maybe there are some laws on which everyone agrees, no matter what their ideology. Everyone agrees there should be a law against murder, for example, and that there should be basic rules of the road. But as soon as we turn to the fine print, it is suprisingly difficult to find a consensus on the detail of any legislative provision. And in many cases, even the fundamental principles are the subject of fierce political dispute. Political parties differ radically about the role of local government, the way the education and health systems should be organized, housing policy, the basic principles of social security, the redistribution of wealth and income, social control and regulation of the economy, national security and official secrets, the privileges and immunities of trade unions, basic criminal procedure, measures for dealing with terrorism, and so on. People sometimes talk about a 'golden age' in British politics (the 1950s perhaps) when there was a broad national consensus on many of these things. Whatever the case then, it is apparent now that there are deep and trenchant divisions, based on principle, world-view, and ideological outlook.

The fact that there is controversy doesn't prevent there being law. Sometimes the laws are ones that have been there for decades – the Official Secrets Act, for example, was passed in 1911 – and their provisions may satisfy nobody; but the parties disagree about how they should be reformed, and so they stay. Sometimes the law may be the product of more recent legislation by one party or the other, and in these cases the opposition may be pledged to repeal it. This is what happened with the Housing (Finance) Act that was the centre of the Clay Cross controversy. Delays in detailed policy-making, drafting, and the shortage of parliamentary time may prevent a party from pushing through its legislative programme as quickly as it might want. But even in determining its legislative priorities, a government will be motivated by partisan values and concerns.

What this model stresses, then, is that legislative attitudes are necessarily partisan attitudes. So long as there is tight party discipline in Parliament, legislative decisions will be taken on the basis of the ideology of the leadership of the party in power. The partisan model stresses the legitimacy of these attitudes and this form of decision-making. The division of opinion between the parties reflects a more widespread division of outlook among the British people. As a society we have to make a choice, for to let matters drift until we achieve unanimity is simply to abdicate choice and let the decision be made by default. To the extent that society makes a choice, it does so crudely on the basis of which outlook commands the greater popular support, and it does that precisely in order to allow those who represent what is, for the time being, the more popular opinion to prevail in the determination of the laws of the land.

(2) *The neutral model of law*

According to the partisan model, our attitude to the law is determined purely by whether we are in favour of its provisions or against them. By contrast, what I call 'the neutral model' enjoins a

13

certain respect for law and law-making which goes beyond purely partisan views. According to this model there is something special about law, and it carries with it special non-partisan responsibilities.

Proponents of the neutral model do not deny that laws are made by party politicans, and that legislation is often motivated by disputed values and ideologies. They do not deny that some laws are Conservative and others Labour in their original inspiration. However, their view is that when a law is being made, something solemn is being decided in Parliament in the name of the whole society. Though it is reasonable for bills to be proposed and debated along partisan lines, the decision procedures of Parliament are designed to indicate not merely which is the stronger party, but what is to be the view of society as a whole on some matter for the time being. The decision procedure itself involves 'divisions': the various sides debate with one another across the floor of the House and in committees, and at the end of the process they divide into two groups and troop through the 'Ayes' lobby and the 'Noes' lobby, respectively. But the *result*, the *outcome*, is a decision of the House as a whole: it is, literally, an act *of Parliament*, not merely an act of the Conservative party or an act of the Labour party, whichever commands the majority. By virtue of the parliamentary process, it transcends partisan politics, and presents itself as a norm enacted for and on behalf of the entire community.

Given this view of political decision-making, the neutral model maintains that legislation is an act which attracts special responsibilities. Even if a legislative proposal is politically partisan, the proponents have a responsibility to ensure that the new law is not so politically extreme as to strain the respect that members of the community – including their political opponents – have for law as such. (This was Anthony Crosland's criticism of the original Housing (Finance) Act of 1972.) And once legislation has been passed, its opponents as well as its promoters have a responsibility to stand by it wholeheartedly. They have a responsibility to ensure that their political opposition to the measure does not weaken their respect for it *as the law of the land*. They will of course campaign for its repeal. But they should not do so in a way that undermines its status as something which stands for the time being in the name of the whole community.

Sometimes the neutral model asks us to think about law in a way that doesn't necessarily involve politically motivated legislation. The model tends to identify law with the framework of rules and principles that make civilized life possible for everyone in a complex society. It is seen as something performing certain social functions (good order, cohesion, justice, and so on), rather than as the expression of particular political or ideological beliefs. Certainly, we can – and should – think about law in both ways. But on the neutral model, the social function idea tends to receive more emphasis than the political provenance. For this reason, the neutral model often focuses on aspects of the legal system that do not involve explicitly partisan initiatives. It focuses on those areas of law where there is something approaching unanimity (such as the fundamental principles of the criminal law and some of the basic tenets of private law). And it focuses particularly on 'the common law' – the body of principles and doctrine that have emerged implicitly from the history of decision-making by courts rather than explicitly from politically motivated decisions of legislators.

I shall have more to say about the common law later on, particularly in Chapter six, which deals with judging. But even at this early stage we should note that judge-made law occupies a crucial role in the English legal system.[7] Many of the main developments in private law (the growth of negligence as a tort, for example) have been entirely judge-made and not the result of parliamentary legislation. When these initiatives take place, when common law doctrine strikes out in new directions, the change is usually presented as the product of reasoning which is independent of politics, as though there were an evolving 'logic' of the law which could proceed untainted by partisan values or ideology. If we buy that story, it is easy to convince ourselves that the basic principles for constituting and regulating the social framework can be arrived at on the basis of pure reason alone.

Now clearly, one cannot say *that* about laws like the Housing (Finance) Act 1972. But the image of the common law – autonomous in its logic, pure in its social function, uncontaminated by party politics – is used in the neutral model to define the status of law. And then politically motivated legislation, once enacted, is seen as acquiring that sort of status despite its political pedigree.

Of course, from the perspective of the *partisan* model, common law is no different from any other law: it is branded with the politics of the people who made it. If some laws are made by judges, then we must look to the politics of the judiciary to discern the true character of those laws. Conservative judges may be expected to enunciate doctrine with a Tory flavour, while judges who incline more to the Left may come out with arguments that are more congenial to Liberals and Socialists. If a judge comes up with a ruling we do not like, we wait patiently (or impatiently) for a contrary holding by another judge more sympathetic to our concerns. Parliamentary legislators are more open than judges about their political concerns, and parliamentary majorities can be changed democratically whereas the judiciary is politically invulnerable. Even so, law in both arenas remains the child of politics, from the partisan point of view.

There is no doubt that the neutral model is an attractive one. It portrays politics not as a brute struggle between factions but as an ongoing debate in the nation about the shape of its social, economic, and political framework. Since law is set apart from power, it can be seen as something capable of curbing and limiting power; the opposite of law is not freedom, but arbitrary rule. Equally, in its common law values, the neutral model presents the legal system as a forum in which anyone may come with a claim and have it heard and determined in accordance with a body of principles that has emerged historically in the community and which is now applied equally to all.

Both models of law – the partisan model and the neutral model – can be seen at work in the Clay Cross affair. No-one denies that the Labour councillors were confronted with a law they sincerely opposed on moral and ideological grounds. The two models differ about how this opposition should have been expressed.

On the neutral model, opposition should have been confined to a campaign to change the law, either by persuading the government to repeal it or by persuading the population to replace the government. As long as that did not happen, the councillors had an obligation to respect it, not merely as a political measure, but as part of the law of the land, as something embodying all the high-minded values we have just discussed. When they chose to defy it, penalties were rightfully imposed on them, not in the name of the Conservative Party or to uphold a Conservative measure, but to vindicate the law as something that, for better or worse, had been enacted in the name of the community.

Even if the Act were repealed, the neutral model would insist that the status that it *had* occupied as law should not be disavowed. The process of legislative repeal should not be like the replacement of leaders in the Kremlin – with the previous incumbent carefully air-brushed out of all the official photographs. We should not pretend that the law had never existed. The penalties for non-compliance during the life of the statute were imposed for defiance of *the law* as such, and they should remain in force (if they were intended, like the councillors' disqualifications, to have a continuing effect) even though the law was subsequently amended. That is what critics of the Labour government meant by 'the rule of law'. To remove the disqualifications would be to undermine the status of law in the community as a whole.

The other model views opposition to a statute in a much more radical light. From a partisan perspective, opposing something like the Housing (Finance) Act is not a game that politicians play for their own entertainment. The issues on which they divide are issues that they think matter. Opponents of this legislation thought it wrong that local authorities should be forced to calculate rents for council houses at market rates; they thought it would be immoral to treat the social provision of housing on the same basis as a commercial investment; they thought it unconstitutional that tribunals set up by central government should oversee that process and local councillors be required to fall in with their recommendations; and they thought it unjust that not raising rents should be the sort of thing that attracted surcharges, bankruptcy, and disqualification. They disagreed with the principles and the ideology which underpinned those requirements and which justified the imposition of those penalties. It was not the opposition of a debating society, for the sake of a good argument; they opposed the legislation bitterly, root and branch.

The point is a general one. To oppose a law on partisan or ideological grounds is to be hostile to all its provisions, including the sanctions that are provided for non-compliance. To oppose a law against abortion, for example, is precisely to think that abortion is not the sort of thing that people should be penalized for. So long as the law exists, opponents will think that those who are penalized under it are suffering a punishment that they shouldn't be suffering. If the opponents of the law plan to repeal it, they will try to make sure that nobody suffers that sort of unjustified penalty in the future. And it is surely a natural extension of the same reforming impulse to ensure at the time of repeal that those who continue to suffer a penalty imposed under the old law should not suffer that penalty any longer.

It is not like an infringement in a game, where one might accept a penalty even though one thinks the rules could be improved. The penalties that flow from legislation can involve loss of liberty, property, even life, as well as stigma and dishonour. For most citizens, a criminal conviction is a catastrophe, and its imposition for acts that do not merit it is a crying injustice. If we recognize as a society that some criminal statute was wrong and unjustified, we ought to do something about the fact that people will have suffered these catastrophic consequences for reasons that are now recognized to be bad ones.

Similarly, for the financial and political penalties imposed on the Clay Cross eleven. They were not playing games either: bankruptcy is catastrophic in anyone's life, and disqualification from office is a very serious matter indeed for someone who has made politics a career.[8] We may accept that they should have considered these risks when they undertook their defiance. But by the same token, if a new government is elected to power and it is convinced that the law under which these penalties were imposed is a bad law, it can hardly view those penal consequences with equanimity. On the neutral model, the penalties are to be viewed simply as an application of *the law*. But from the partisan view, they are part and parcel of the wrongness of the measure under whose auspices they were imposed.

Those are two extreme views of the matter. Are there any positions in between? Do we have to see law *either* as partisan expression *or* as transcendent structure? One point was made a number of times in the Clay Cross dispute: how can Labour politicians expect Conservatives to put up with Labour legislation if they will not, in their turn, put up with Conservative legislation? As the parties alternate in power, the legislation of each is sometimes anathema to the other. Conservative governments require Labour councils to raise rents. Labour governments require Conservative councils to abolish grammar schools.[9] If neither party is prepared to swallow the other's legislation, then both will be frustrated in their objectives. Maybe there is room for some sort of common ground in this idea of reciprocity: you respect our laws (until you've repealed them in the proper way) and we'll respect yours.

Democracy, dominance and class

In describing the partisan model, I presented it in a democratic light. Law-making is the activity of representatives whose partisan opinions find favour with the majority of the people. The party in power has a right to pass legislation that reflects its own ideology and to expunge all traces of the laws of its predecessors, because society has now opted for its policies and its outlook in an act of collective choice.

Nobody needs to be told that this model of democracy is somewhat Utopian in the context of British politics, and that the real processes of social choice are much messier and more complicated than that. Voters hardly ever have the opportunity to endorse or condemn any particular law or policy directly. Occasionally, some proposal will be 'made an issue' in the political contest leading up to an election: an opposition party will pledge itself to repeal some measure passed by the incumbent government, and the latter will mount a spirited defence; or one or other party will 'promise' to enact a certain law, and their opponents will try to convince the electorate that this would be undesirable. But even when legislative issues are posed like that, they are still entangled with all the other measures put before the people on each side. Obviously it is hard to infer support for a particular measure from a vote cast in favour of a party candidate who stands by a whole series of policies packaged as a relatively indivisible whole.

Those are not the only complications. Electors vote for particular candidates, not for a party programme as such. They vote under a 'plurality' system which allows a government to acquire majority control of the House of Commons with a minority of the popular vote (sometimes with fewer votes overall than the main opposition party), and which poses almost insuperable difficulties for any new party seeking entry to the political system. The result is that political and ideological contests tend to be as much intra-party as inter-party. Each of the major parties is in fact a broad coalition of factions, and its avowed policies and its legislation when in office reflect the outcome of power struggles within the party which are certainly not correlated precisely with the popular support that exists for each shade of opinion.

These are familiar points about the British political system. They do not impugn the partisan model of law-making, but they affect the way we view partisanship in our society. The struggle for control of Parliament, the struggle for the right to legislate, is still a struggle between rival factions, with rival policies, values and commitments; but it is not necessarily a struggle related directly to the will of the people.

Some legal scholars, particularly on the Left, take a much more jaundiced view of the political basis of law-making. Electoral politics, they say, is just a veneer. The real determinants of legislation are the powerful interests that control and influence any government and the formal and traditional ways of thinking built into the structures and attitudes of the British establishment.[10] Ultimately, the real struggle, they say, is not between parties or even within parties. The real struggle is between classes, between those currently in control of society and its resources and those who, since they have no means of production of their own, must work for a living on terms dictated by the others. It is, in short, a struggle between capitalists and proletarians (complicated, in ways that are controversial, by racial conflict, gender oppression, and the growing number of those who have no role in the economy at all except one of pure dependence and helplessness).[11]

Among those who take this approach, there are many shades of opinion about law, partisanship, and politics. Most people on the

Left share Karl Marx's view that political disagreements and disagreements about what the law is or ought to be do not stand on their own as intellectual debates, but are driven by deeper forces of class and economics.[12] Even if they don't accept his views about economic determinism and the inevitability of working-class revolution, they believe that if we want to know what is *really* going on in a society, we should look at what is happening in the factories, in the relations of production, and in the struggle for economic power.

In its crudest form, this view seems to entail that a capitalist society (as Britain is supposed to be) is bound to have capitalist law. Parliamentarians may make all sorts of proposals, but the only laws that will survive and flourish in the economic conditions of capitalist society are laws that facilitate and sustain capitalist enterprise, capitalist economy, and the exploitation and control of the working people. Law is partisan alright, but as long as the capitalist class remains dominant, the law will have a capitalist flavour no matter what happens at the level of electoral politics. The differences I have described as partisan – between Labour and Conservative – are really only differences at the margin. Labour's legislation may have some impact – shoring up the shaky edifice of the welfare state here, or adding a little bit of economic regulation there – but it is powerless to change the broad structure of society or the way wealth and resources are distributed and controlled. There can be no real hope of laws which reflect working-class values until that class has risen successfully against its oppressors. In the meantime, the rule of law is the rule of capitalism, and the sort of sporadic defiance of the law that we find in incidents like the Clay Cross affair is nothing but the continuation of class struggle at a relatively superficial level.

If we take this approach, then the neutral model of law, the idea of the rule of law, and even the reciprocal compromise of 'You obey our laws and we'll obey yours' all seem like gigantic frauds. The ideology of *the law* is a way of dressing up class dominance so that it seems to be embedded in a framework of relations that transcends the interests of any particular class. The capitalist class rules most of the time not by brute force but by getting its ideas accepted as 'neutral' or 'objective' and as part of 'the way things have to be'. So it presents institutions like property and the market as though they were in the interests of everyone in society. That way, people can submit to class control without having to think that this is what is going on. They can be gulled into thinking that they are submitting to an independent and objective order called 'the law'.

Much of the work done in what has become known as the 'Critical Legal Studies' movement (CLS) proceeds on assumptions such as these.[13] In American law schools, CLS was first presented as a way of debunking what I have called the neutral model. Law students in America are traditionally taught to think of legal doctrine in a way that stresses its rational development and its lofty independence of partisan interests. Concentrating on common law and constitutional interpretation, they are taught that legal reasoning is a process that is logically compelling and ideologically neutral. CLS scholars, by contrast, try to get students to look at legal history and the development of doctrine as processes that are intimately connected to class interest and economic change. They present law and legal doctrine as a social framework designed to make economic and other forms of exploitation morally and intellectually respectable. They reject the ideological basis of the neutral model as 'liberal'; their interest in it is confined to looking at the way it has mystified and duped us in the past.[14]

The partisan model and the rule of law

If the partisan model is correct – either in its party version or in its class version – is there any reason for us to waste time thinking about the rule of law or legal philosophy? If law is just a matter of who controls the means of production in British society, why worry about jurisprudence? If legal ideology is a fraud, a way of masking the reality of one's power, why waste time on the fine details of the mystification? Why not focus on the social reality instead?

There are three ways of responding to those questions: one rather cynical, one less so, and one not cynical at all. The most cynical response is to say that we are interested in dissecting legal ideology because we want to confront the reality of class power with the content of its own pretensions. By pretending to take seriously the idea of the rule of law and so on, we might be able to embarrass our opponents by showing in the light of day how far short of their ideal their own practice falls. The masses will no longer be fooled once they see the contrast between the smokescreen of legal rhetoric and the reality of class struggle.

The less cynical response is to focus on the specific role that law has to play if it is to help sustain a system of class domination. Nowadays few on the Left view the state as merely a 'committee' of the bourgeoisie. In its ethos, its personnel, and its social function, the state stands somewhat apart from the interests of business and capital. One of its specific jobs is to maintain some sort of order in the midst of class conflict – to mitigate the struggle as it were, so

21

that production and economic life can proceed. Marx's collaborator, Frederick Engels, is often cited here:

> In order that these opposites, classes with conflicting economic interests, shall not consume themselves and society in fruitless struggle, it became necessary to have a power seemingly standing above society that would moderate the conflict and keep it within the bounds of 'order.'[15]

Although he believed that the state was ultimately a tool of 'the most powerful, economically dominant class', Engels thought it was a tool that would work only if it avoided being comprehensively identified in everyone's mind with the interests of the dominant class. People must have some reason for regarding the state as an independent force (even if that is, in the last analysis, an illusion), otherwise the ruling class gains no advantage from dominating through the state as opposed to dominating through brute economic force. Now, to put it bluntly, in order to be perceived as an independent source of order, the state must some of the time actually be an independent source of order. And in its institutions and personnel, it will develop practices and attitudes oriented towards that end.

The point was sometimes made by saying that the state is 'relatively autonomous' from society and determined by economic forces only 'in the last resort'.[16] What this means is that the state has some degree of independence: it can act on its own initiative, though of course it is subject to constraints. Given those constraints, there is some room for the *political* partisan model to operate, and perhaps some room also for a view of the state as neutral. If the state is partly independent of the ruling class, then it makes a difference how that independence is exercised by the people working within it, and we may be interested once again in the party-political provenance of various laws, and in the aspiration of legality and reciprocity in politics.

Much the same can be said about the role of law. Even if its contribution to bourgeois dominance is to mystify the people and make them think in terms of a neutral or transcendent order, it has got to give them some *reason* for thinking in that way. The point has been powerfully stated by the historian E.P. Thompson in response to the claim made by some 'structuralist' Marxists that law is *simply* a device for mystifying the masses and masking the reality of class dominance:

> People are not as stupid as some structuralist philosophers suppose them to be. They will not be mystified by the first man

who puts on a wig. It is inherent in the especial character of law, as a body of rules and procedures, that it shall apply logical criteria with reference to standards of universality and equity. It is true that certain categories of person may be excluded from this logic (as children or slaves), that other categories may be debarred from access to parts of the logic (as women or, for many forms of eighteenth-century law, those without certain kinds of property). All this, and more, is true. But if too much of this is true, then the consequences are plainly counterproductive. Most men have a strong sense of justice, at least with regard to their own interests. If the law is evidently partial and unjust, then it will mask nothing, legitimate nothing, contribute nothing to any class's hegemony. The essential precondition for the effectiveness of law, in its function as ideology, is that it shall display an independence from gross manipulation, and shall seem to be just. It cannot seem to be so without upholding its own logic and criteria; indeed, on occasion, by actually *being* just.[17]

Two points follow. First, it is always possible for members of the ruling class, and certainly the personnel of the state, to become caught up in their own rhetoric. Thompson notes that a ruling ideology cannot usually be dismissed as mere hypocrisy: 'even rulers find a need to legitimize their power, to moralize their functions, to feel themselves to be useful and just.' Moreover if their ideology is something as complex as law, 'a discipline that requires years of exacting study to master', many of its practitioners are bound to become so immersed in its logic that they take seriously and in good faith its substance and its reasoning.

The other point is more subtle but even more important. The ideology of the rule of law, legality, and so on can help sustain class power only if it is – considered in itself – a morally appealing set of ideas. We may overlay something nasty with something sweet in order to make the nastiness more palatable, but then the something sweet must really *be* sweet, considered in itself, or else it will contribute nothing to the palatability. Law helps to legitimate class power by presenting it to all concerned masked in a form which, if it actually *did* correspond to reality, would be the form of a society that was good and fair and just. The idea of a set of rules that apply the same to everyone, the idea that anyone, whatever her class, may come to an impartial tribunal and ask that justice be done, the idea that force may not be used even by those in authority except in pursuance of a general principle – these ideas may be a misdescription of what actually goes on in modern Britain (or in the England that Thompson was writing about), but they are attractive nevertheless and a society which really did conform to them would be a good society.

If this is true, and if the earlier point is true – that a ruling class must actually submit to the rule of law some of the time in order to sustain the general *pretence* of legality – then it seems to follow that law and legality, even if they are instruments of class domination, do also make a positive contribution to society. There is a difference, as Thompson notes, between 'direct unmediated force (arbitrary imprisonment, the employment of troops against the crowd, torture, and all those other conveniences of power with which we are all conversant)' and the rule of law, even if both are modes of class domination. It is hard to give an account of what that difference is and what it means without concluding, as Thompson does, that, considered in itself

> the notion of the regulation and reconciliation of conflicts through the rule of law – and the elaboration of rules and procedures which, on occasion, made some approximate approach towards the ideal – seems to me a cultural achievement of universal significance. The rule of law itself, the imposing of effective inhibitions upon power and the defence of the citizen from power's all-intrusive claims, seems to me an unqualified human good.[18]

All this points in the direction of an approach to law that may not be cynical at all. If we agree that legality and the rule of law are *capable* of modifying class conflict and oppression in desirable ways, then maybe we should think favourably about the concept of a society actually ruled by law, not as a description of our society, but as a social ideal, something to be aimed at. Maybe, as things stand at present, legal rules are used to serve partisan ends. We need to be realistic and clear about what is actually going on. But we also need an ideal or an aspiration for political life – some sense of what it would be for things to be better. For this purpose, even in the midst of its partisan embroilment, the image that law projects is an attractive one.

That may be an important point even in the context of Marxist argument. Many have followed Karl Marx's lead in thinking that the inevitability of social and economic change excused them from having to think very much about the structure of post-revolutionary society. Their comments on law and the state under communism have been confined to a vague sense that with the disappearance of class conflict, these forms would simply 'wither away'.[19] But clearly more needs to be said, if only because the experience of actually existing socialist states shows how much contingency and variety there may be. Though some Marxists regard the old principles of respect for rights, universal laws, and legality as irredeemably tainted, others are less certain. And some have started to argue that the idea of the rule of law, in some form and connected with a concern for real human need and community, might actually express in an attractive way an image of human dignity, an image of a society where 'the free development of each is a condition of the free development of all'.[20]

What is this image? It is the image of a land where everyone is subject to the same set of rules, where they are applied scrupulously and impartially by officials who take that as their vocation, and where people can look one another in the eye and know that they are co-operating openly in a framework on terms that apply equally to them all. We shall discuss various conceptions of the rule of law in much more detail in Chapter three, and one of the things we shall be looking at there is whether the rule of law can serve as a complete social ideal or just an essential part of one. Some may think that the idea seems altogether too squeaky clean when compared to the sordid reality of political legislation, biased officials, and exploitative institutions that we see around us. But that is to be expected: as I have said, our ideals seem squeaky clean precisely because it is their job to give us a measure of what it would be for things to get better. Their distance from reality doesn't disqualify them as ideals, nor should it discourage us from considering their nature and their structure.

Clay Cross again

We have come a long way from the story of the fight against rent increases in a small Derbyshire town. But I think we are now in a position to use what has been said to make some sense of what was at stake in that conflict.

The Clay Cross eleven and their supporters saw the Housing (Finance) Act as a purely partisan measure. Some perhaps saw it in class terms – a bourgeois bill, the sort of thing to be expected in a capitalist society. Others, a little more optimistic, saw it as merely a Tory bill, something that the Labour party could repeal when it gained control of Parliament. Either way, their defiance was simply participation in a partisan struggle, and the Labour party's vindication of their defiance was itself nothing more than another phase in the same old conflict.

Among those who were troubled by the defiance and alarmed by Labour's actions, there was a wider variety of perspectives. The simplest view was that the statute, being part of the law of the land, deserved unconditional respect. On this view, the rule of law ideal was threatened the instant the councillors took their stand, and the ideal was in the direst peril once a political party was seen to be offering them comfort and encouragement in that stand.

A more balanced view saw the whole episode as an unhappy one for the rule of law. The readiness of the councillors to dismiss the measure simply as a partisan act showed an insensitivity to the aspiration inherent in the idea of law and legislation. It implied that unless and until laws congenial to them were passed, the ideal of the rule of law didn't matter. On the other hand, one could argue that, as long as legislation has a manifestly partisan character, its claim to unconditional respect is going to be tenuous anyway. If parties insist on passing laws without consultation and without any sense that they embody terms of co-operation that are widely acceptable, then they cannot be surprised if people treat them as purely partisan measures and respond to them accordingly. One cannot claim to be serving 'the rule of law' by passing any old measure one likes; instead, doing that may be a way of undermining it, if the measures simply exasperate and enrage many of those who have to live with them. If we assume the rule of law is important, then everyone, *including legislators*, must do what they can to sustain it. If people have a responsibility to respect the law, then equally politicians have a responsibility to pass bills that encourage and elicit such respect. If the rule of law matters, it ought to matter enough to serve as a norm for legislation as well as a guide to individual behaviour.[21]

What is wrong with the neutral model of law on this account is that it confuses the ideal with the reality. We would like our laws to command respect in a way that transcends partisan differences, and it is a good thing when they do. But the mere fact that a political measure like the Housing (Finance) Act is presented as part of *the law* doesn't show that we have succeeded in that aspiration; it shows only (and at most) that that is what we are aspiring to. And, of course, what's wrong with the pure partisan model is exactly the converse. Taking laws simply as they are and treating them as class or political triumphs, they neglect the special character of law-governed domination and the attraction of the aspirations implicit in it. On the most cynical Marxist view, those ideals are tainted hopelessly by the purposes they have served. But for others, who wonder how they could possibly have served those purposes if they didn't capture something important, the ideals of law and legality might be worth some further exploration.

Notes

1 Austin Mitchell, 'Clay Cross', *Political Quarterly*, 45 (1974), p. 166.
2 This view was expressed in leading articles in *The Times*, 20 October, 1973 and 20 March, 1974, noting that the government could have put in a Housing Commissioner to collect the increased rents at an early stage.
3 He referred in private to the party's undertaking to the Clay Cross eleven as 'this miserable promise', and when he introduced the Bill to remove their disqualification, the *Daily Telegraph* lamented the spectacle of 'the finest intellect and what was the finest sensibility in the Labour Party, reduced to mouthing things which others may believe to be true but he must know to be false'. (Susan Crosland, *Tony Crosland* (London: Jonathan Cape, 1982), p. 282.)
4 I have drawn this account mainly from contemporary reports in *The Times*. There is a somewhat more sympathetic account of the end of the affair in David Skinner and Julia Langdon, *The Story of Clay Cross* (London: Spokesman Books, 1974), Chs. 9–10.
5 The term '*ideology*' is sometimes a problem. Often it is used pejoratively ('I have my principles; you have an ideology'). Throughout this book, however, it is used in the following sense: an *ideology* is any organized body of values and beliefs about the social, economic, and political world which forms the basis for political commitments.
6 The Parliament Act of 1911, as amended in 1949, provides that a bill passed by the Commons in two consecutive sessions separated by at least a year may be presented for Royal Assent and become law even despite the opposition of the Lords. (The Parliament Act of 1949, reducing the waiting period to one year from two, was passed despite the House of Lords voting against it.) If a bill deals purely with fiscal matters, it may be passed despite the opposition of the Lords after only one month. These powers, however, are rarely invoked, and the House of Lords still often succeeds in modifying government legislation. The issue of Royal Assent is discussed a little more fully in Chapter Four.
7 I stress 'English' here, because common law is somewhat less central in the legal tradition of Scotland.
8 Though this has not deterred similar actions (leading to the imposition of similar penalties) by Labour councillors in the 1980s.
9 In the case of *Secretary of State for Education v. Tameside Metropolitan Borough Council* [1976] 3 WLR 641, the boot was almost exactly on the other foot: a Labour minister complained that a Conservative council was frustrating government policy (on comprehensive education).
10 See, for example, Paddy Hillyard and Janie Percy-Smith, *The Coercive State: The Decline of Democracy in Britain* (London: Fontana, 1988).
11 See Ralph Miliband, *Marxism and Politics* (Oxford University Press, 1977); John Dearlove and Peter Saunders, *Introduction to British Politics* (Cambridge: Polity Press, 1984).
12 Confronted with accusations about his hostility to the rule of law and so on, Marx responded: 'Your very ideas are but the outgrowth of the

conditions of your bourgeois production and bourgeois property, just as your jurisprudence is but the will of your class made into a law for all, a will whose essential character and direction are determined by the economic conditions of existence of your class.' (Karl Marx and Frederick Engels, *The Communist Manifesto* (1848; Harmondsworth: Penguin Books, 1967), pp. 99–100.)

13 See Mark Kelman, *A Guide to Critical Legal Studies* (Cambridge, Mass.: Harvard University Press, 1987) and Peter Fitzpatrick and Alan Hunt, *Critical Legal Studies* (Oxford: Basil Blackwell, 1987).

14 For an initial 'liberal' response to CLS, see Ronald Dworkin, *Law's Empire* (London: Fontana, 1986), pp. 271–5 and 440–1.

15 F. Engels, *The Origin of the Family, Private Property and the State* (1884; Peking: Foreign Languages Press of Peking, 1978), Ch. IX, pp. 205–6.

16 See Nicos Poulantzas, *Political Power and Social Classes* (London: New Left Books, 1975), pp. 253 ff. There is a clear introductory discussion in Hugh Collins, *Marxism and Law* (Oxford: Clarendon Press, 1982), pp. 47 ff.

17 E.P. Thompson, *Whigs and Hunters: The Origin of the Black Act* (Harmondsworth: Peregrine Books, 1977), pp. 262–3. This is mainly an historical work examining conflict between landowners and poachers in the eighteenth century. The quotation is taken from Part IV of Thompson's chapter 'Consequences and Conclusions', which has become something of a classic in Marxist controversies about the rule of law.

18 Thompson, *Whigs and Hunters*, p. 266.

19 F. Engels, *Anti-Duhring* (1878; London: Lawrence & Wishart, 1940), p. 315; V.I. Lenin, *State and Revolution* (1917; Moscow: Progress Publishers, 1965), pp. 18 ff.

20 The quotation is from Marx and Engels, *Communist Manifesto*, p. 105. These lines of thought have been pursued recently, for example, in Steven Lukes, *Marxism and Morality* (Oxford: Clarendon Press, 1983) and Ernest Bloch, *Natural Law and Human Dignity*, translated by Dennis Schmidt (Cambridge, Mass.: MIT Press, 1986).

21 For a criticism of British political practices along these lines, see Douglas Ashford, *British Dogmatism and French Pragmatism* (London Allen & Unwin, 1982).

Chapter three

The Rule of Law

Pedro v. Diss

Late one night in 1979, a man called Ya Ya Pedro was standing by
the door of his brother's house in London. Another man, Martin
Diss, came up to him, identified himself as a police officer, and
asked Pedro what he was doing there. Pedro walked away without
answering. When Constable Diss repeated his question, Pedro told
him to 'fuck off'. Eventually he allowed himself to be searched,
but when the policeman began to question him about some keys
that he found in his pockets, Pedro walked away again. Constable
Diss grabbed him by the arm and said, 'Do you live here?' Pedro
replied with another obscenity and swung backwards, striking the
constable in his chest with an elbow. As he did this, the constable
took hold of his clothing, and Pedro punched him. He was eventually restrained with the assistance of two other officers, and they
arrested Pedro and charged him with assaulting a constable in the
execution of his duty.

When Pedro appeared before the Highbury magistrates, he was
convicted and fined £50. But he appealed to the High Court, and
the Chief Justice, Lord Lane, with one other judge, overturned the
conviction and sentence. They said that when Pedro punched
Constable Diss, the officer was *not* acting in the lawful execution
of his duty. The police, said Lord Lane, do not have an unlimited
power to detain people for questioning: their powers of legitimate
detention and arrest are set down and governed by law. If they go
beyond those powers, the person they have got hold of is entitled to
strike back in self defence, just as he may resist *any* other person
who attacks him. Lord Lane went on:

> It is matter of importance, therefore, to a person at the moment
> when he is first physically detained by a police officer, to know
> whether that physical detention is or is not regarded by that
> officer as a formal arrest or detention. That is one of the reasons

why it is a matter of importance that the arresting or detaining officer should make known to the person in question the fact that, and the grounds on which, he is being arrested or detained.[1]

Constable Diss claimed that he had thought Pedro was a burglar, and that he was authorized by Section 66 of the Metropolitan Police Act 1839 to 'stop, search and detain any person who may be reasonably suspected of having or conveying in any manner anything stolen or unlawfully obtained'. The problem was he didn't tell Pedro that that was what he was doing; he didn't say this was the power he was exercising and these were the grounds of his suspicion. So Pedro had no way of distinguishing the situation from one in which he was being unlawfully attacked. That was why Lord Lane held that he was entitled to defend himself, even against a police officer.

It is tempting to say that Pedro got off on a 'technicality'. In some countries, you are not allowed to resist a police officer even if his attempt to detain you is unjustified; moreover the officer has no obligation to say why you are being detained and you certainly have no entitlement to resist him if he does not.[2] I don't want to argue that the rule in *Pedro v. Diss* is necessarily better. But the case illustrates a couple of broader points of principle.

First, it involves a determination to subject members of the police force, as far as possible, to the same basic rules of law as every other citizen. Ordinary members of the public are not normally allowed to detain one another forcibly and they are entitled to resist anyone who tries to do that to them. The police are subject to that basic framework of rules along with everyone else.

Second, it embodies a particular attitude towards any *special* powers that may be thought necessary for the police to be able to do their job. The special powers of the police are to be limited and governed by rules – not just any rules, but rules which are known and publicized rather than hidden away in the Police Training Manual. Indeed, the striking thing about the case is the judges' insistence that Diss ought to have told Pedro the particular rule on which he was relying. Members of the public shouldn't have to submit to a general sense that the police are simply 'special' and can interfere with their lives in ways in which they may not interfere with one another. They are entitled to know what's going on, and to know by what authority the constable is acting in what would otherwise be an objectionable (and resistable) way. Otherwise they will be at the mercy of unpredictable arbitrary power.

Of course, it is idle to pretend that very many members of the public know the rules that govern the police, and it's doubtful that when Pedro struck out he knew he was acting within what would turn out to be his legal rights. Still, even if Pedro and others like him don't know the exact rules, and don't know how far they are entitled to resist, they do know that there are *some* limits and that those limits can be found out by their lawyers and invoked for their benefit. That may sound like technicality or even legal sharp practice. But as you think about it, imagine living in a society where citizens widely and correctly believed that there were *no* limits on what the police could do, or at any rate no limits that could be invoked and relied on by ordinary people like them.

The rule of law, not men

For many of us, the policeman on patrol is the most visible expression of the power of the British state. He represents an organization that has the ability to overwhelm any of us us with physical force if we resist its demands, and he can call on that force any time he wants.[3] Though there is no national police force in Britain, events like the Miners' Strike of 1984-5 have shown that the police forces will co-operate to whatever extent is necessary to overwhelm those who defy them. Similarly, although the police in Britain are not armed as a matter of course except with truncheons, they do have access to firearms and, as events in Northern Ireland have shown, they can ask political leaders to deploy military force if that is necessary to resist some challenge to their authority. Their potential power, like that of any government official, is enormous for in the last resort they can call upon all the organized force of the state. And the same is true of other officials as well – from taxation officials to social welfare clerks. They are all the agents of an immensely powerful organization.

When you put it like that, it is hard to resist the image of one group of people – the organized agents of the state – wielding power over another, much larger group of people – the rest of us, relatively powerless in ourselves and abjectly vulnerable to their demands. Some are powerful, some are not. The state is the rule of one group of people by another. And that, of course, is an affront and an indignity to the people who are in the subordinate position, since it leaves us unfree and evidently unequal.

Ever since Aristotle, political philosophers have tried to mitigate or qualify that image. Politics, they have argued, need not be the arbitrary rule of man over man. Perhaps we can imagine a form of political life in which everyone is a subject, and everyone is ruled, not by a person or by any paticular group of people but by a shared set of abstract rules. If I am subject to another person, then I am at the mercy of his whims and passions, his anger and his prejudices. But if we are both subject to the law, then the personal factor is taken out of politics.[4] By subjecting everyone to the law, we make ourselves, in a sense, equals again.

That is the message of *Pedro v. Diss*: the police officer has no special privileges; just like the lowly suspect, he is equally subject to the law of the land.[5] Similarly, other officials, even politicians and ministers of state, must follow the law along with everyone else, even when they think they are acting high-mindedly in pursuit of the common good or the will of the people. As much as any of us, they should all be subject to legal constraint. It is only on this basis that we can characterize the British state in terms of the phrase 'the rule of law'. This is why people think it is possible to be free and to be governed at the same time: they say they are subject to the rule of laws, not men. This is the idea which we said at the end of Chapter Two might bear some further consideration.

Legal positivism

On the face of it, the idea that laws rather than people rule Britain, or should rule Britain, sounds stupid. Without some human agency to enforce it, without constables like Martin Diss, a law is just a piece of paper or, worse still, an idea in someone's head. Before we can be ruled by law, the law needs people to promulgate it, people to detect offences against it, and people to prevent and punish those offences. But then it looks as though it is those people who are ruling us after all. They may rule us with laws or without laws, but it is certainly they, and not the laws by themselves, that do the ruling.

More important perhaps, the old slogan about 'the rule of laws, not men' seems to ignore the fact that laws are made by people. We may point proudly to rules like the Metropolitan Police Act which govern the behaviour of police constables and regulate their powers. But laws like that are not – like the law of gravity – part of the fabric of the universe, independent of what any human decides. The Metropolitan Police Act was passed by a group of powerful *people*: Queen Victoria and the members of the two Houses of Parliament in 1839. Law is not an alternative to rule by men, for it is man-made law. That is what the partisan model stressed in Chapter Two. We have the laws we do – allowing the police to detain suspected burglars, for example – because a number of powerful people have got together to decide that that is what the law should be. They could have decided otherwise, and their legislative decisions are as much instances of the rule of men as the arbitrary activity of a tyrant.

It is natural for us to think of law in this way – as something that particular people *make*, and therefore not a genuine alternative to rule by men. Law-making is what goes on at Parliament. We call our MPs 'legislators', and we know we are at their mercy because the agents of the state (the police etc.) will enforce whatever standards they enact. In a familiar sense, law is an expression of human power.

In legal theory, this familiar way of looking at law is embodied in an approach known as *legal positivism*. Legal positivists believe that laws are nothing but the edicts and commands *posited* by the most powerful group or organization in society. Law is recognized in terms of its human sources. It may be worth saying a little bit about this approach and how it works.

In English jurisprudence, the great legal positivists were Thomas Hobbes, Jeremy Bentham, and John Austin. They believed that in every law-governed society, it was possible to identify one entity which occupied the position of *sovereign*. The sovereign was the person or group whom almost everyone else was in the habit of obeying. Thus they believed the king in medieval England was a sovereign – his word was law – but that in modern Britain, the sovereign was a more complex entity consisting of the king or queen together with the two Houses of Parliament. Since the people of Britain typically comply with the edicts and commands of that entity – since most people do what the Queen-in-Parliament says – then we define the edicts and commands of that entity as law. On the positivist definition, law *is* simply whatever is commanded by whoever happens to have the attention and obedience of most of the population.[6]

To put it slightly differently, positivists say we can identify law as a *fact* of social and political life. People happen to be in the habit of obeying certain individuals or agencies. Sociologists can note that fact, and if it seems a reasonably stable and striking feature of a society they will call it 'law'. By describing it that way, they are not saying they approve of the situation, nor are they saying that the commands of the sovereign they have identified are necessarily good. To call something law, on the positivist view, is to offer a description not an evaluation. So legal positivism is perfectly compatible with the partisan and Marxist views of law we talked about in Chapter Two. Positivism defines law as the command of the sovereign, and the partisan model tells us something about the nature of the sovereign and its ideological or class bias. On the positivist account, particular laws are imbued with the values and concerns of the people who issue them. It may be possible to *identify* and *describe* the law even though I do not share the values that it embodies; in that sense the science of law can be 'value-free'. But law itself is never value-free, for law is an emanation of human power and humans characteristically exercise power in the pursuit of principles and values.

Law, then, for the positivist, is a human enterprise through and through. Positivism is a secular image of law. Law doesn't come from God or out of the sky, nor is it implicit in nature or morality. It is something powerful people make and something they use their power to enforce.

There are difficulties with this simple theory of sovereignty and obedience, and we shall consider some of them in later chapters. But let's stay with the simple positivist picture for a little, and see exactly what threat it poses to the idea of the rule of law.

The rule of law is the idea that we are ruled by laws not by particular people. The positivist response is: no, laws are made by people, so ultimately people rule us after all. Even if the detail of the positivist account is inadequate, still something like it is true. There is clearly *some* sense in which *people* make the laws; so the contrast between being ruled by other people and being ruled by laws seems a false one. If the contrast is false, what can philosophers who talk about 'the rule of law' possibly have in mind?

A higher law?

Some people disagree with the positivist view that all law is laid down by human beings and human organizations. Christian thinkers, down the ages, have often talked of the law of God: a body of fundamental precepts governing our personal and social lives laid down for us by our Creator. They refer to this as 'higher law' or 'the moral law', though the term most commonly used is 'natural law'. Clearly, if the idea of divinely ordained natural law makes sense, then that law should be accorded much greater authority than the feeble and fallible efforts of human legislators. Perhaps the idea that we should be ruled by laws not men involves an appeal to a form of legality that is higher than that constituted by the commands of those who dominate us.[7]

Not all theories of natural law are religious. For some, natural law is simply a set of objective moral truths about man and society. Though the idea of moral objectivity has its problems, it need not rest on theological foundations.[8] The secular and theological versions of natural law share a conviction that it is possible for humans to use their reason and their moral insight to work out the best way to live and the best way to order society. Those moral standards then serve as a criterion for evaluating human law. Many believe that the very *concept* of law – the concept we use in the day-to-day operation of the legal system – is an evaluative concept imbued with these standards. If the commands of a sovereign depart too far from these moral criteria then they become (in Aquinas's phrase) 'not law at all in the true and strict sense, but a perversion of law'.[9] They forfeit any claim to the respect which the idea of law normally elicits.[10]

The idea of natural law is an intriguing one. Something like it was appealed to in the Nuremberg Trials after the Second World War, when high Nazi officials were charged with crimes recognized as such by the general conscience of civilized humanity. In a somewhat less dramatic way, the same idea is involved, as we shall see, in the way cases are decided at common law, as judges follow their collective sense of what justice requires even when there are no posited statutes to guide them; and also in the way jurists in civil law systems think of legal rules as unfolding rationally and logically from the articulation of first principles. In all these ways, 'the rule of law' may involve the application of moral standards that go beyond the particular decrees and commands issued by legislating sovereigns.[11]

The controversy between positivism and natural law is one that dominates modern jurisprudence. Yet it is often hard to avoid the impression that the two sides are not really disagreeing. Both sides agree that statutes passed by human legislatures can be judged morally good or morally bad. They may even use the same moral criteria (though *some* positivists have worries about the objectivity of those criteria). Where they disagree is in their use of the concept of *law*. A legal positivist sees no tension or contradiction in the idea of a morally bad law; it still counts as a law provided it is issued by a sovereign in the way we described earlier. A natural lawyer, on the other hand, does see a tension in that idea, for he regards the concept of law as a sort of moral aspiration and not merely a descriptive concept of social science. I find it hard to regard all this as anything more than a verbal dispute, particularly since neither side dissents from the practical conclusion that a bad statute is not necessarily entitled to our respect or obedience.

The rule of law and the way we legislate

'Natural' law is one explanation of this contrast between rule by laws and rule by man. But when modern theorists talk of 'the rule of law', they sometimes have a different set of ideas in mind. They accept that we are talking about human laws, the laws posited by politicians and legislators, laws which may be good or bad, right or wrong. But, they say, the rule of law means that legislators and officials ought to go about their task in a certain way or a certain spirit. They distinguish between two different ways in which we can evaluate legislation. We can evaluate it in terms of its *content*, or we can evaluate it in terms of its *form*. The rule of law is an ideal which evaluates legislation in terms of its form.

To evaluate a law in terms of its content is to look at what it says. What actions does it prohibit? Are those actions really wrong? What actions does it require? Are those actions really obligatory from a moral point of view? Are its requirements reasonable? Who gets what benefit under the law, and who suffers what penalty? Is that what they really ought to get and what they really ought to suffer?

The idea of evaluating the *form* of a piece of legislation is a little more subtle. It means looking, not only at what it says, but how it says it. When we evaluate laws in terms of their form we say things like: laws should be general and apply equally to everyone; laws should not be retrospective; laws should be intelligible and easy to follow; laws should be publicized; the law should not be changed too often; and so on. Even if the content of a law is bad, we may say, 'Well, at least it applies equally to everyone, and everyone knows where they stand.'

By themselves formal criteria are probably not enough; we want laws that are just as well as laws that apply equally to all. But even if they are not sufficient for good law, formal criteria are usually regarded as necessary. If you want to get anywhere in the art of legislation, you have got to follow certain forms.

In modern discussion, 'the rule of law' is almost always associated with these formal criteria of evaluation. When we talk of a society ruled by law rather than by men, we are not contrasting human governance with rule by God or reason. Instead we are contrasting a society ordered by settled general rules, which apply equally to everyone, with a society dominated by the arbitrary whims of a dictatorial sovereign. Both are cases of human rule, but in the former case human rulers submit themselves to a certain legislative discipline which they simply ignore in the latter case. Theories of the rule of law are attempts to articulate and defend what that discipline requires. It is worth noting at the outset that not every legal system, or not everything that claims to be a legal system, lives up to these requirements. Ours falls short in a number of ways and for a number of reasons, some of them good reasons and some of them bad. The rule of law doctrine is a critical and demanding standard for *evaluating* the form of positive law. It tells us something (though not everything) about the sort of law we want.

One law for all

Think back for a moment to Ya Ya Pedro and Constable Diss. Diss grabs hold of Pedro, and Pedro punches him in the struggle to free himself. The magistrates say he is guilty of assault. On appeal, the High Court says (in effect): 'No. Unless the arrest is lawful, Pedro is entitled to defend himself against Martin Diss just as if he were any other citizen who tried to grab hold of him. Once they go beyond their specified powers, the police have no special privileges. The ordinary rules of self-defence apply. If it's wrong for me to attack Pedro, it's also wrong for Constable Diss to attack Pedro. The law is the same for everyone.'

This requirement of universality – the idea of 'one law for all' – is a prominent feature of the normative ideal of the rule of law. But why is universality a good thing? Why is it desirable that there should be one law for everyone, irrespective of who they are, or what their official status?

One obvious application of universality is that we don't, on the whole, allow personalized laws; we don't have laws that make exceptions for particular people. In medieval England, there used to be things called 'Bills of Attainder', announcing that someone in particular (the Earl of Warwick, or the king's brother for example) was thereby banished from the realm and his estates confiscated. The idea of the rule of law is that the state should not use personalized mechanisms of that sort.[12]

Moral philosophers link this requirement of universality with morality and with rationality. They say that if you make a moral judgement about someone or something, your judgement can't be based simply on that person or that incident in particular, or if it is, it's arbitrary. It must be based on some feature of the person or action – something *about* what they did, something that might in principle be true of another person or another situation as well. In other words it must be based on something that can be expressed in a universal proposition. For example, if I want say, 'It is all right for Diss to defend himself', I must say that because I think self defence is all right in general in that sort of case, not merely because I want to get at Pedro or say something special about Diss. So I must also be prepared to say that it would be all right for Pedro to defend himself in a similar circumstance. Unless I can point to some clearly relevant difference between the two cases, then I must accept that the same reasoning applies to both.

Another way of putting it is that universalizability expresses an important principle of justice: it means dealing even-handedly with people and treating like cases alike. If I am committed to treating like cases alike, then I ought to be able to state my principles in a universal form. If I cannot – that is, if I can't find a way to eliminate references to particular people from my legislation – that is probably a good indication that I am drawing arbitrary distinctions based on bias or self-interest or something of that sort.[13]

As well as these philosophical reasons, there are also pragmatic arguments in favour of universality. We are less likely to get bad laws or oppressive laws, if the burden of any law falls as much on those who make it as on the rest of the population. The king might think twice about banning tobacco, if it means that he can't have a cigarette. An MP may be reluctant to impose heavy penalties on adultery when he remembers what he was doing last week. If our legislators are human in their inclinations and temptations, they may be less likely to enact laws that are inhumanly demanding if they know that the legislation may be applied to their conduct as well.

Notice I say you are *less* likely to get oppressive laws. There are no guarantees. An ascetic sovereign may be perfectly willing to subject his own conduct to the same harsh discipline he imposes on his subjects. When the Iranian parliament enacted amputation as a penalty for repeated offences of theft, its members presumably welcomed the possibility that they too should have their hands cut off if they offend against Allah in that way. The idea of the rule of law usefully prohibits legislation which singles somebody out for special treatment. But being singled out is only one way of being oppressed. People may be oppressed as members of a group or because they possess some general characteristic, such as being a black or being a woman, and it is much more difficult to rule out this sort of legislation on the basis of the ideal of the rule of law. As soon as we recognize that, then we recognize that the idea of universality – the idea of 'one law for all' – is not nearly as straightforward as it looks. It rules out one type of discrimination: discrimination against (or in favour of) named individuals. But it doesn't rule out discrimination against (or in favour of) certain *types* of people. It doesn't, for example, rule out the sort of discrimination that we find in the South African Group Areas Act, since that discrimination is stated in terms that make no reference whatever to particular individuals.[14] It is true of course that the Group Areas Act treats different people differently: apartheid applies one set of standards to blacks and another set of standards to whites. But if that *by itself* were enough to rule out apartheid legislation, it would also rule out an awful lot of legislation which we regard as desirable and necessary.

The trouble with the purely formal idea of 'one law for all' is that, if it is interpeted absolutely literally, it becomes really far too simple to capture the requirements of good legislation in a modern state. When you think about it, it seems crazy to say we should apply literally the *same* legal rules to everyone in all circumstances. Do we want to enforce the same standards of cleanliness in a paint-shop as in a restaurant? Is there to be one law to govern children and adults? Must ambulance drivers observe the same speed limit as the rest of us? No-one thinks that ought to be the case.

There is an important point of logic here. Most of our laws do not have the form 'No-one is to do X' or 'Everyone must live up to standard Y.' Instead, most of them are formulated in a conditional way: 'If you are engaging in activity X, then you must live up to standard Y.' So the law says things like: '*If* you are running a restaurant, *then* you must maintain these standards of hygiene' and *If* you are under 16, *then* you must attend school' and '*If* you are driving an ambulance to an emergency, *then* you may go faster than 70 m.p.h.', and so on. The statute considered in *Pedro v. Diss* had this form. It didn't say 'Anyone may be detained': it said, '*If* you are a constable and *if* you suspect someone of carrying stolen property, *then* you may detain them.' These conditional propositions are still universal: *everyone* under 16 must go to school, *any* ambulance driver on the way to an emergency may exceed 70 m.p.h.; it doesn't matter what your name is. They don't refer to any person in particular. But they don't apply simplistically across the board to everyone, and we wouldn't want them to. We don't want our commitment to universality to blind us to those distinctions and discriminations that are morally or pragmatically justified.

Special rules for officials?

As a matter of fact, this point has important implications for the way law applies to politics. The simple idea with which we began was that the same rules should apply to officials like Constable Diss as apply to citizens like Ya Ya Pedro. There should be one law for all, and no special law for officials of the state. But now if it is reasonable to apply different standards of hygiene to paint-shops and restaurants, if it is reasonable to allow a higher speed limit for ambulances than for private motorists, why isn't it also reasonable to apply rules of behaviour to police officers that are different from the ones we apply to ordinary citizens? After all, don't the police – like ambulance drivers – have a *special* job to do?

It is amazing what a grip the simple idea of 'one law for all' has had in British law and legal theory. For a long time, it was fashionable to pretend that a police officer was nothing but 'a citizen in uniform' – that his powers to question suspects and arrest felons were no greater than that of the ordinary 'man in the street'. It was simply that he did this for a living, and was trained at it, whereas the ordinary citizen had better things to do. This has long since become a fiction. The police have a whole array of powers to arrest people, to detain them for questioning, to break, enter and search their homes, and so on, which are conferred on them specifically by legislation. And the same is true of many other state officials – from the VAT-man to the social worker. They have a job to do, and Parliament has given them special powers to do it. These special powers may or may not be excessive; the issue is politically controversial. But few deny that state officials need *some* special powers (and also *some* special protections) if they are to be able to do their job.

Equally important, we may also want to say that state officials need to have special *restrictions* on their conduct (that are different from, and additional to, the ones that apply to the rest of us), as well as special powers. I will use a case to illustrate this point.

In a 1979 case, *Malone v. Metropolitan Police Commissioner*, an antiques dealer, James Malone, who was suspected of handling stolen property, sued for an injunction to restrain the London police from tapping his telephone. The judge refused to give an injunction. He held that the police had a perfect right to do it, not because there was any specific legal authorization, but simply because telephone-tapping did not involve any trespass or other unlawful act.

> The subscriber speaks into his telephone, and the process of tapping appears to be carried out by Post Office oficials making recordings, with Post Office apparatus on Post Office premises, of the electrical impulses on Post Office wires provided by Post Office electricity. There is no question of there being any trespass on [Malone's] premises for the purpose of attaching anything either to the premises themselves or to anything on them: all that is done is done within the Post Office's own domain.[15]

In other words, since the ordinary law of trespass has not been violated here, the action of the officials does not require any specific authorization. Malone's case, the judge said, rested on the assumption 'that nothing is lawful that is not positively authorized by law'. But England has always been a country where anything not expressly forbidden by the law is permitted: that is the basis of our liberty. It seems to follow that, since there is no law on the matter, the police have the right to tap telephones.[16]

We have already seen the absurdity of holding that the police should have no more powers than the ordinary citizen. Now we are seeing the absurdity of the converse proposition – that the police should not be subject to any special restrictions that don't apply to other people. They should have as much freedom as the rest of us. That proposition is absurd, because the power (both legal and physical) that the police have makes them especially dangerous *as well as* especially useful. Acting within the state apparatus, officials can do things to citizens which are quite different in character from the sort of things citizens can do to one another. It is a mistake for us to think that the laws we use to deal with one another will necessarily be adequate for our dealings with the officials of the state.

Something like the view that I have been describing as 'simple' and 'mistaken' was extolled as the essence of the rule of law in England by the great nineteenth-century jurist, A.V. Dicey. He said that one of the things we mean by the rule of law is

> not only that with us no man is above the law, but that here every man, whatever be his rank or condition, is subject to the ordinary law of the realm and amenable to the jurisdiction of the ordinary tribunals.[17]

He contrasted England in this respect with systems like France, which subjected officials not to ordinary law but to a specialized body of *droit administratif* (rather in the way that soldiers are subject to a specialized body of military law – special rules, special tribunals, special procedures – distinct from that applied to civilians).

Dicey acknowledged that the responsibilities placed on officials are necessarily more extensive than those of the rest of us, but insisted that this was in addition to their normal legal burdens. The main grounds on which a citizen could challenge an official were the same as those that could be invoked to challenge the actions of any other citizen.

The point makes sense if it is stated carefully: though we may concede that different rules are appropriate for different types of activity, it doesn't follow that there has to be, in effect, a different legal system for officialdom. Or – if there are to be specialized procedures and tribunals in this area – we might still want to insist that they be governed by the same ethos of legality that permeates the rest of the legal system.

In other words, we might talk in terms of a *modified* 'rule of law' doctrine to be applied to the conduct of officials. The simple principle of 'one law for all' holds that state officials should be bound by exactly the same rules as everyone else. That's the version we have to give up. The modified version, however, insists that official conduct should be governed by *the same sort* of legal rules, even if they are not literally the same rules, as the rest of us. We may take the simple version as our default position. State officials (police officers etc.) are to be governed by the ordinary law of the land, unless there is a specific legal provision to the contrary. If, however, there is a need for a special provision (because the police, for example, have a special job to do), we should not simply make an exception in the ordinary law of the land; we should lay down *rules* to govern the conduct of the officials.

Moreover, the rules which govern official conduct (whatever they are) should be made known to the general public, not just hidden away in a police manual. When they are dealing with ordinary citizens, officials should be required (as Martin Diss was required) to make it clear what the basis of their authority is. As in the legal system generally, the rules governing official conduct ought to be rules that citizens can invoke and on the basis of which they can initiate legal proceedings. One of the objectionable things about the image of *droit administratif* (as Dicey portrays it) is the sense that the regulation of official conduct is a matter for the officials, of the officials, and by the officials – in short, none of the citizen's business. There is a deep and underlying principle in our law that someone harmed by another's unlawful conduct can initiate proceedings himself without necessarily having to wait for the state to act. There can be private suits, and even private criminal prosecutions. The same principle ought to govern administrative law. Those who are affected by official action or inaction should be able to bring actions on the basis of the official rules to protect their interests. As I have said, even if the rules are different in their contents, still the way in which they govern relations among different groups in society ought to be the same. And there are other points of underlying principle – the procedural idea of natural justice, for example – that can give some sense to the idea of 'one law for all' even when the detailed legislation is different.[18]

Relevant differences

The special role of officials provides one set of relevant reasons for legal discrimination. What about others? One difficulty with the rule of law doctrine is that it does not provide much of a basis for telling us when different laws should apply to different types of activity. It tells us that laws should be universal, but we saw it concede, at the same time, that they may be conditional in form: '*If* you are engaged in activity X, *then* you must abide by standard Y.' It insists that the application of the special standard Y to activity X should not be arbitrary – it must be based on some *relevant reason* which distinguishes X from other activities to which standard Y does not apply. But it does not give us any guidance as to what would count as a relevant reason and what would not. It doesn't tell us why ambulance-driving is a legitimate basis for legal differentiation, whereas race (as in the South African example) is not.

Some have argued that the rule of law doctrine permits discriminations between types of activity, but not discriminations between types of people. Special hygeine requirements for restaurants may be all right because people don't *have* to run a restaurant if they don't want to, and they can avoid the rigours of the special regulations by going into some other line of business. But, for example, laws discriminating on the basis of race or gender seem particularly offensive because the discriminations are based on features or characteristics that people cannot help. There is nothing that a black or a woman can do to avoid the rigours of a racist or a sexist law. What is wrong with something like the South African Group Areas Act is that it attaches a special restriction, not to an activity which people may choose not to engage in, but to racial characteristics which are immutable.

That distinction between voluntary activities and immutable characteristics helps a bit, but it doesn't explain everything. There are cases where we do make justified discriminations based on immutable characteristics: the law insists that children not adults must attend school, but being a child at a given time is not something that a person can help. There is nothing a child can do to avoid the rigours of that rule (except grow up). In other words, the formal distinction can't do everything; what seems to matter is whether in the end the legal discrimination is substantially justified. Some discriminations between immutable characteristics are justified. And some discriminations between avoidable activities (like the choice between political apathy and political agitation, for example) are not. We are left again in the same position: the rule of law tells us there must be a universalizable reason for any

43

permissible discrimination, but it leaves it to our wider moral theory to tell us what a morally relevant reason would be.

In his book *The Constitution of Liberty*, F.A. Hayek proposes a test of a different sort for whether a discrimination is morally relevant:

> The requirement that the rules of true law be general does not mean that sometimes special rules may not apply to different classes of people if they refer to properties that only some people possess. Such distinctions will not be arbitrary, will not subject one group to the will of others, if they are equally recognized as justified by those inside and those outside the group.[19]

If both the public and the restaurateurs recognize the need for special hygiene requirements in restaurants, then the legal difference between restaurants and other places of business does not count as arbitrary discrimination. If ordinary motorists as well as ambulance drivers recognize the need for special dispensations for emergency vehicles, then the ambulances' right to exceed the ordinary speed limit will not seem like an arbitrary privilege. And even if we can't convince the twelve-year-old truant now that he ought to be in school, we expect that as he gets older and wiser he will recognize the justice of our having imposed this rule upon him and not his nineteen-year-old brother. What condemns a measure like the Group Areas Act, then, on this account, is that there is no way we can imagine the South African blacks recognizing the validity of the racial restrictions on land-owning imposed specifically on them. The differentiation doesn't seem to be one that could be justified equally to members of either group.

Hayek's argument does not have to rest on the idealistic assumption that a justified differentiation is one that literally *everyone* agrees to:

> This does not mean that there must be unanimity as to the desirability of the distinction, but merely that individual views will not depend on whether the individual is in the group or not. So long as, for instance, the distinction is favoured by the majority both inside and outside the group, there is a strong presumption that it serves the ends of both. When, however, only those inside the group favour the distinction, it is clearly privilege; while if only those outside favour it, it is discrimination.[20]

In other words, it gives us a sort of litmus test. We should be alerted to the possibility of arbitrary discrimination if and when it seems to be the case that all the support for the special restriction comes from outside the specially restricted group.

I believe that something like Hayek's approach is an important part of the rule of law doctrine as a political ideal. In Chapter One, we saw that there has got to be some reciprocity between the way laws are made and designed and the way that everyone is required to respect them. We cannot credibly demand universal respect for law if law and law-makers themselves do not, in some sense, universally respect those whom they purport to govern. Similarly, to say (in either the simple or the modified version) that we want 'one law for all' is to say not merely that the same body of law is to be *applied to* everyone, but also that it is, in a deeper sense, a law *for* everyone – a law that takes everyone into account. Without this deeper commitment, the doctrine will look formalistic and heartless – as though there were some obsessive virtue in uniform regulation as such.

Law and official discretion

I have said that 'the rule of law' provides a norm or an ideal for legislators to live up to. If they are going to make laws, our legislators must do so in a universalizable and non-discriminatory way. But what if state officials decide to exercise their power in a way that *doesn't* involve law-making? Does that mean they are exempt from the demanding requirements of the rule of law ideal?

The question is an important one, because in the modern administrative state there are very many officials and agencies who are entrusted with discretionary authority. A city Housing Officer has authority to determine the allocation of scarce housing resources to needy cases. The Civil Aviation Authority supervises fares and routeing in the airline industry. And so on. These officials work under broad statutory authority, but their particular decisions are often made on a case-by-case basis, responding to the particular features of the circumstances in front of them.

In its broader application, the idea of the rule of law is sometimes applied to this sort of activity as well. Those who believe in developing standards of *administrative* legality argue that, as far as possible, officials and agencies ought to make and publish detailed rules to govern the exercise of their powers – rules which satisfy the same tests of universality and non-arbitrariness that we apply to Parliamentary legislation. And they argue that, when these rules are applied to particular cases, they should be applied in a manner analogous to the application of a statute in a court of law. The people affected should be given notice of what is being done, and they should be entitled to a hearing at which they can make representations before an unbiased tribunal. They argue also that the regular law courts should exercise an active and inquisitive supervision of these agencies to see that their rule-making and rule-applying procedures are fair and rational.

We cannot go into the detail of these views; that would take us far afield into the realm of administrative law. But it is worth noting that many students of public administration are sceptical of this sort of legalism. They believe it interferes unduly with the capacity of state agencies flexibly to pursue social goals in changing and difficult circumstances. And they suspect lawyers and courts of engineering some sort of 'take-over bid' in public administration, trying to recast all state decision-making agencies in their own image, as though legalistic procedures were the be-all and end-all of moral and political rationality.[21]

There is certainly some substance to these suspicions. But 'creeping legalism' is not the only explanation of the modern trend towards judicial control of administrative decision-making. Many administrative lawyers are concerned with accountability: they worry that, unless administrators are forced to be open and explicit about how they make their decisions, society as a whole will never be able to hold them rationally accountable for the decisions they make.[22] And many are genuinely worried about the effect on citizens of the wide discretion vested in state officials. As we shall see in the next section, many of the concerns associated with the 'rule of law' ideal are concerns about freedom and predictability in the lives of ordinary people.

I hope this brief discussion has helped to indicate that 'the rule of law' is not a trivial matter. It is actually a very demanding and difficult ideal to live up to, and it is therefore politically quite controversial. Government in Britain is carried out in a variety of ways: sometimes through Cabinet and ministerial decision-making; sometimes through legislation; sometimes through the courts; and sometimes through the decision-making of expert officials. At best, 'the rule of law' embodies a commitment to accountable and articulate government in accordance with universal standards of equal concern and respect. But at worst it can sometimes seem like an unacceptable narrowing of the tools of government, and an attempt to assimilate a variety of state procedures to a single model of statutory rules and legalistic tribunals.

Knowledge of the law

We have talked at great length about the idea of 'one law for all'. I want to conclude this chapter with a discussion of a slightly different aspect of the rule of law. One of the things we thought important in the case of *Pedro v. Diss* was that the special rules governing the police and the special powers that they have should be, as far as possible, publicized and well-known to the ordinary citizen. They should not be hidden away in secret rule-books known only to the initiates of the constabulary. The citizen should be in a position to know what he can expect and what is expected of him.

In an important book *The Morality of Law*, the American jurist Lon Fuller developed an ethic of law-making that respected this principle. Laws, he said, should not only be general in form and apply equally to citizen and official alike. If they are to be used as a way of guiding and governing human behaviour, then the following requirements must also be observed. First, the laws must not impose impossible demands: they must lay down guidelines for behaviour which citizens are capable of following. Second, the laws should be prospective not retroactive: they should be oriented to guide conduct for the present and future, not to penalize past conduct that was perfectly lawful when it was performed. Third – and still connected with this general requirement of practicability – the demands that the law makes on us should be consistent with one another. We must not have one rule telling us to do one thing and another rule telling us to do the opposite, so that we cannot avoid a violation no matter what we do. Fourth, the laws should be be made public: they should be promulgated, so that people know what's required of them. They shouldn't be hidden away in the official archives so that prosecution for some offence comes as a complete surprise. Fifth, they should be promulgated in a form that is clear, so that it is apparent from reading the law what one must do. And sixth – on the same sort of basis – the laws should be constant over time, so that one is not always having to learn, month by month, a completely new body of regulations.[23]

Many of those requirements sound innocuous. Why would anyone want to have laws that weren't promulgated or laws that required the impossible? The answer, unfortunately, is that some regimes pass laws, not so much to govern behaviour, but as as a device for terrorizing the population, keeping everyone in a general state of apprehension, so they precisely do *not* know where they stand, so far as the state and its officials are concerned. This is certainly one of the purposes for which secret laws and retroactive laws were used in Germany in the Nazi era.[24]

But we don't actually need to appeal to such dramatic examples. There are many ways in which Fuller's requirements might be neglected even in a legal system that was comparatively benign. In a complicated regulatory state, there are thousands of different rules and regulatory schemes, and it may not be known at any given time how consistent these are with one another, or how practicable are the demands of a particular rule in relation to the system as a whole. Fuller's requirements may seem straightforward enough when applied to particular laws, but they may become very demanding when applied to the web-like apparatus of an entire system of legal regulation.

It is also worth remembering that most of the time the average person has only the haziest idea of what the law actually is. We say that the rule of law requires clarity, promulgation, and constancy in the laws. But the details of legislation are mostly *not* promulgated directly to those whose lives are governed by them. Check through the following questions. What is the legal definition of murder? What are the categories of people who cannot be witnesses to a valid will? Do the police in Glasgow have the right to demand that people in the street tell them their names and addresses? Can I be sued if I pump ground water from my land, causing my neighbour's property to subside? Are coin-operated video games subject to the requirements of the Cinematograph Act 1909? Why does it matter whether a trust is set up for charitable purposes or not? What does your inability to answer these questions correctly tell you about the idea of the rule of law?

The problem is not merely that these are technicalities, familiar only to professionally trained lawyers, whom we must pay for advice. For some of these questions, there are no agreed answers. The precise rules that will be enforced in particular cases await the decisions of judges who are, in effect, having to decide what the law is to be in these areas. We will consider all this in Chapter Five. But the importance and difficulty of these issues should shatter any easy complacency about the idea of a society ruled by law. We live with a society in which most people *don't* know in detail what the law requires of them, and in which often even the members of the legal profession can't predict what rules will be enforced against their clients. If we think, nevertheless, that promulgation, clarity, constancy and so on are important, then we should prepare ourselves to use the doctrine of the rule of law as a basis for criticizing, rather than as a basis for admiring, the legal culture with which we are familiar.

Freedom and predictability

Before using them to condemn our system, we ought to work out why these standards are important. The obvious answer is that law is self-defeating if it is incapable of governing people's conduct. People can't follow the rules if they don't know what they are.

But there is also a deeper argument about freedom. Most of us accept that the state should carry out certain tasks associated with the pursuit of the common good (though people disagree about how extensive this should be). In accepting that, we have to recognize that it may involve a certain amount of interference by the state and its officials in the running of our lives. The police are going to have to be able to stop and question people, if they suspect some offence has been committed. Revenue officials are going to have to be able to examine our accounts from time to time, if the burden of state activity is to be borne fairly in the community. Social workers and health professionals may want to uphold miniumum housekeeping and child-rearing standards, and may occasionally have to break down doors to do that, if there is to be any concern for basic welfare. And so on. Those constraints and interruptions are part of the price of the pursuit of the common good, and most people are prepared to put up with them. But they are prepared to put up with them only because they know, broadly speaking, where they stand. They know the sorts of occasions or the sorts of situations in which they can expect state interference, and they know roughly what they can do to minimize its disruptive impact. The basis of that knowledge is, first, the awareness that official action is governed by rules and, second, an understanding of what those rules permit and require.

By contrast, there would be something shocking and horrible about a situation where officials could simply descend on someone or break into a home, doing things and commanding things in a way that was completely unexpected. The problem need not be one of arbitrariness: the official action might be completely justified in terms of the social goals it was trying to promote. It's the abruptness, the unexpectedness that matters. People like to be able to plan their lives, to know what they can count on, to know what things they can do without inviting official intervention and what are the sort of things or situations that *will* call down the forces of the state upon them. State officials are always in a position to disrupt our lives, whether they are acting for good or evil ends. They have the power that we discussed at the beginning of this chapter. That threat is mitigated (though of course never removed) if at least we know the sort of circumstances in which they are likely to interfere. Then we have some idea of what we have to do in order to avoid the official disruption, and can plan accordingly. Or – if the interference is universal and unavoidable, like taxes, say, or speed limits, or conscription – we can plan around it, taking it into account, like the cost of living or the possibility of rain.

Maybe it is a good thing that Metropolitan Police constables like Martin Diss should have the right to stop and search loiterers after dark; but then it is equally a good thing that ordinary people – not only burglars but innocent insomniacs as well – should know this, and know the situations they may face when they wander the deserted streets at night. It is certainly a good thing that the state maintains a factory inspectorate with powers to close down factories or machines that are unsafe. But equally it is desirable that factory owners should know in advance what the safety requirements are going to be, so that they can adjust their workshops accordingly, and count on uninterrupted production runs without the unpredictable interference of an inspector. Without this sort of knowledge, plans cannot be laid, investments made, or long-term projects carried through with any degree of confidence.

The background values here are undoubtedly liberal ones. On the liberal philosophy, each individual is taken to have a life of his own to lead, and it is thought important for him to be able to determine its overall shape and direction.[25] Each person faces an array of decisions through time, each of which will contribute to the overall shape of his life (in his own eyes and those of others). The liberal idea is that, at each of these points, the individual should be in a position to make a choice on the basis of the view he then holds about the shape he wants his life to have and the purposes he wants it to embody. The liberal defence of the rule of law is that a person cannot do this unless he knows the sort of social environment he faces, for without that knowledge he won't have any idea which decisions of his will have what effect on his life. Since the social environment is partly constituted by structures of power, he needs some familiarity with those in order to be able to pursue his own autonomy. The idea is not the libertarian one that social power can be dispensed with altogether. Instead, liberals insist that people can make nothing of their lives unless they know what the social parameters of their decision-making are going to be.

F.A. Hayek, in his work, has taken those arguments one step further. He argues that freedom consists in the general ability to plan your life around known obstacles, and therefore that the rule of law is not only a necessary but a sufficient condition for freedom. If the laws of the state are constant and predictable, says Hayek, they are no more a threat to the freedom of the individual than the laws of nature:

There is little difference between the knowledge that if he builds a bonfire on the floor of his living room his house will burn down, and the knowledge that if he sets his neighbours' house on fire he will find himself in jail.[26]

I believe this takes the point too far. Someone locked up in solitary confinement for life knows exactly what he can count on, and exactly what he can plan around; yet no-one would regard him as free. Even known and predictable obstacles can be threats to freedom. The point to hang on to is that if it is ever necessary for the government to restrict our freedom or to interfere in our lives – and almost everyone thinks it *sometimes* is – then it's better that the interference should be predictable than that it should come like a bolt from the blue. The attraction of the predictability argument is that it helps to explain what I have emphasized several times in this chapter: that the rule of law is a necessary but not (as Hayek suggests) a sufficient condition for a well-governed society.

Hayek is also famous for another point about the rule of law, which is more controversial from a *political* point of view. He argued in his book *The Road to Serfdom* that as the state began to interfere more and more in our lives and in the economy, as it began to take on more and more social and economic responsibilities, it was moving inexorably away from the ideal of a society governed by fixed and constant rules and more towards a society governed by the ubiquitous whims and enthusiasms of officials. The problem is one of *discretion*. You cannot run a planned economy, he argued, nor insulate everyone against the vicissitudes of economic life (unemployment, poverty, etc.), unless officials are empowered to make decisions day-by-day and case-by-case: decisions to adjust quotas, examine circumstances, make changes, and make all the decisions on behalf of rest of us which, in a market society, we would each make individually, for ourselves. If official discretion were bound by known and settled rules, it could not involve economic planning, for this requires a form of detailed and flexible decision-making that responds pragmatically to circumstance, not slavishly to principle.[27]

In its time, this argument of Hayek's was seen as a *laissez-faire* attack on the nascent welfare state in Britain and America. But many of its themes find resonances on the Left as well as the Right. For example, many of the people who are poor and unemployed in Britain today find it very distressing that they are not allowed to know the detailed rules for the administration of Supplementary Benefit by the DHSS. They are kept in the dark about the contents of the departmental 'Black Book' which officials use to distinguish deserving from undeserving cases. The first thing they know about it is when an official behind shatterproof glass tells them that they are not entitled to some benefit they are seeking. This can be very nerve-wracking because it means that people have less opportunity to plan, less knowledge in advance of what they can count on. The campaign – more vociferous and successful in the United States than in Britain – to have welfare payments defined as formal *rights* rather than discretionary privileges is, in effect, an attempt to apply the doctrine of the rule of law to the whole area of welfare.[28]

So once again, the rule of law turns out to be quite a demanding ideal. It recognizes that our lives are vulnerable to the actions of state officials, both in the way they enforce certain standards and in the way they control government largesse like welfare, licences, and facilities of various sorts. It demands that as far as possible those actions should be governed and structured by rules, not by the unpredictable exercise of discretion, so that people know where they stand. The rules that govern official actions should be *promulgated* rules, not locked in some secret manual for the eyes of civil servants only. They should be made known so that people can take them into account. The argument also requires that the law be relatively straightforward, so that people can work out for themselves what it is likely to demand of them. It should not contain too many nasty surprises hidden among the fine print and technicalities in a place that only a lawyer would know where to look. Finally – and this is more or less the same point – the law should remain relatively constant over time, and not change every other month, or even after every other election. The plans that people want to make are often long-term ones. They cannot ask of course for absolute predictability in a changing world. But on the whole, it would be desirable if law made things better, not worse, in that regard.

Our aim in this chapter was to explore the doctrine of 'the rule of law' as an *ideal*. We were not going to assume complacently that it worked in British society, and we have seen now that this diffidence was justified. The rule of law is neither a simple ideal nor an easy one to live up to. It expresses a number of principles and requirements, based on various grounds. They look attractive enough when they are expressed as slogans, but they prove to be strikingly difficult to apply in any straightforward way to the governing apparatus of modern society. That does not mean we should abandon the rule of law. But we should recognize that it is an ideal that has its costs, and we ought to be as clear as we can about the reasons why those costs ought to be borne.

Notes

1 *Pedro v. Diss* [1981] 2 All ER 59, at 64. (The conventions for referring to legal materials are explained in Chapter one.)
2 In the United States, for example, a police officer must have reasonable grounds for suspicion before he can stop or detain anyone, but he is not obliged to tell the detainee what his grounds are.
3 The German sociologist Max Weber said that the definitive character of the modern state was that it was an organization possessing a monopoly on the use of legitimate force or violence in a territory, and this definition has been widely accepted. See Max Weber, 'Politics as a Vocation' in H.H. Gerth and C. Wright Mills (eds) *From Max Weber: Essays in Sociology* (London: Routledge & Kegan Paul, 1970).
4 Aristotle put it like this in his book *The Politics* (c. 335 BC; Harmondsworth: Penguin Books, 1962), Book III, Ch. 16, p. 143: 'He who asks the Law to rule is asking God and Intelligence and no others to rule; while he who asks for the rule of a human being is bringing in a wild beast; for human passions are like a wild beast and strong feelings lead astray rulers and the very best of men. In law, you have the intellect without the passions.'
5 In a recent case (the Court of Appeal decision in *Gouriet v. Union of Post Office Workers* [1977] 1 QB 761–2), Lord Denning cited the words of a seventeenth-century jurist to make exactly this point: 'Be you ever so high, the law is above you.'
6 You will find a discussion of legal positivism in any textbook on jurisprudence. The references to Hobbes, Bentham, and Austin are: Thomas Hobbes, *Leviathan*, edited by C.B. Macpherson (1651; Harmondsworth: Penguin Books, 1968), especially Chapters 17, 18, and 26; Jeremy Bentham, *Of Laws in General* (London: Athlone Press, 1970); John Austin, *The Province of Jurisprudence Determined* (London: J. Murray, 1861–3). The most famous (and most readable) modern book of positivist jurisprudence is H.L.A. Hart, *The Concept of Law* (Oxford University Press, 1961), but his theory is much more sophisticated and sensible than the crude view of sovereignty sketched here. Hart, like the others, stresses the man-made character of law, but replaces the idea of sovereignty with the idea that, as a matter of fact, certain types of procedure are 'recognized' in society as law-making. We shall discuss Hart's theory of 'the rule of recognition' in Chapter Four.
7 The classic proponent of this view was St Thomas Aquinas. There are readable excerpts from Aquinas's *Summa Theologica* (c. 1260) in A.P. D'Entreves, *Aquinas: Selected Political Writings* (Oxford: Basil Blackwell, 1959), esp. pp. 55–76.
8 For a critical discussion of 'moral objectivity' see J.L. Mackie, *Ethics: Inventing Right and Wrong* (Harmondsworth: Penguin Books, 1977).
9 *Aquinas: Selected Political Writings*, p. 60. See John Finnis, *Natural Law and Natural Rights* (Oxford: Clarendon Press, 1980), Ch. 2, for an excellent discussion.

10 What respect is due to law as such will be considered in Chapter seven.

11 For a positivist response to the natural law idea, see H.L.A. Hart, 'Positivism and the Separation of Law and Morals' in Ronald Dworkin (ed.) *The Philosophy of Law* (Oxford University Press, 1977).

12 Actually, though Bills of Attainder are used as examples of personalized laws, historically it is more accurate to see them as verdicts passed by Parliament acting in its capacity as a court, rather than as statutes in the modern sense. Though they applied only to specified individuals, almost all Bills of Attainder referred for their justification to the general law against treason.

13 This maxim is at least as old as Aristotle's discussion of justice in the 4th century BC, in *Nicomachean Ethics*, Bk. V, Ch. 3.

14 The Group Areas Act 1950 (South Africa) prohibits any blacks from holding property in areas designated for whites (and vice versa).

15 *Malone v. Metropolitan Police Commissioner* [1979] Ch. 344, at p. 369.

16 The decision was a little more complicated because Malone had also alleged that telephone-tapping infringed Article 8 of the European Convention on Human Rights (the Article which protects privacy). The judge held that the right of privacy in the ECHR did not confer any legal rights in England, despite the fact that Britain was bound to the Convention by treaty, and that if Mr Malone's case was to succeed it had to succeed in English law. We shall consider the application of the ECHR in Chapters four and five.

17 A.V. Dicey, *Introduction to the Study of the Law of the Constitution*, (1885; London: Macmillan, 1961), p. 193.

18.The term 'natural justice' is a way of referring to elementary requirements of fair procedure (what Americans call pleonastically 'procedural due process'). These include the requirements that a complaint be heard by an unbiased tribunal and that a person affected by an official decision should have notice that this is going to take place and an opportunity to make representations, etc.

19 F.A. Hayek, *The Constitution of Liberty* (London: Routledge & Kegan Paul, 1960), p. 154.

20 Hayek, *Constitution of Liberty*, p. 154.

21 Various views along these lines are discussed in Carol Harlow and Richard Rawlings, *Law and Administration* (London: Weidenfeld & Nicholson, 1984).

22 There is an excellent discussion in Ian Harden and Norman Lewis, *The Noble Lie: the British Constitution and the Rule of Law* (London: Hutchinson, 1986).

23 Fuller, *The Morality of Law*, Ch. 2.

24 See Hannah Arendt, *The Origins of Totalitarianism* (New York: Meridian Books, 1958), Ch. 12.

25 For discussion of this idea, see John Rawls, *A Theory of Justice* (Oxford University Press, 1971), p. 408 ff.; Robert Nozick, *Anarchy, State and Utopia* (Oxford: Basil Blackwell, 1974), p. 49; and Joseph

Raz, *The Morality of Freedom* (Oxford: Clarendon Press, 1986), p. 370.

26 Hayek, *Constitution of Liberty*, p. 153. (See generally his discussion on pp. 142–59.)

27 F.A. Hayek, *The Road to Serfdom* (London: Routledge & Kegan Paul, 1944).

28 See the discussion in Desmond King and Jeremy Waldron, 'Citizenship, Social Citizenship and Welfare Provision', *British Journal of Political Science*, 18 (1988), pp. 415–43.

Chapter four

The Constitution

The choice of a Prime Minister

In 1963, the Conservative government led by Harold Macmillan
was in disarray. Set back by De Gaulle's 'Non!' to British entry
into the European Community, rocked on its heels by the Profumo
affair, and facing a vigorous Labour opposition under the comparatively youthful leadership of Harold Wilson, the Conservatives
were confronting the prospect of a protracted and messy leadership
struggle as Macmillan's health declined and his reputation waned.
There were a number of plausible contenders: in the House of
Commons, Iain Macleod, Reginald Maudling, and Macmillan's
deputy, R.A. Butler; and also the peers Lord Hailsham and Lord
Home (later Alec Douglas-Home) whose way to the Commons
leadership had been cleared that year by an Act of Parliament
faciliating the renunciation of his title by Antony Wedgwood-Benn.

The contest, such as it was, proved inconclusive, largely because
Macmillan refused to concede the premiership until it became
physically impossible for him to carry on. In October 1963, he was
suddenly taken ill, and he authorized Lord Home to announce to
the party conference (then in session) that the Prime Minister
would have to resign and that he should initiate 'the customary
processes of consultation ... within the party about its future leadership'.[1]

In consultation with his advisers, and on the basis of their reports
about feeling in the party, Macmillan became convinced that the
leadership, and with it the job of Prime Minister, should pass to
Lord Home. 'Rab' Butler was perhaps a natural successor, but
Macmillan appears to have been determined to exclude him, and
Butler was in any case slow to mobilize his support.[2] Even so,
when Macmillan's position became apparent on 17 October,
through rumours and press leaks, the other contenders met and
expressed their concerted opposition to Lord Home's bid for the

premiership. Their reasons were varied. Home was to the right of the party. He was a member of the House of Lords, and not at all 'a reluctant peer' like Hailsham or Wedgewood-Benn. As Macleod pointed out, 'we were now proposing to admit that after twelve years of Tory government no one amongst the 363 members of the party in the House of Commons was acceptable as Prime Minister'.[3] Above all, there seemed to be an emerging consensus in favour of Butler. Two of the other strongest contenders were now willing to serve under him, and if Home was presented by Macmillan as the only candidate who could break the deadlock and unite the party, then it was clear that that ground was rapidly being cut from under his feet. The emergence of this consensus was widely known and widely publicized on the evening of the 17th and the following morning.

Macmillan, however, was adamant, and bolstered Home's flagging confidence by telling him, 'Look, we can't change our view now. All the troops are on the starting line. Everything is arranged.' On the morning of 18 October, he sent a letter of resignation to Buckingham Palace from his hospital bed. The resignation was announced from the Palace at 10.30 a.m., and some thirty minutes later, the Queen visited him in hospital. From his bed, Macmillan read her a memorandum announcing the results of soundings that had been taken in Cabinet and in the party by his advisers, and urging the appointment of Lord Home to replace him. It is clear that Macmillan and the Queen were both aware of the 'organized revolt' by the other candidates against the prospect of Home's leadership. The Queen listened to Macmillan's advice, and on the account he recorded in his diary,

> She expressed her gratitude, and said that she did not need and did not intend to seek any other advice but mine. She agreed that Lord Home was the most likely choice to get general support, as well as really the best and strongest character. But what of the revolt? ... I said that I thought speed was important and hoped she would send for Lord Home immediately – as soon as she got back to the Palace. He could then begin to work. She agreed.[4]

When she returned from the hospital, the Queen summoned Home to the Palace and invited him to try to form a government.

The invitation angered many in the Conservative party and in the country at large, who thought Macmillan and the Queen had acted with improper alacrity to exclude Butler and ensure the appointment of their favourite. Iain Macleod argued in the *Spectator* that Macmillan's advice had been 'magisterial' and that 'presented with such a document, it was unthinkable [for the Queen] even to consider asking for a second opinion'.[5] But other commentators were more critical. Paul Johnson in the *New Statesman* argued that Macmillan should not have ventured to offer authoritative advice on such a delicate matter from his sickbed, and that the Queen should not have accepted such advice without question. The choice of a Prime Minister is a matter of royal prerogative subject only to the requirement that the person chosen can command a majority in the House of Commons. All the constitutional precedents, he argued, make it clear 'that the role of a Prime Minister in choosing his successor is limited or non-existent, and that, in any event, his advice is never mandatory'. Once Macmillan had resigned he had no status to offer binding advice to the monarch. Moreover, the Palace had been contacted by the opposing faction early on the morning of the 18th and informed of the support coalescing around Butler. There can be no doubt that the Queen was aware of the opposition to Home's appointment. Johnson continued:

> She can read, and she must have seen in the newspapers circumstantial information that the impression of unanimity conveyed by [Macmillan's memorandum] was open to doubt. Had Mr. Macmillan been tendering formal and constitutional advice to her, she would of course have had no choice but to accept it. But his advice was, in the constitutional sense, informal, and her acceptance of it optional. If there was any question of its validity, to take a second opinion, far from being unthinkable, was her positive and compelling duty.[6]

The disturbing suggestion that Johnson makes is that, in virtue of his background, lineage, and opinions, Home was the favourite of the Palace as well as Macmillan. 'If there was a conspiracy to foist Lord Home upon the nation, it is hard to escape the conclusion that the Palace was a party to it.'

On Macmillan's advice, the Queen did not appoint Home Prime Minister immediately, but invited him to try to form a government, to see what support he could get. With the imprimatur of the Palace and his predecessor, he faced down the opposition of Butler and the others and was able to persuade them to accept Cabinet office under him. He then resigned his peerage and became Prime Minister. In the 1964 election, the Labour Party won what most regarded as an inevitable victory (though Harold Wilson had himself doubted his ability to defeat a Conservative government if it had been led by Butler).[7] Butler retired embittered to the Mastership of Trinity College, Cambridge a few years later.

'The British way of doing things'

The episode illustrates some fascinating aspects of British constitutional practice. Everyone agrees that it is for the Queen to make the formal appointment of a Prime Minister. They agree too that she should normally choose the leader of the party commanding a majority in the House of Commons (if any party can). If the leader of the majority party resigns or dies, she should appoint his successor as Prime Minister. But in 1963, though the Labour Party had a settled procedure for electing a new leader in those circumstances, the Conservative Party did not. It was generally agreed that, on the resignation of a Conservative premier, the Queen should choose the person most likely to command the support of a Commons majority (which means, in effect, most likely to command the support of all Conservative MPs). It was understood that in practice she should take soundings among Privy Councillors, senior politicans, and party whips if it was necessary for her to choose among competing contenders for the office, and that, although he might be consulted along with the others, the retiring Prime Minister had no automatic right to nominate his successor.

Now I don't want to be pedantic, but notice the language of this previous paragraph. The procedure for the appointment of a Prime Minister by the Queen is expressed in phrases like 'It is generally agreed that...' and 'It is understood that...' and 'Everyone agrees...'. The striking thing is that there is no written law on the matter – no statutes, no constitutional provisions laying down who the Queen may select and how. Even the view that this is her job – one of her 'prerogative functions' – is just something that is 'generally accepted'. You won't find it written in any Act of Parliament. Nor will you find it expressed by a judge as a principle of common law. It is simply one of the understandings we work with, and the rules about how a constitutional monarch ought to exercise this power are nothing more than a part of that understanding.

To say that we have no written rules on these issues is not to say that they are trivial or matters of only academic concern. When we say that the Queen should choose as her Prime Minister the politician capable of commanding the greatest support, we are obviously saying something very important. Who gets to be Prime Minister matters enormously for the country, since the Prime Minister has considerable power and the ability to stamp the force of his or her personality on the whole range of public policy. Nor is it just a matter of party; different personages within the same party can make an enormous difference, and once entrenched a Prime Minister is very hard to shift. Because the issue is one of public importance, we would not be happy with the monarch exercising her own personal preference in the decision – choosing the contender she found most congenial in terms of personal favour or her own political beliefs. The idea of democracy would be flouted if there were not some connection between the will of the electorate and the choice of Prime Minister. Short of an explicitly presidential system, the custom of designating the person who can command a majority of elected representatives seems both fair and fundamental to the British constitution.

But though the issue has this democratic importance, we have not embodied it in any written charter or any statute and there is no reason to believe that the courts would ever enforce it. So what *is* the status of this custom or understanding? And why do we expect the Queen and her advisers to take any notice of it?

Similar questions can be asked about other 'ways we have of doing things' in British politics. Though the Conservative Party regularized their succession procedures after 1963, there are still grey areas in the appointment of a Prime Minister, particularly in the context of multi-party politics. In February 1974, Edward Heath lost his Conservative majority in the Commons; but the understanding appears to have been that he was entitled to soldier on as Prime Minister until such time as he was actually defeated in the House, whereupon it was accepted that the Queen should invite (as she did) the Leader of the Opposition to form a government. But what if there are several Opposition parties? Is the Queen to make a guess about which coalition under which leadership is most likely to succeed?[8]

Once you start looking, these unwritten understandings start cropping up everywhere. There is an understanding that the Queen will give Royal Assent to any bill passed in both Houses of Parliament, but there is no written rule to this effect. There is an understanding that the monarch will not enter into treaties, declare war, dissolve parliament, dismiss ministers, or appoint peers, on her own initiative, even though these are royal powers: she will follow the advice of her ministers. Similar understandings govern the activities of Parliament itself. There is an understanding that a parliamentary majority will not be used, for example, to pass laws abolishing or postponing regular elections or authorizing taxation other than through annual Appropriations Bills; but there are no written rules to this effect. Nothing, except this general sense of what it is 'appropriate' to do, stands in the way of a parliamentary majority prolonging its authority through such measures. A party that had a Commons majority at present but doubted its ability to sustain this in an upcoming election could use that majority to amend the Representation of the People Act, and nothing except the political opposition of its own backbenchers or the *de facto* opposition of other officials or of the people at large, organized around an implicit understanding that this action was wrong, would stand in its way. So far as the enforcement of any explicit constitutional prohibition on such conduct was concerned, the courts and the law would be helpless.

Our whole system of responsible government, our whole structure of political accountability, seems to be built on foundations that involve nothing more robust than the unwritten sense of these shadowy and ambiguous understandings.[9]

To many outside observers, this reliance on tacit 'understandings' is quintessentially British. A game like cricket, for example, is governed not only by the explicit rules of the game, but by certain unwritten principles of good sportsmanship and gentlemanly conduct. But the tacit understandings of British politics are not – like the spirit of cricket – secondary and supplementary to a body of written laws that constitute and regulate the game. The United Kingdom has no written constitution at all. In the most fundamental and important aspects of our political structure, the unwritten understandings, the tacit principles of 'gentlemanly conduct', are *all we have*.

Britain is among a handful of countries in this regard (the others include New Zealand and Israel), for almost every people in the world can point to some authoritative document which gives expression to the aspirations of their community, sets limits on what the state can do, and lays down a structure for the processes and institutions of their government. Of course, it is not that there is *nothing* enacted on any of this in British law. There is a series of historic documents ranging from Magna Carta in 1215 to the Parliament Act of 1911 which do many of the things that constitutions are supposed to do. There are also charters like the Treaty of Rome (to which we acceded in 1972) and the European Convention on Human Rights which, as we shall see, have a considerable impact on relations between the state and the citizen in this country. But they are all things that have been produced in our political life *along the way* and could equally well be dropped by the same processes that produced them. There is no great document in Britain comparable, for example, to the Constitution of the United States of America and its twenty-six amendments, to lay the *foundations* of our political life, to set the terms on which it is to be conducted, and to bring our diverse and disparate sources of constitutional authority into some sort of order and coherence.

To say that the United Kingdom has no *written* constitution is not to say that it has no *constitution*. On the contrary, our political system is highly structured and fairly stable, and its framework is discussed in a great many books bearing titles like *The British Constitution*, *English Constitutional Law*, and so on. Anyway, even in those countries where there is a written document, constitutional lawyers must go beyond the text and consider the rules implicit in political practices that have grown up since the document was drafted. For example, the American Constitution makes no mention of political parties or presidential primaries, despite the enormous role they play in political life. The difference is that where there is a written charter, there is a starting point and point of orientation for this enquiry; whereas British constitutional lawyers have to grope their way unguided through a disorganized maze of statutes, treaties, and precedents, united – if they are united at all – only by the spirit of these unwritten understandings.

Constitutional conventions

The term used to describe the sort of customs, practices and understandings that were at stake in the succession to Harold Macmillan is 'conventions'. They are not written rules but 'conventions' of the constitution. Or sometimes we are told helpfully that they are 'conventional' and not 'legal' rules. So what is a 'convention'?

It is important to say first that a convention is not just a regularity in political behaviour; it is not just a prediction of what reliably happens. Every year the Prime Minister moves to Chequers from Downing Street for Christmas. We can predict that she will do this, and we would be surprised if she didn't. But surprise is all that would be occasioned by such an 'irregularity'. We wouldn't criticize the Prime Minister for not spending Christmas at Chequers. We don't see it as a principle or norm to judge her by. It is a regularity we have discerned in Prime Ministerial behaviour, not a standard Prime Ministers are supposed to live up to.

Now constitutional conventions are not like that. They are normative. They are used for saying what *ought* to be done, and, as we saw, they are used as a basis for *criticism* if someone's behaviour does not live up to them. We use them to *judge* behaviour not merely to predict it.

But although they are norms, they would never be enforced by a court: you could never get a judge to declare that a convention ought to be followed as a matter of law, and if someone decided to flout a convention the only remedy would be political not legal. (Either those in possession of political power – the people, the other office-holders, the military perhaps in the last resort – would put up with what had happened or they wouldn't. If they did, the convention would in effect have been changed. If they did not, there would be something akin to a revolution.) Most writers have said that since these are norms but not legal norms, the only conclusion possible is that they are *moral* norms – norms of political morality. A.V. Dicey, for example, wrote that conventions 'consisting (as they do) of customs, practices, maxims, or precepts which are not enforced or recognized by the courts, make up a body not of laws, but of *constitutional or political ethics*'.[10] And Geoffrey Marshall says that they 'simply spell out the *moral duties, rights, and powers of office-holders* in relation to the machinery of government'.[11]

But calling them 'moral' or 'ethical' doesn't really help. There are all sorts of different views about 'constitutional or political ethics' and about 'the moral duties, rights, and powers of office-holders'. Pacifists may think that MPs have a moral duty not to authorize expenditure on nuclear weapons. Radical democrats believe that no law should be passed without a referendum. Christian fundamentalists may believe that atheists should not be allowed to hold public office. All these are held by their proponents as moral norms, but I take it none of them would regard their principles as conventions of the constitution. Certainly, we think or we hope that there are moral justifications for the conventions we have. But there is no reason to be confident that they capture the *best* political morality. It is not their moral justification that makes them conventions of the British constitution. We have got to say something more specific.

Sir Kenneth Wheare once wrote that a convention is 'a rule of behaviour accepted as obligatory by those concerned in the working of the constitution'.[12] That is an interesting definition because it suggests that, in the last resort, these rules have no other basis than the fact that the people involved accept them as standards for their behaviour. They follow them in most cases; they feel guilt or compunction when they don't; they criticize deviations from them by others; and, what's more, everyone knows what is going on when these criticisms are made, for everyone has in mind roughly the same set of standards. They are not merely habits or regularities of behaviour; they enter into people's consciousness and become the subject-matter of reflection and of a sense of obligation. But they are not merely subjective views about morality either. They have a social reality, inasmuch as they capture a way in which people interact, a way in which people make demands on one another, and form attitudes and expectations about a common practice with standards that they are all living up to. They get mentioned in newspapers, in periodicals, and in learned treatises. Politicians refer to them when they are evaluating one another's behaviour. They are social facts, not mere abstract principles, because they bind people together into a common form of life.

All this sounds very fragile compared with the robust reality of a statutory law or a written constitution. I have made it sound as though constitutional conventions are rules that pull themselves up by their own bootstraps. They are rules because they are accepted as rules by those they bind, and if they weren't accepted by those they bind they wouldn't be rules at all. They have no other validity, no other force, than their common acceptance by the people they govern. If the Queen were quietly to abandon the practice of picking a majority leader as Prime Minister and started picking Court favourites instead, and if politicians and journalists ceased to criticize her for that, the convention would have disappeared. It is only the fact that politicians use it as a standard for practice and criticism that gives it its social reality.

But there is an interesting point of theory here. Though conventions seem terribly fragile when we describe them in this way, many jurists believe that *every* legal system is based in the end on something as fragile as this. Let me expand the point.

Rules of recognition

In Chapter two, we briefly considered the simple philosophy of legal positivism: law is the command of a sovereign; and a sovereign is whoever the people happen to be in the habit of obeying. Though this theory sounds hard-headed and realistic – law is the command of the person who gets obeyed – the position of sovereign rests on nothing more substantial than the fact that ordinary people are willing to defer to her. If they weren't willing to do that, there would be no sovereign and no legal system, or perhaps the sovereign (and therefore the legal system) would be different. In Britain, most of us happen to be willing to obey the edicts of the Queen-in-Parliament; we respect their word as law. If we were to change our attitudes in this regard, if we were to start routinely defying or ignoring the edicts of our Parliament, then those edicts would not be law on the positivist account (however highminded and moral they were in themselves). They would either be futile gestures or at most commands backed with bayonets (and even then they would need the willing obedience of those who wielded the bayonets, or of those who commanded *them*, and so on). Even the most hard-headed theory has to concede that political power can never be based entirely on force: it has to begin with the voluntary acceptance by some of the right of others to command them.[13]

In modern theories of legal positivism, the simple image of sovereignty is no longer accepted. Part of the problem is that even sovereignty can't be understood except in terms of rules that specify what is to count as a sovereign command. (For example, the US Congress acting together with the President counts as a legal sovereign only if its edicts conform to the conditions laid down in the US Constitution.) The most influential positivist theory of law in recent times has been that of H.L.A. Hart. Hart argued that what makes a system of edicts a legal system is not a simple matter of command-and-obedience. What matters is that enough people accept what he calls 'a rule of recognition'. A rule of recognition tells us what makes a rule a legal rule; it distinguishes legal rules from, for example, rules of etiquette, rules of the church, ex-legal rules that have been abolished, and so on. It is a way that citizens, or at least officials in the system, have of identifying the rules and requirements that are to count as part of the law.[14]

Why is a rule of recognition necessary? The members of a tribal group might just get by with a small set of generally accepted social rules, with no need for a master-rule telling them how to identify the rules. But a complex modern society needs a master-rule for two reasons. We have many different communities and practices in our society – ranging from churches to sports clubs to informal practices of etiquette. They all make rules and they all make demands on us. The difference with *law* is that, ultimately, these are the rules that will be *enforced* with all the power of the state. The rule of recognition tells us how to identify the rules which will be enforced in this way.

The other reason is that in modern society, we often want to change the rules and if there are many rules and many changes, we want a way of keeping track of which rules are currently in force and which are not. The rule of recognition gives us criteria for doing that.

In Britain, the rule of recognition says (among other things) that a bill passed (in the appropriate way) by the two Houses of Parliament and assented to by the Queen has the force of law, and prevails over any earlier law or any other rule that conflicts with it. It tells us, in effect, to look at the *institutional pedigree* of a norm to see if it is a legal rule: look at its date, the process of its enactment and the formalities associated with it, and that is all you need to know about its legal status.[15] Other countries have more complicated rules of recognition: in the United States, one has to look not only at how and when the Bill was passed (by both Houses of Congress, and with the President's assent or a fresh majority of two-thirds or more in each house of Congress) but also at its compatibility with the Bill of Rights embodied in the 1787 Constitution. And a full statement of the American rule of recognition would have to include the procedures for amending the constitution as well. Whatever the complexities, Hart's argument is that a legal system needs some such rule of recognition to identify what are to count at any time as its laws.

What gives the rule of recognition *its* legal force? What makes it the authoritative way of determining what the law is? The question does not really have an answer. It's a bit like asking what makes the US Constitution constitutional. The rule of recognition is just there. It is a social fact about the way people involved in the workings of our society – particularly lawyers, parliamentarians, judges, policemen, and so on – behave, and above all it's a fact about how they think they ought to behave. No doubt, judges and so on have their reasons for thinking they should defer to the edicts of Parliament. Some of them may be democratic reasons; some of them may be reasons of tradition. But their practice of doing so – their practice of deferring to Parliament, their practice of taking this as their standard – is not consecrated by any further authority. Their practice, their readiness to regard themselves as bound by this rule, is what makes our society a legal system: it's the fulcrum or the foundation of the rest. Without some social practice of this kind, there would be no legal system in Britain – that is, no shared sense among officials and people of which rules and commands they should expect to be upheld.[16]

I brought up positivism and Hart's rule of recognition because I wanted to illustrate a general point about the foundations of political life. There is tradition, there is morality, there is affection, there is charisma, there is ideology, there is mystification, there are lies and – ultimately – there are bayonets and bullets. All of these are important in the analysis of politics, and all of them – *including* the last two (think of Northern Ireland) – have a part to play in explaining the stability of our political system. But there is also law and there is political order, regulating authority, succession, and the transfer and exercise of power. Law and political order matter an awful lot to us. But in the end they amount to an interlocking system of rules and practices that depend on nothing more concrete and nothing more secure than the readiness of those involved in political life to regulate and judge their own and others' behaviour by certain standards. Hart's theory of the rule of recognition implies that something no more secure than this lies at the foundation of every legal system. What we have said about constitutional conventions – the norms that were in play, that were allegedly broken in the transfer of power from Macmillan to Lord Home – indicates that they fall into this category as well. It is the fragile readiness of those involved in political life to order their conduct by certain implicit standards that forms the basis of whatever claim Britain has to be a constitutional regime.

What is different, then, about the British constitution is not that it rests in the last resort on a set of fragile understandings; that is true of *every* legal and constitutional system. Rather, the distinguishing fact about Britain is that *so much* of its constitutional law has that status. In other countries, there is a written charter whose authority rests implicitly on such a presupposition. Americans tacitly presuppose the authority of the delegates at the 1787 convention who began their document with 'We the People of the United States...' when they accept that document as binding. In Britain, however, the whole thing is a structure of tacit presuppositions from start to finish. There is no great charter whose authority is tacitly presupposed. There are just tacit presuppositions. That is the peculiar feature of our political life.

Constitutions and the structure of power

I said earlier that, though Britain has no written document comparable to the Constitution of the United States, it is wrong to infer that it has no constitution. We are described as a 'constitutional monarchy'; there is a settled order of representative democracy in our political process; and there is widespread agreement that British politics and government are more fully and reliably constrained by considerations of constitutional principle than many regimes that can point to the expression of those principles in a piece of parchment exhibited in a glass case in a marble building.

I do not want to be complacent about this. Later in this chapter and also in Chapter five, I will discuss the shortcomings as well as the advantages of having an unwritten constitution. But we can't get very much further without asking a very basic question. What is a constitution? For what do countries have constitutions (whether they are written or unwritten)? What is the role of a constitution in political life?

Broadly speaking, a constitution is a set of rules, principles, and understandings about how a country will be governed. S.E. Finer in his book *Five Constitutions* defines them as follows: 'Constitutions are codes of rules which aspire to regulate the allocation of functions, powers and duties among the various agencies and officers of government, and to define the relationships between these and the public'.[17] Of course, it is not only countries that have constitutions. Clubs, trades unions, and other organizations may have them too, and in that context they perform an analogous function: they define and regulate positions of authority within the organization and they set out its aims and the various purposes for which its powers are to be exercised.

It is important to notice that constitutions are not usually taken to include every last detail of the organization of the state – from the procedure for coronation down to the statutory responsibilities of the Duck Marketing Board. A constitution is usually understood as a broad statement of the *fundamentals* of public power, not a comprehensive codification of every rule that regulates every last action of every agency and officer of the state. Of course this boundary is necessarily a fluid one. In Britain, there are some people who get up and talk sonorously about 'constitutional issues at stake' when the slightest modification is made to the taxing powers of local authorities; and there are others who call this just an alteration of detail in the fabric of administration. There is no way of deciding who is right or who is wrong about that: we can use the term 'constitutional' more or less as we please.

One useful suggestion might be the following. Not everything in the fabric of government and administration is a matter of constitutional importance. But 'constitutional' is not a word that distinguishes the more important *institutions* and *agencies* (like Crown, Cabinet, and Parliament) from the less important ones (like the Duck Marketing Board). It is a term that distinguishes *issues* in terms of their importance. Some issues about the workings of Parliament (such as who gets what office space) are not of constitutional moment. And some issues about the workings of the Duck Marketing Board (such as whether the Board's actions are reviewable by the courts) are. The question is always: is there an important issue here about the fundamental balance of political power? We have an idea that it *matters* how far the power of the state extends over the life of the community and the lives of the individuals who make it up, and it certainly matters how far the community and the people it comprises can control those who exercise power over them. These issues of power are the real concerns of constitutionalism.

From this point of view, one of the most important things about the structure of British government is its claim to be a form of representative democracy, and the laws and conventions we have to provide for elections and representative accountability are no doubt the most important part of our 'constitution'. Now, most written constitutions make some gesture in their provisions towards democratic forms. In Britain, however, the whole business of voting and representation is governed by ordinary statutes. It is only by virtue of Acts of Parliament, technically capable of being repealed by a parliamentary majority, that we have a new parliament installed on the basis of popular voting at least every five years. An act could be passed in a matter of weeks to change that – to extend the life of Parliament or to abolish elections altogether – if a government had the will and the parliamentary support to do it. No doubt there would be resistance in the Commons and in the country, and some officials might be reluctant to accept the changes. But if that resistance found no political voice, it would have no constitutional law on which to ground itself. The democratic basis of our political system in Britain is as secure as the rest of our constitution, and rests on nothing more substantial than people's sense that it would be wrong to repeal statutes like the Representation of the People Act.

Even if the democratic character of our constitution were assured, there would be other structural matters to be concerned about. Since the emergence in late eighteenth- and early nineteenth-century thought of the concept of 'tyranny of the majority', constitutionalists have been convinced that democratic control of government is at most a necessary, and certainly not a sufficient, condition for society free from oppression.

> If it be admitted that a man possessing absolute power may misuse that power by wronging his adversaries, why should not a majority be liable to the same reproach? Men do not change their characters by uniting with each other; nor does their patience in the presence of obstacles increase with their strength. For my own part, I cannot believe it; the power to do everything which I should refuse to any one of my equals, I will never grant to any number of them.[18]

Apprehensions of this kind have led many constitutional theorists in the direction of individual human rights as constraints on democratic decision-making. We shall consider this in Chapter Five. But there may also be ways of designing the structure of government which can reduce the chances of power being exercised tyrannically, either by a majority or an elite.

The conviction that *how the state is organized* makes a difference to what it does is as old as Aristotle and has been a central focus for political science and political theory for hundreds of years.[19] The leading idea has been that the power of a society becomes more dangerous to its members to the extent that it can be exercised by a single organization or by a single group of people acting together. If, on the other hand, power is distributed among a number of agencies, then maybe their respective efforts to control the life of the society will cancel one another out and their mutual antagonisms may operate as checks and restraints on their individual actions. As James Madison put it, 'Ambition must be made to counteract ambition.' If we could utterly trust the motives of our rulers, these checks would not be necessary. But since we can't, we need what Madison referred to as a 'policy of supplying, by opposite and rival interests, the defect of better motives'.[20]

Various ways of ensuring a plurality of power centres have been suggested. One way stresses the importance of local as well as central institutions, and the balance of power between central government and local authorities is often regarded as a matter of fundamental concern. Thus, for example, when central government tried a few years ago to limit the amount that local councils could raise from property taxes ('rate-capping'), a number of MPs on both sides of the House objected to the new law claiming that it was 'contrary to the spirit of our unwritten constitution'.[21] By that they referred, not to any explicit rule that local authorities should be independent in this regard, but rather to the broad constitutionalist value of the dispersion of power and to certain tacit understandings predicated upon that.

Another way of dispersing power concerns the structure of the central institutions themselves. In Britain, the legislature is not a single institution but – in theory at least – a triad of institutions: the Commons, the Lords, and the monarchy. In the final analysis the Commons will prevail in any trial of strength between them.[22] But the House of Lords remains an independent power centre to a certain extent. It can delay bills that have been passed in the Commons, and a defeat in the Lords can be politically embarrassing for a government even though there are constitutional mechanisms for overcoming it. So the bicameral (literally 'two-roomed') structure of our legislature provides some check on the dominance of any one organization.

A third idea is what is known as 'the separation of powers'. The notion is that in any government there are at least three jobs to be performed: the making of laws (the *legislative* function); the application of those laws to particular cases (the *judicial* function); and the enforcement of the laws and of the decisions of the courts (the *executive* function). The separation of powers holds that these functions should be performed by different people with relatively independent political careers, so that their ambitions can act as brakes on one another.

Though the doctrine has been greatly influential in the United States, it is in fact achieved only imperfectly in the American Constitution. Members of Congress (the legislature) and the President (the chief executive) are elected through different channels, but the highest echelons of the judiciary are appointed by the President subject to the approval of the Senate. And of course there is a sense in which the agencies could not possibly be utterly isolated from one another. They are, after all, functionally related: the judiciary must decide cases at least sometimes on the basis of laws passed by the legislature and it is those laws and those determinations that the executive must enforce. Moreover, the different departments of government could hardly act as 'checks and balances' on one another's ambitions if they were utterly distinct.

If anything, the separation of powers doctrine runs into the criticism that it works too well – that by giving distinct institutions independent roles in the process of government, it gives each the power to frustrate the purposes of the other, leading sometimes to a deadlock in which recriminations flow back and forth and the political power of the community is simply not exercised at all. This may be music to the ears of those who fear strong government as a threat to individual liberty. But many believe there are other things to be done in society besides protecting individual freedom from the state. The constitutionalist strategy of playing distinct institutions off against one another may be a good way of preventing political oppression, but it is also a good way of ensuring the paralysis of government and the neglect of social policy.

Part of the problem is that the doctrine gives no account of the relation between the formulation of social and economic policy, on the one hand, and its implementation, on the other. The experience of modern government is that social problems are chronic and complex and any possible solutions need to be thought through and formulated by a specialized body of experts under coherent political direction. The solutions may still take a legislative form, but there needs to be reasonably tight co-ordination between those who are responsible for their formulation, those who are responsible for their implementation, and those who are responsible for their authoritative passage into law. On a number of occasions in the past 100 years – and the present debate about the federal budget deficit is one of them – there has been a widespread feeling in the United States that the constitutional separation of powers in effect prevents this co-ordination.[23]

Are things any better in Britain where the separation of powers – to the extent that it exists at all – is much less rigid? The judiciary in Britain is, of course, independent of the legislature: we shall discuss that in Chapter six. But the system of 'cabinet government' ensures a much more intimate relationship between the legislature and those responsible for formulating and implementing public policy. If there is an 'executive' branch of British government, it is to be identified politically with the Cabinet which – at one and the same time – controls the bureaucracy and operates as a dominating committee of the House of Commons. In strict theory, the British executive is the Crown, but the convention that the monarch acts only on the advice of her ministers and selects as her ministers only those who can command the confidence of a Commons majority means that in effect these powers belong to the Prime Minister and her colleagues. When you add to this the fact that the Civil Service is under the direct authority of ministers, then you see that there is nothing remotely approaching a 'functional' separation between those who make policy, those who administer it and those who pass the laws.

It may well be that this parliamentary approach, with its blurring of the traditional boundaries between the separate types of 'power', is a more efficient and realistic type of political structure. Maybe it can cope better with the exigencies of modern government and public administration than a system in which there is a jealous stand-off between those who make law and those who implement it. The problem is that we have not, in Britain, evolved any *other* way of addressing the concerns that motivated those who originally called for the separation of powers. They did not propose separation as some sort of functional fetish – or because they liked the tidiness of a distinction between the legislature, the executive, and the judiciary. They did it because they feared the prospect of political power accumulating under a single centre of decision. The fact that the particular solution they proposed seems obsolete and baroque in the modern world doesn't mean that there is any less reason for apprehension about that prospect.

It is supposed to be a virtue of an unwritten constitution that it does not bind us to institutional structures that might seem appropriate in one age but inappropriate or outdated in another. We are not bound even to pay lip-service to formulae laid down in 1787 in the way the Americans are. Our unwritten conventions give us flexibility in this regard: we can, if we want, address old problems in new ways. But that advantage is easily lost if it is taken as an excuse for not addressing the problems of power and its accumulation at all, and that has been for too long the experience in Britain. The flexibility of our political institutions – the lack of structural constraint – has worked greatly to the advantage of the executive in its quest for more efficient administration and more centralized control. Indeed, this cherished flexibility is itself somewhat 'inflexible' in the way it resists the introduction of constraints and mechanisms for scrutiny.[24] We do not need to say that this is a sinister process: mostly it has been done with the best will in the world, to better achieve the goals of public policy. But whether the intentions are sinister or not, the fact is that there is something dangerous – for the future – about the shift of power from periphery to centre, from Parliament to the committee that controls it, from a functionally articulated structure to a unitary state. Our lack of a written constitution has allowed that to happen without forcing anything like a public debate about the fundamentals of power and liberty. Once again, we feel the lack most sharply not for the actual constraint that it might exercise but for the way it might force us to face up honestly to the principles and concerns of constitutionalism.[25]

Constitutional constraints

Structural features like bicameralism and the separation of powers work indirectly; their object is to make it less likely that authority will be exercised oppressively by laying down institutional obstacles. In addition, most of the written constitutions of the world impose certain direct constraints on the exercise of political power. They lay down that there are certain things which are simply *not to be done*, no matter how laudable the purpose for which people undertake to do them.

The best known example of a set of direct constraints is the so-called 'Bill of Rights' comprising the first ten amendments to the American Constitution. For example:

> *First Amendment*: Congress shall make no law respecting an establishment of religion, or prohibiting the free exercise thereof; or abridging the freedom of speech, or of the press; or the right of the people peaceably to assemble, and to petition the Government for a redress of grievances.

The point of this and the other amendments is to ensure that neither the law-makers (in this case, Congress) nor the executive officials (from the President down to the police officer on the beat) nor the judges will act in a way that encroaches on certain individual rights. It is worth noting, however, that not all constitutional constraints concern the rights of the individual. In the 1937 Constitutution of the Irish Republic there are constraints on legislation which are based on religious doctrines about desirable social policy:

> *Article 41 (3) 2*: No law shall be enacted providing for the grant of a dissolution of marriage.

And in some other countries, there are constraints based on historical experience and international law; the modern Japanese Constitution, for example, provides for the renunciation of war and directs that 'land, sea, and air forces ... will never be maintained'.[26] Still, partly because of our liberal traditions, and partly because of the immense influence of the American example in our thinking about constitutionalism, constraints of individual rights have been the main focus of interest.

The topic of rights looms so large in modern discussions of law that I am going to devote a whole chapter to it – Chapter five. There I shall talk about what rights are – legal rights, moral rights, human rights – and why people think they should operate as substantial constraints on governmental and legislative action. In the present section I want to concentrate on the broader idea of constitutional constraint as such, and on what it would be for the British Parliament or government to be constrained rather than, as we sometimes say, 'sovereign'.

The American Bill of Rights is the best-known example of set of constitutional constraints. Anyone affected by a piece of legislation or by some executive action may bring suit in a federal court to challenge its constitutionality, and the courts have taken upon themselves the power to declare various pieces of state and federal legislation unconstitutional and invalid if their contents seem at odds with the provisions of the Bill of Rights, suitably interpreted. Thus, for example, a Texas statute restricting abortion was struck down by the Supreme Court in the landmark case of *Roe v. Wade* because it conflicted with what the court regarded as 'the right to privacy' implicit in the Fourth and Fourteenth Amendments.[27]

However, the American model is not the only way that constitutional constraints can work. Instead of stipulating that certain laws are not to be passed, period, a constitution may insist that certain types of provision may be passed only with a special majority (say, two-thirds rather than a simple majority) in the legislature, so that the legislation requires bi-partisan support. Or maybe the laws that it constrains can be passed only after ratification through a popular referendum, or only after the legislature has voted twice on the issue with a General Election in between, or only after some other specified period of time (for reflection, or for the mobilization of opposition) has passed. The weakest forms of constraint are things like a set of guidelines for legislation which are said explicitly to be unenforceable in the courts, or a Bill of Rights embodied in an ordinary statute which may be repealed explicitly or implicitly by subsequent legislation. Though these latter models don't seem like genuine constraints at all, still they might be better than nothing if they serve as a focus for political argument and concern. The bare fact that they were being overridden might provide a basis for mobilizing political opposition, and for awakening public debate.

Of these modes of constraint, all but the last would involve the imposition of substantial restrictions on what Parliament could do. Before going any further, then, we should look at the so-called doctrine of 'parliamentary sovereignty'. When people think, for example, about a Bill of Rights for Britain, they think of it as a way of limiting the sovereignty of Parliament, and there are a number of people who base their opposition to the idea on just this ground.

The sovereignty of parliament

The phrase 'parliamentary sovereignty' can mean a number of things, and some of them are misleading even as descriptions of the *status quo*. It is certainly misleading if it is taken to mean that Parliament is, considered in itself, the most powerful institution in the land. Everyone knows that the actual power of Parliament as an institution has diminished throughout the twentieth century, and its members now exercise only minimal control over legislation, public policy, taxation, and spending. If we want to talk about real power, if we want to know which body usually gets its way, or whose initiatives are most likely to succeed, we should focus on the Cabinet or perhaps on the office of Prime Minister and her small coterie of aides. Parliamentary sovereignty may indicate, however, not that Parliament is in control, but that those who are in control must exercise certain of their powers *through* Parliament. (That is true of legislation and taxation, though it is not true of ministerial exercise of the prerogative powers of the Crown.) It may also be a way of indicating that those who exercise these powers are recruited from Parliament and occupy their offices by virtue of their ability to command a Parliamentary majority. But it is not the way to locate real political power.

Nor, in the modern world, is the doctrine of parliamentary sovereignty a way of expressing the independence of Britain as a sovereign state. We remain basically a self-governing nation. But sovereignty is now somewhat limited through the impact of European Community EC law. Rules and regulations made in Brussels and Strasburg are enforced in the United Kingdom, and our politicians are often required to accept and put up with EC policy or EC regulations that they do not like or would not pass for this country by itself if they had a free hand. In legal terms, the law of the European Community (i.e. the Treaty of Rome, and the various laws, regulations, and judicial decisions made under its authority) has been incorporated into British law by a local statute – the European Communities Act of 1972. Theoretically, then, it might seem as though parliamentary sovereignty is undiminished since EC law has authority here only by virtue of an Act of Parliament. In fact, matters have gone beyond that. Though Parliament could explicitly repeal the European Communities Act, it is no longer treated as an ordinary statute. European regulations incorporated under its authority prevail even against *subsequent* British legislation. In other words, we have abandoned, in regard to European law, the doctrine of implicit subsequent repeal that is usually taken to characterize the sovereignty of each Parliament *vis-à-vis* its predecessors.

I imagine our rulers could always pull out of Europe if they pleased, and so we remain sovereign to that extent. But we are increasingly and in such complex detail bound into the European Community, that such a step would have something of the character of a revolution. And in that sense parliamentary sovereignty is no longer a constitutional doctrine, but simply a concession that in the end a country or a people if they have the power may repudiate any limitation if they want to.

There is a third sense of sovereignty that comes closer to the heart of the matter. The most common sense of parliamentary sovereignty is the sense of 'omnicompetence': the idea that there are no restrictions on what Parliament can do. Now, to be picky and semantic, the word 'can' is a bit of a problem here. There are certainly enterprises Parliament might embark upon and not succeed: it might try, for example, to change racial attitudes through legislation and fail miserably. The 'can' is supposed to be an institutional one: crudely, there is nothing that Parliament is *not allowed* to do (or try). There are no rules against it doing certain things in the way that there are rules (such as the First or Fifth Amendment) limiting the American Congress.

Even this does not state the point carefully enough. There *are* rules prohibiting the British Parliament from doing certain things, and like the American First Amendment they are based on individual rights. The European Convention on Human Rights (ECHR)[28] requires the states which have ratified it (and Britain is one) to 'secure to everyone within their jurisdiction' rights and freedoms such as the following:

Article 10 (1): Everyone has the right to freedom of expression. This right shall include freedom to hold opinions and to receive and impart information and ideas without interference by public authority...

Now this rule certainly prohibits the British Parliament from passing laws permitting the censorship of mail or from banning politically controversial publications. What is more, it is an official rule, and there is a court (in Strasburg) which we help run and pay for, to determine when it and the other rules of the ECHR are broken.

What, then, does it mean to say that the British Parliament is sovereign and unrestricted? It means, in the end, not much more than the expression of a certain deference to Parliament on the part of *British* courts. Whatever the ECHR lays down, whatever the European Court of Human Rights may say, *our* courts will never question the validity of an Act of Parliament.

In this sense, sovereignty as a legal doctrine is fairly well established. In a number of cases, the courts have held that they will not allow litigants to rely on the provisions of the European Convention (except possibly as aids to interpretation where there is more than one way of reading a British statute). In *Malone*'s case (the antique dealer whose telephone was tapped), which we discussed in the previous chapter, the judge held that the legality of police phone-tapping was to be determined by British law not by the European Convention, which, he said, had the status only of a treaty.[29] (There is nothing equivalent to the European Communities Act 1972 for the ECHR.)

I have said that parliamentary sovereignty does not mean that there are no rules or principles by which legislation can be assessed, only that there are none that the courts are prepared to enforce. The point can be put another way in terms of the tacit understandings of our constitution. Early in this chapter, we saw that at the level of structural decision-making (who gets chosen as Prime Minister, what role the monarch plays, etc.) there are certain implicit principles which everyone mostly follows but which are never raised to the status of explicit legal rules. The same may be said about the protection of rights and civil liberties in this country. Parliamentary sovereignty does not mean that our legislators think they can do as they please where the rights of the citizen are concerned. They probably do think of themselves as following certain principles like free speech and 'an Englishman's home is his castle'. What is more, those principles may be regarded by all concerned not merely as moral ideals, but as norms which (like the norm about who gets to be Prime Minister) are partly constitutive of political life in this country. Just as the Queen doesn't think of herself as having the power to choose whoever she likes as her ministers, so parliamentarians may not think of themselves as having the power to abrogate basic civil liberties.

But, however deeply entrenched these constitutional attitudes are, they do not undermine parliamentary sovereignty as a legal doctrine, for parliamentary sovereignty in that sense is nothing more than a doctrine about what the *courts* should be expected to do.

So long as our judges continue to have a deferential attitude towards legislation, it is difficult to see how any explicit constraints on parliamentary power could ever be introduced into our constitution. One of the paradoxes of parliamentary sovereignty is this. The omnicompetence of Parliament means that there is one thing no Parliament is ever in a position to do – namely, bind its successors. Suppose Parliament in 1994 were to pass a Bill of Rights including among other things a British version of the American First Amendment: 'Parliament shall not pass any law abridging the freedom of speech.' And suppose that a year or two later, in 1996, a government were to introduce and push through a bill that prohibited the publication of any left-wing magazine. While some judges might spend time wondering whether or not such a ban should be interpreted as an attack on free speech, others might say simply that when an act of 1996 conflicts with an act of 1994, the one which is later in time must prevail. Precisely because Parliament must be free in 1996 to do anything it pleases, Parliament in 1994 cannot possibly be free to impose constraints on what its successors may do. So it looks as if, no matter how solemnly a Bill of Rights was enacted in Parliament, it would always be open to our judges to treat it as just another statute, subject to the same doctrine of implied repeal as any other legislation. It looks, in other words, as though there is no way of getting *behind* parliamentary sovereignty to alter the basis on which parliamentary power is exercised.

The difficulty is a real one, but we should not be too pessimistic about it. Some jurists have written as though it were a dilemma of logic, as though it would be simply *impossible* to entrench a Bill of Rights or anything like it in this country. But that is not so. I have said it would be open to our judges to take this negative approach, but there is nothing to imply that this is the approach they *must* take. The members of the judiciary might decide to treat our imagined 1994 Bill of Rights as authoritative and constraining; they might decide to strike down the 1996 ban as unconstitutional. If they did that, no doubt one or two diehard defenders of parliamentary sovereignty would write letters to *The Times* and articles in the *Law Quarterly Review* saying that they were mistaken and were exceeding their authority. But if the judges stuck to their guns and continued to strike down legislation that was incompatible with the Bill of Rights, and if officials and citizens continued to take notice of their decisions, then eventually we would have to say that the traditional doctrine of parliamentary sovereignty had disappeared.

In the last resort, as we have seen, the issue of legal sovereignty and the rule of recognition that lies at the basis of our legal system are a matter of what gets accepted and what rules get followed. If judges will not recognize laws that are incompatible with the Bill of Rights, and if officials refuse to follow or enforce those laws once the judges have declared them invalid, then we have no choice but to say that the rule of recognition has changed. Instead of it being the rule that 'whatever the Queen-in-Parliament enacts is law', the rule of recognition will now be 'whatever the Queen-in-Parliament enacts is law unless it infringes the Bill of Rights'. There will have been a quiet revolution in the basis of legal validity. We can see that as a possibility as soon as we become aware that, ultimately, legal validity is simply a matter of how citizens, officials, and agencies approach the traditional sources of law anyway. And that was the lesson we drew from the story of the Macmillan succession.[30]

The constitution as a framework for politics

In our discussion of structures and our discussion of constraint, the issue has been the balance of power in society. The aim of a constitution is to regulate that balance in a way that is regarded as fair and favourable to liberty, order, and responsibility as they are understood in the society. But there is also one other aspect of constitutionalism that is worthy of mention.

The idea of positive law, as it has emerged in these chapters, is the idea that we can make and remake our society and our politics more or less as we please. Of course, there are limits to our success: we may try to make Britain fairer or more prosperous and fail. But in principle there is nothing in the way we organize things that we cannot change (though we may not achieve what we were trying to achieve in doing so). If there is a statute we can repeal or amend it. If there is an institution, we can restructure it. We can have two parties or several parties, proportional representation or the plurality system, quinquennial or triennial elections, nuclear weapons or conventional weapons only, a welfare state or no welfare state, a poll tax or local rates, and so on.

That sense – that *everything* is up for grabs – can sometimes be unnerving. Partly this is the giddy sense of nausea that existentialists have pointed to: our fear of freedom. Partly it is the sense of disorientation that we mentioned in our discussion of the rule of law: if everything or anything can be changed, then people cannot plan and they do not know where they stand. But it is also partly a sense that we are never quite sure about the terms on which a political issue is being debated. We think we are talking about welfare and how to maintain the welfare state; but suddenly we are talking about Parliament and how its procedures obstruct radical initiatives. We think we are talking about taxation and the rating powers of local authorities; and suddenly we find that it has turned into a debate about whether central government should have the power to abolish metropolitan authorities. Since everything is up for grabs, any difficulty we have in pushing a particular proposal through some process can suddenly be transformed into a proposal to alter that process itself. And that, we may think, makes any particular political debate somewhat more fluid and evanescent than participants may want it to be.

One thing about a constitution is that it tries to redress that sense of the excessively mercurial character of politics. The idea is that certain aspects of the political process should be made stable and put somewhat beyond the challenge of ordinary politics, precisely so that there can be a known and predictable framework for substantial political debate. If we know that the electoral process cannot be challenged, then we know that a debate about radical economic policy is not suddenly going to turn into a debate about the validity of 'bourgeois' politics. And that may make it easier, not more difficult, to debate the economic policy in full, because the participants will share a common sense of what has to be shown, who has to be convinced, what sort of a majority has to be established and so on.

Of course, the framework for political action and discussion can never be put wholly beyond challenge – as we have seen, any invulnerability it has rests in the last resort on the common willingness of participants to respect the rules that surround it – nor should it. As circumstances change, it may be sensible to focus on and debate changes in the political process. The idea of a constitution is simply that there should be a deliberate and distinguishable way of doing this: deliberate and distinguishable in the sense that we know *when* that issue is being raised, and that it is not necessarily tangled or implicated in the discussion of every other issue we address. The shape and existence of the structure may be an issue, but it should be an issue that is clearly separable from the other great issues of politics.

I don't think this question of the need for a stable framework is the be-all and end-all of constitutionalism. The substantial need for constraints on power and for a proper balance between the state and the individual, which we discussed in previous sections, explains most people's concern about the lack of a clear and discernable constitutional tradition in the United Kingdom. But I think the uneasy feeling that everything is up for grabs at all times is also part of our suspicion about the balance of power. We are concerned about the power of the government or the majority, not only because there is no limit on the extent of their reach, but also because there is no limit on the type of decisions they may make. They may change the law of elections as easily as they change the traffic regulations; they may alter the structure of the courts as readily as they lower the rate of taxation. And that can leave us wondering whether there are any processes we can rely on in voicing our political concerns.

A written or an unwritten constitution?

Throughout this chapter, I have insisted that every constitution and every body of law rests on something that is, in the last resort, a matter of what gets *accepted* in a political system. There is no question of making everything explicit or putting everything in writing, for there would still be the issue of whether and why *that text* was taken as authoritative. Still, there is much less that is explicit in British constitutional law than in most other countries. So we need to consider, finally, the reasons for and against embodying at least some of our more important constitutional understandings – whether at the level of structure or constraint – in a more formal document.

There are two well-known arguments against doing this. People say that the *implicit* law of our constitution is more powerful, and also that it is more flexible and less dependent on the vagaries of textual interpretation than an explicit constitution would be.

Like many distinctively English doctrines, the idea that an implicit constitution is more powerful than an explicit one was put forward by A.V. Dicey. In Chapter Three, we discussed Dicey's version of the principle 'one law for all'. His view of the rule of law also covered another principle which sums up much of the hostility to Bills of Rights and the like in English thought:

We may say that the constitution is pervaded by the rule of law on the ground that the general principles of the constitution (as for example the right to personal liberty, or the right of public meeting) are with us the result of judicial decisions determining the rights of private persons in particular cases brought before the courts; whereas under many foreign constitutions the security (such as it is) given to the rights of individuals results, or appears to result, from the general principles of the constitution. There is in the English constitution an absence of those declarations or definitions of rights so dear to foreign constitutionalists.[31]

In logical terms, the claim that an Englishman has the right to liberty of the person arises *inductively* from all the decisions pronounced by courts on particular occasions when wrongful arrests have been challenged. In other countries (Dicey takes France and Belgium as examples), the inference works the other way round: the legislature proclaims an explicit principle of personal liberty, and the courts *deduce* particular decisions from that. Now, as it stands, this is not an important distinction. Provided liberty is equally well protected in both systems, it does not particularly matter whether we infer the right to liberty from a mass of court decisions or whether we base the decisions on some prior statement of the right. But Dicey saw two particular advantages in the English way of doing things.

First, if we infer our rights from actual court decisions, then we can be pretty confident that the rights are not mere *paper* rights but will actually be enforced. Since our rights are inferred from what the courts actually do, we do not hold out any expectations of protection that may later turn out to be groundless. The old maxim '*ubi ius ibi remedium*' (loosely translated: 'don't say there is a right unless there is a real procedure for enforcing it') counsels against any general abstract formulation of individual rights in a special charter set aside from the rest of the law:

[T]he Englishmen whose labours framed the complicated set of laws and institutions which we call the Constitution, fixed their minds far more intently on providing remedies for the enforcement of particular rights or (what is merely the same thing looked at from the other side) for averting definite wrongs, than upon any declaration of the Rights of Man or of Englishmen. The Habeas Corpus Acts declare no principle and define no rights, but they are for practical purposes worth a hundred constitutional articles guaranteeing individual liberty.[32]

The other advantage Dicey claimed was that it would be much more difficult for the English government to suspend civil liberties (in a political crisis, for example) than it would be, say, for the Belgian government:

> [W]here the right to individual freedom is a result deduced from the principles of the constitution, the idea readily occurs that the right is capable of being suspended or taken away. Where, on the other hand, the right to individual freedom is part of the constitution because it is inherent in the ordinary law of the land, the right is one which can hardly be destroyed without a thorough revolution in the institutions and manners of the nation.[33]

Is there anything in these arguments? My hunch is that Dicey's arguments work only if you accept that the principles in question *are* in fact embodied in our common law and the conventions of our constitution. If it is true that all this is implicit in the ethos of our legal and political practice, then it probably does offer more security to the citizen and is more difficult to overturn than the explicit text of a written charter would be. But people nowadays are much less complacent about that than Dicey was. In the next chapter, we shall raise a number of questions about common law protection for human rights. Certainly so far as broad principles of political structure are concerned, the legacy of our implicit constitution has been a facility in accommodating the requirements of centralized power rather than the robust embodiment of constitutionalist principles.

We can see this if we move to the second argument in favour of the British way of doing things – the argument about flexibility. The argument has some force, particularly when we contrast it with the American way of doing things. What happens there is that many of the great issues of public life are debated now by lawyers almost entirely within the narrow framework of the phraseology adopted by those who drafted the Bill of Rights almost 200 years ago. In Britain we can debate issues like abortion, religious tolerance, hanging, racial discrimination, and so on, in a flexible and open-ended way, experimenting with a variety of approaches and formulations, in the way morally sensitive people do when they are dealing with complex issues. In America, by contrast, the whole debate has to be oriented towards the interpretation of a particular text, so that what counts is whether a particular proposal can be squeezed under terminology like 'equal protection of the laws', or 'free exercise' of religion, or 'cruel and unusual punishments' and so on. The Americans have committed themselves to certain formulas and they have to make what they can of them; this lends a rather scholastic tone to many of their constitutional debates. With our less articulate heritage of constitutionalism, we can make what we please of our affection for rights or our desire for limited government.

Still, as we saw earlier, the existence of a potential for flexibility does not necessarily mean that potential is exploited in ways that are conducive to freedom or open government. Too often the flexibility of·our political system means that the concerns of our constitutional heritage are simply overlooked. Since Britain has failed to take advantage of the creative opportunity afforded by the implicitness of its commitment to freedom, it might be better off accepting the costs of a more text-bound approach. At least, on that approach, we would be less able to evade the issues at stake, and we would have a clearer shared sense of what exactly was at stake in the actions and organization of our government.

Anyway, we do not have to choose between explicit constitutional rules and 'implicit ways of doing things', any more than we have to choose between a Bill of Rights and the spirit of the common law. (The American experience shows that these last two are not mutually exclusive.) In any political system there is going to be a fairly loose fit between the official principles of constitutional structure and the way that the government of the country is actually carried on. Walter Bagehot introduced a famous distinction between the 'dignified' and the 'efficient parts of a constitution, the former being 'those which excite and preserve the reverence of the population' and the latter 'those by which it, in fact, works and rules'.[34] In England, the monarchy, the House of Lords, and increasingly the House of Commons (regarded as an independent centre of authority) are relegated to the 'dignified' category, while the Cabinet, Whitehall, and Downing Street might be regarded as the 'efficient' powers in the land. In America, a number of 'efficient' parts of the political system, like the political parties and their structures of primary elections, find no mention in the 'dignified' terms of the written constitution. This is what we should expect: political systems evolve much faster than the trappings of authority and legitimacy. The difference is that in Britain the evolution of political forms is relatively unconstrained, for even the 'dignified' rules are in the last resort just informal understandings, while in the United States there is necessarily constant reference back to the ideas and principles embodied in constitutional formulations. That may mean that the Americans are stuck with the frozen formulas of 1787. But at least there is something for them that can operate as a relatively constant point of reference for evaluating the course that political evolution is taking. In Britain, by contrast, the points of reference seem to be moving as well.

In all of this, I have tried to stress more the role that the provisions of a constitution can play in wider political debate – the way they serve as landmarks and rallying points in a fluid environment – rather than the actual constraints that they impose upon power. We must concede that a sufficiently powerful and determined group could always choose to treat a written constitution as nothing more than a useless piece of parchment and brush it aside casually with a bayonet. But political power is not like brute strength – something that people are born with. It is the ability to mobilize and retain the support of others, to get enough of them to go along with you, so you can overcome any other resistance. The provisions of a written constitution are unlikely to prevail in the face of potentially tyrannical power if that exists; but their currency among officials and in the wider population may make it less likely that such power can come into existence. If people are familiar with the formulated standards of constitutionalism, they have a given basis for thinking about them and talking about them – something they can hang on to apart from what anyone else says. There will not be the giddy sense that when political structure changes, the criteria for evaluating the operations of government change also, so that there is never anything constant in the norms of political life.

The job of a constitution is to provide a framework for politics. If we think of this purely in terms of a framework for government and administration – a framework that defines a *modus operandi* for the state – it may not matter much whether it is explicit or implicit, embodied in a written charter or in the shared understandings of political practice. But if we think of politics in the wider sense of political life and political debate, the need for an explicit framework is more evident. No formulation is ever perfect, for none can capture exactly and for all time the standards that we would want to deploy. But if there *is* a formulation, then there is something that can be used as a focus for interpretation and reinterpretation, and that itself will provide a landmark for common debate about the purposes and principles of political life.

Notes

1 Harold Macmillan, *At the End of the Day: 1961-1963* (London: Macmillan, 1973), p. 506.
2 The best account of the process so far as Butler was concerned is in

Anthony Howard, *RAB: The life of R.A. Butler* (London: Jonathan Cape, 1987), particularly Ch. 15.

3 Iain Macleod, 'The Tory Leadership', *The Spectator*, 7073, 17 January 1964, p. 66.

4 Macmillan, *At the End of the Day*, p. 515.

5. Macleod, 'The Tory Leadership', p. 66.

6 Paul Johnson, 'Was the Palace to Blame?', *New Statesman*, 715, 24 January, 1964 pp. 113–14.

7 Howard, *RAB*, p. 339 and p. 401 n. 39.

8 See the discussion in Geoffrey Marshall, *Constitutional Conventions: the Rules and Forms of Political Accountability* (Oxford: Clarendon Press, 1984), pp. 33–5.

9 There is an excellent survey of other similar principles in Marshall, *Constitutional Conventions*.

10 A.V. Dicey, *Introduction to the Study of the Law of the Constitution* (1886; 10th edition, London: Macmillan, 1967), Chapter XIV (emphasis added).

11 Marshall, *Constitutional Conventions*, p. 216 (emphasis added).

12 K.C. Wheare, *Modern Constitutions* (Oxford University Press, 1966), p. 179.

13 See Dennis Wrong, *Power: Its Forms, Bases and Uses* (Oxford: Basil Blackwell, 1979), Ch. 5.

14 H.L.A. Hart, *The Concept of Law* (Oxford: Clarendon Press, 1961), especially Chs. 5–6.

15 A full statement of the rule of recognition in Britain would have to say something about the common law and about judge-made law also. This is discussed more fully towards the end of Chapter six.

16 Similarly, the Austrian jurist Hans Kelsen has argued that every legal system logically presupposes the validity of something he called a *Grundnorm* or 'basic norm' – a rule which establishes procedures for the valid positing of other rules, but which is not itself validated by any more authoritative source. See Hans Kelsen, *The Pure Theory of Law* (Berkeley, Calif.: University of California Press, 1967). There is an accessible discussion in J.W. Harris, *Legal Philosophies* (London: Butterworths, 1980), Ch. 6.

17 S.E. Finer, *Five Constitutions: Contrasts and Comparisons* (Harmondsworth: Penguin Books, 1979), p. 15. (This is an excellent little book setting out and comparing the constitutions of Britain, France, West Germany, the USA, and the USSR.)

18 For this concern, see Alexis de Tocqueville, *Democracy in America* (1835; New York: Mentor Books, 1956), Part One, Ch. XV, p. 114. See also *The Federalist Papers* (1788; New York: Mentor Books, 1961), No. 10, and J.S. Mill, *On Liberty* (1859; New York: Bobbs-Merrill, 1956), Ch. 1.

19 Book III of Aristotle's *Politics* is still one of the greatest and most readable works of constitutional theory.

20 James Madison in *The Federalist Papers*, No. 51.

21 Second Reading of the Rates Bill, *Hansard*, January 17 1984. (The

quotation is from a speech by the former Conservative minister, Geoffrey Rippon.)

22 See the discussion in Chapter two, at footnote 6.
23 There is an excellent discussion in M.J.C. Vile, *Constitutionalism and the Separation of Powers* (Oxford: Clarendon Press, 1967).
24 I am grateful to Susan Sterett for this point.
25 This argument is hammered home in Nevil Johnston, *In Search of the Constitution* (Oxford: Pergamon Press, 1977), Ch. 3.
26 *Constitution of Japan*, 1946.
27 *Roe v. Wade* 410 U.S. 113 (1973).
28 Notice that the ECHR is distinct from the European Community; it is part of a different supra-national structure of law in Europe.
29 *Malone v. Metropolitan Police Commissioner* [1979] 1 Ch. 345.
30 There is a good discussion in A.W. Bradley, 'The Sovereignty of Parliament – in Perpetuity?', in Jeffrey Jowell and Dawn Oliver (eds) *The Changing Constitution* (Oxford: Clarendon Press, 1985).
31 Dicey, *Introduction to the Study of the Law of the Constitution*, pp. 195–6.
32 Ibid., p. 199.
33 Ibid., p. 201.
34 Walter Bagehot, *The English Constitution* (1867; Oxford University Press, 1952), p. 4.

Chapter five

Rights

The five techniques

It is time for some exercise. Find a wall and stand facing it. Raise
your arms above your head as high as you can, and place your
fingers against the wall. Spread your legs and move your feet back
away from the wall so that you are standing on your toes with the
weight of your body mainly on your fingers. Try maintaining this
posture for, let's say, five minutes.

In August 1971, a number of men were detained and brought by
the British Army to an unidentified interrogation centre in Northern
Ireland. There, for four or five days, they were required to spend
long periods in a room 'at the wall' in the posture just described.
They stood in this position for a total of between twenty to thirty
hours, and though it was not continuous, they sometimes spent four
hours at the wall at a time without interruption. If they tried to
move, sit down, sleep, arch their back, or rest their weight in some
other position, they were forced back into the posture by the
soldiers who were guarding them. If they collapsed they were lifted
up again. To add to the experience, they were made to wear dark
hoods over their heads, and were subjected to a continuous hissing
noise loud enough to mask any other sounds or speech. They were
not permitted to sleep during the two or three days that this went
on, and they were fed only a piece of bread and a cup of water
every six hours. Hooding, posture, noise, and deprivation of food
and sleep became known as 'the five techniques'.

From time to time, the hoods would be taken off, the noise
stopped, and the men permitted to sit down. They would then be
interrogated by police officers of the Royal Ulster Constabulary
(RUC). When the interrogations stopped, the five techniques would
begin again. And so on for two to three days. This 'interrogation in
depth' led to 'the obtaining of a considerable quantity of intelligence information, including the identification of 700 members of

[the Irish Republican Army] and the discovery of individual criminal responsibility for about 85 previously unexplained criminal incidents'.[1]

These events took place in the course of a massive detention and internment operation known as 'Operation Demetrios', conducted early in the morning of August 9, 1971 by the British army under the direction of the RUC Special Branch. In a very short space of time, the army arrested some 340 people suspected of involvement in, association with or knowledge of IRA activities. Many were released within forty-eight hours. The rest were detained and about a dozen of them were taken for 'interrogation in depth' using the five techniques. The policy of detention and interrogation without trial continued in various forms, and under the authority of various laws, until 1975.

The decision to launch 'Operation Demetrios' was taken against the background of a dramatic escalation of the level of terrorist violence in Northern Ireland during 1970 and 1971. Between January and July 1971, 304 bombs were detonated in the Province, including 94 in July alone. By 9 August, 13 soldiers, 2 policemen, and 16 civilians had died in bombings or shootings. No one denies that the IRA mounted the bulk of those attacks. The Northern Ireland Government (direct rule from Westminster was not introduced until 1972) came under great political pressure to 'do something' about this unprecedented terrorist campaign. The possibility of a sweeping internment operation had been canvassed for many months, and, although the authorities sought to avoid using special powers, it was clear that conventional methods of enquiry, arrest, and prosecution were yielding only limited intelligence and a very low conviction rate.[2]

The conduct of the security forces towards detainees was governed by general regulations prohibiting 'violence to life and person, in particular, mutilation, cruel treatment and torture' as well as 'outrages upon personal dignity, in particular humiliating and degrading treatment'. However, it was also official policy to seek information 'while it is still fresh so that it may be used as quickly as possible to effect the capture of persons, arms and explosives and thereby save the lives of members of the security forces and of the civil population'. An official document noted that 'information can be obtained more rapidly if the person being interrogated is subjected to strict discipline and isolation with a restricted diet'.[3] Experts thought the five techniques, sometimes also termed 'disorientation' or 'sensory deprivation' techniques, would contribute to the sense of discipline and isolation, as well as preventing contact between detainees and enhancing security in the holding centres.

Their use was authorized at 'high level' in the British government, and was taught to RUC officers by the English Intelligence Centre at a seminar held in April 1971.

As a result of what happened during that August, a number of detainees made complaints about the behaviour of the security forces. Some complained about 'the five techniques'; some alleged brtuality in the course of interrogation; and there were other allegations of unrelated assaults and deprivations during the initial arrests. Some complaints were made to the RUC at the time, or shortly after release; others circulated in British newspapers; and others were taken up by the government of the Republic of Ireland. On 31 August, the British Government set up a Committee of Enquiry to investigate under the chairmanship of Sir Edward Compton. Its report was published in November, and it concluded that, while there was no evidence of 'physical brutality, still less of torture or brain-washing', the use of each of the five techniques constituted 'physical ill-treatment' and it raised 'certain questions about the detailed application of the general rules governing inter-rogation'.[4]

The furore that followed the release of this report led quickly to the setting up of another Committee under the chairmanship of Lord Parker to consider 'whether ... the procedures currently author-ised for interrogation of persons suspected of terrorism ... require amendment'. The Parker Report concluded that the use of the five techniques would probably have been held unlawful under English law, but a majority of the Committee argued that the application of the techniques in the circumstances prevailing in Northern Ireland need not be ruled out on moral grounds. (A minority disagreed with that.)

After the Parker Report was published in March 1972, the British Prime Minister stated in Parliament that the Government 'having reviewed the whole matter with great care and with reference to any future operations, have decided that the techniques ... will not be used in future as an aid to interrogation'. Directives were immediately issued to the RUC and to the army specifically prohibiting further use of such methods.

In the meantime, the Irish Government had made application to the European Commission on Human Rights in Strasbourg, alleging that internment without trial and the British interrogation tech-niques violated human rights. The Commisssion is an agency set up under the European Convention on Human Rights (ECHR) to investigate petitions from individuals or member countries about violations in Europe of the rights laid down in the Convention, and to report its findings to the Committee of Ministers of the Council of Europe.[5] The Irish complaint related to a number of ECHR provisions including the right to liberty, a fair trial, and non-discrimination. Its most prominent complaint, however, concerned Article 3 of the Convention, which says simply:

> No one shall be subjected to torture or to inhuman or degrading treatment or punishment.

Article 15 provides that 'in time of war or other public emergency', a state may 'take measures derogating from its obligations under this Convention', and the Commission found that the British government did face such an emergency at that time. However, the ECHR expressly specifies that no derogation may be made from Article 3 under this exception; in other words, the prohibition on torture and inhuman treatment is absolute.[6]

When the Commission's report was published, the Irish government took the next step in the ECHR procedures and referred the report to the European Court of Human Rights for a formal determination that the United Kingdom had violated the Convention. Britain along with most other countries in Europe recognizes the compulsory jurisdiction of the court, and even allows its citizens to make individual petitions complaining of human rights violations.[7] We have already seen that British judges do not treat the ECHR as part of our law; but the government nevertheless usually accepts the decisions of the European Court of Human Rights as binding and responds accordingly.[8]

When Ireland moved to bring the case before the Court, the British government responded in an interesting way. Though it contested a number of the Irish claims and some of the Commission's conclusions, it conceded the justice of the complaint that was made under Article 3. Indeed Britain argued that the matter should not be brought before the Court, precisely because the complaint *had* been conceded and measures taken to prevent any recurrence of the abuses. The British Attorney-General gave the following formal and solemn undertaking before the Court:

> The Government of the United Kingdom have considered the use of the 'five techniques' with very great care and with particular regard to Article 3 of the Convention. They now give this unqualified undertaking, that the 'five techniques' will not in any circumstances be reintroduced as an aid to interrogation.[9]

The Court, however, insisted on entering a judgement, holding that it had a responsibility not only to decide cases brought before it, but 'more generally, to elucidate, safeguard and develop the rules instituted by the Convention, thereby contributing to the observance by the States of the engagements undertaken by them'.[10]

In fact, the Court came up with a judgement that was slightly less damning than the Commission's report. The Commission had condemned the use of 'the five techniques' as *torture*. But the Court felt differently:

> The five techniques were applied in combination, with premeditation and for hours at a stretch; they caused, if not actual bodily injury, at least intense physical and mental suffering to the persons subjected thereto and also led to acute psychiatric disturbances during interrogation. They accordingly fell into the category of inhuman treatment within the meaning of Article 3. The techniques were also degrading since they were such as to arouse in their victims feelings of fear, anguish and inferiority capable of humiliating and debasing them and possibly breaking their physical and moral resistance. [However] although their object was the extraction of confessions, the naming of others and/or information and although they were used systematically, they did not occasion suffering of the particular intensity and cruelty implied by the word torture.[11]

Still, torture or not, they were violations of Article 3, and judgement was entered against the British government accordingly.

Rights as moral constraints

I want to devote this whole chapter to the topic of *human rights* and their place in our legal and political morality. Over the past couple of decades, there has been a wide-ranging debate in Britain about the desirability of establishing a Bill of Rights, and every so often there are legislative initiatives along these lines. To date they have been unsuccessful. But the issue remains alive, particularly because of the influence that the ECHR has anyway in our politics.

So what is the argument for a Bill of Rights? What are human rights and why should they be taken seriously in politics? What are they based on? What values do they promote and what values (if any) do they threaten? These are the questions I want to discuss.

Let me begin with the ECHR and the ideals that that charter expresses. We have seen that the Convention sets up various institutions like the European Commission and the Court of Human Rights. But let's forget the institutional machinery for a moment; indeed let's forget the law, and just concentrate on the aspirations expressed in the document itself. What is it trying to say? What is the idea of human rights to which the signatory states (or, in the quaint language of the Convention, 'the High Contracting Parties') are committing themselves?

The basic idea that the ECHR expresses is that there are certain things (such as detention without trial, interference with privacy, or censorship of the press) that ought not to be done in the course of normal political life, and there are certain things in particular (such as torture) which ought not to be done at all, under any circumstances, whether in normal times or even in war or public emergency.

Stated in this way, these are moral ideas. They are normative claims about what should and should not happen, what a government should and should not do. They represent the moral commitments and concerns of those who framed and signed the Convention. For example, it was because they believed, morally, that torture and deliberate ill-treatment were always wrong, that they were prepared to draw up and ratify a document including something like Article 3. Now opinions might differ on this. Some people might think that torture is not always morally wrong, that it should not be ruled out in every circumstance in this sort of absolutist way. Since that is a possible challenge, we have to ask how the view embodied in the ECHR can be defended. *Why*, exactly, is no-one to 'be subjected to torture or to inhuman or degrading treatment'?

Some readers may think it strange that we have to give *reasons* for not torturing people, or that we have to give *reasons* for not interfering with other rights like freedom of speech, privacy, and personal liberty. Surely, they will say, the moral wickedness of torture and these other interferences is self-evident. Only monsters, tyrants, and bullies interfere with human rights in that way. The modern popularity of human rights is partly a response to the horrors and outrages that have afflicted the world in this century: Hitler's genocide of the Jews of Europe, Stalin's purges, massacres and terror-famines, and so on. Can't we take it for granted that everyone is against that sort of thing? The job of human rights is to prevent it from ever happening again. Why, then do we call for justifications? Reason and moral argument are not going to affect a Nazi. If we consider who the audience is when we are writing moral philosophy, is there anything here that needs to be defended? Anything that is seriously in dispute?

One useful thing about the Northern Ireland case is that it helps us respond to that impatience. Maybe some of the officers involved in Operation Demetrios were bullies and sadists. Maybe some of the officials who authorized the five techniques were 'little Hitlers' or bureaucrats who were too lazy and morally inept to distinguish right from wrong. But the fact that we have to recognize is this: most of those involved in the detention and interrogation of IRA suspects believed they were acting for the best. They knew they were facing a very difficult and dangerous situation, and they thought they were responding to it in the best way – the morally best way – they knew how. I don't just mean the soldiers who may have thought they had no alternative but to follow the orders they were given. I mean the people who planned the operation, commanded it, developed the interrogation techniques, taught them, authorized them and put them into practice. As far as we can tell, in August 1971, these people – who ranged from Cabinet ministers to RUC officers – thought they had no alternative. They couldn't think of any other way to stop the bombings and the shootings that seemed to be escalating out of hand.

We will not spend time here debating in any detail the Irish problem, the British responsibility for it, or the options open to the security forces. You don't have to be a supporter of British policy or an opponent of the IRA to understand the point of view of someone who believed honestly and in good faith that detention and 'interrogation-in-depth' represented the best response, or at least, the least bad response, to the crisis they were facing. In fact, the operation exacerbated the violence, rather than ameliorating it, and maybe that was predictable. But it yielded intelligence that gave the security forces a fuller knowledge of the IRA and enabled them to secure a large number of convictions.[12] We can imagine someone believing (even if we disagree with them, especially if our disagreement is based only on hindsight) that these benefits would outweigh the costs, that ultimately more harm would be prevented than occasioned by the operation. If a politician or a responsible official honestly believed this at the time that action was called for – honestly thought they knew a way to bring about a net reduction in the level of terror and suffering – what were they supposed to do? If they thought that ultimately more suffering would be prevented as a result of interrogation with the five techniques than would be involved in or occasioned by their use, then surely it was sound public policy – indeed, surely it was moral – to go ahead with the exercise in those circumstances?

It is in one way too easy, and in another way too difficult, to justify human rights as against tyrannical or sadistic exercises of power. It's too easy because everyone who wants to think in moral terms already agrees that power should not be abused in the way tyrants and bullies abuse it. And it's too difficult, because of course tyrants and bullies are usually unresponsive to moral argument, and uninterested in the sort of reasons that are laid out in literature like this.

The hard cases for human rights, the cases where moral argument *as such* really matters, are cases where there seem to be good moral reasons on both sides of the equation. Where lives might be lost if we don't put pressure on suspects under interrogation, there are moral reasons and respectable moral motivations pulling us both ways. If we are really concerned about human rights, we have to be prepared to stand by that concern in this sort of case as well; and we have to be prepared with reasons to convince an official acting in good faith that she must let people's lives be put at risk and let crime go unpunished if the only alternative to that is ill-treating a terrorist suspect.

Another way of putting this is to say that rights are *costly* for a community to uphold, and we shouldn't wonder that the representatives of the community sometimes try to avoid those costs. If we cannot put physical pressure on terrorist suspects during interrogation, then more lives may be threatened by the bombs their comrades have planted, and the job of the security forces made that much more difficult. Those are the costs of accepting that sort of prohibition. Similarly with other human rights. Respecting the right of free assembly may make it more difficult to run an orderly traffic system and may frustrate countless commuters, if week after week various protest groups want to march the serried ranks of their supporters with banners along the streets. If governments, courts, and other agencies are not allowed to restrict the freedom of the press, it may be more difficult to protect national security from various breaches of confidence, to protect juries from bias, or to implement controversial programmes. Since rights place limits on what we may do in the pursuit of public policy, they are inevitably going to be seen as irksome restraints by those who make policy and carry it out. Committing ourselves to individual rights is committing ourselves to forego the use of certain means in pursuit of our social goals; if those happen to be the most efficient means available, then the commitment to rights involves the social cost of having to pursue alternative means that may be less efficient, less reliable, and more cumbersome.

The implications of this point about the cost of rights have been spelled out by Ronald Dworkin:

> The institution of rights against the Government is not a gift of God, or an ancient ritual, or a national sport. It is a complex and troublesome practice that makes the Government's job of securing the general benefit more difficult and more expensive, and it

would be a frivolous and wrongful practice unless it served some point.[13]

If we expect our officials and politicians to respect individual rights, we have got to be prepared to articulate the values and concerns that underlie them. Otherwise, rights will be seen as mere nuisances, to be shoved aside as irrelevant in the pursuit of policy objectives. In the following section, I will try and say something about those underlying values and concerns.

Rights and respect for individuals

Social policy is supposed to be oriented towards the well-being of the whole society and everyone in it. But since different people have different interests, policies for society as a whole often involve striking a balance between the interests and wishes of different individuals and groups. As we pursue goals like prosperity, order, economic growth, and so on, we accept that some people will suffer losses while others benefit. For example, some people lose the enjoyment of their property when a new motorway or airport is built, and though they can use the new facility along with everyone else, they may sometimes still be left worse off overall in the long run. Similarly, in a campaign to maintain order in fraught circumstances like those of Northern Ireland, we may impose inconvenience on shoppers and motorists, requiring them to stop and be searched, and we may even have to detain some people who turn out to be innocent of any terrorist involvement and deprive them of their liberty while their credentials are checked. Very few social goals can be pursued without cost. And often some people bear more of the costs than others.

One way of looking at the idea of human rights is as follows. People who believe in rights believe that there are *limits* on the losses that any individual should have to bear in the pursuit of social policy; they believe that there are *limits* on the sacrifices that may reasonably be demanded of any person in society.[14] We must abandon any social goals that require us to impose losses or harms that exceed those limits. The job of declarations like the ECHR is to mark those limits and to caution us against transgressing them.

On this account, what went wrong in Operation Demetrios was that a policy of gathering intelligence about the IRA involved the imposition of an unacceptable level of harm on certain individuals – the suspects who had to be ill-treated if the information was to be obtained. No-one, according to the human rights view, should have to bear that much of a share of the costs of a nation's security policy. The officials and politicians should have abandoned that particular exercise rather than impose that level of harm on any individual.

Where do these limits come from and why do we believe in them? They cannot be regarded as God-given, for we no longer share the sort of consensus about divine revelation or natural law that would enable us to establish any claim about what God permits us to do to one another. The religious conception of 'natural' rights is no longer politically available.

One possible view is that our convictions are based on a deep *ethical* view about the respect we owe to one another in virtue of our common humanity, and in virtue of our potential to act morally. Individually and in our political life, we believe that people have got to be able to retain their dignity, their self-esteem, and at least the basic capacity to make a life for themselves in the society we are organizing. Human dignity is violated when someone is tortured, their home-life thrown open to surveillance, their culture denigrated, their political voice taken away, or their needs treated with indifference. You cannot do that to people and expect them to retain the basis of self-esteem that they must have in order to live a human life. If the price of prosperity, security, or social utility is that we deprive some people of this basic respect, then prosperity, security and utility cost too much.

Those ideas remind us that, though we tend to think of the community *as a whole* when we think about social policy, it is in fact composed of nothing but men and women each with their own life to lead, and it is ultimately *their lives*, considered one by one, that give community and social policy whatever moral importance they have. When we talk about imposing costs on people for the general good or the good of society, we are apt to think carelessly of some entity which transcends individual men and women and benefits from their sacrifices. But that is a mistake. As Robert Nozick put it:

> There are only individual people, different individual people, with their own individual lives. Using one of these people for the benefit of others, uses him and benefits the others. Nothing more.[15]

Because individuals are vulnerable to a government that has the power to require sacrifices of some for the sake of others, it is important to ensure that nobody is exploited as a pure resource for others. The philosopher Immanuel Kant stated the fundamental premise of morality this way: 'Act in such a way that you always treat humanity, whether in your own person or in the person of

another, always as an end and never simply as a means'.[16] The idea
of rights can be seen as an expression of that concern, for if
someone bears too great a share of social costs it will seem as if
he is being treated simply as a means and not respected as
someone who intrinsically matters in the great scheme of things.

The ideas just discussed may seem a little too *individualist* for
some people's taste; they stress the overwhelming importance of
the individual person at the expense of the community as a whole.
Theorists of rights are often accused of this – of denigrating
community, exalting egoism, and celebrating claims of the isolated
individual.[17] But we don't have to denigrate community in order to
see the importance of individual respect. Of course people grow up
and are nurtured in communities, and owe their community all the
social and cultural resources they use in developing their sense of
self. And it is true that the best life is a life led together with
others, in love, friendship, society, and political involvement. But a
person's dignity and self-respect still matter even as she joins with
others in making a common life. There is still a difference between
involvement and exploitation, between being loved and being used,
between free association and a sense of being trapped in a framework that is indifferent to one's fate. No plausible communitarianism can require us to ignore those differences.

The utilitarian argument against rights

The idea of human rights, I have said, is an expression of the
respect owed to each individual in the pursuit of social policy.
Some philosophers argue, however, that respect for the individual
is already embodied in the way social policy is formulated, and that
there is no need for any special constraint based on rights.

The most powerful view of this kind is *utilitarianism*. Utilitarians
say that the overall aim of social policy is to bring about the
greatest amount of happiness or satisfaction summed (and on some
versions averaged) over the whole population, and to minimize the
amount of suffering and dissatisfaction, again summed (or averaged)
across the whole population. Suppose we have to decide where to
site a new London airport. We look at the alternatives; we make a
list of everyone who will benefit from its being sited at location A
and how much they will benefit; we make another list of everyone
who will suffer from its being sited there and how much they will
suffer; we sum the amounts and take the second away from the
first. We do the same for location B and we choose the location that

will yield the highest positive balance of benefit over suffering. The point of this cost-benefit analysis is to make sure that the interests of everyone who is affected are taken into account. Everyone's benefit and everyone's suffering are treated equally, and nobody's interests are simply shoved aside as being of no consequence. Once we have taken everything into account, we use the only fair procedure that seems to be available – namely, to try to create the most benefit and the least misery we can. If we do this scrupulously and carefully, and a decision is reached which involves the imposition of a certain amount of hardship on some individuals, they can hardly complain that they are merely being *used*; because their interests and their hardship have been taken fully and fairly into account along with those of everyone else.

Utilitarianism is often decried as nasty or amoral, but here it is parading its merits as a theory of fairness and respect, denying that anything more in the way of human rights is required to capture the importance of those values.

The Northern Ireland case with which we began can be analysed in utilitarian terms. Those who planned Operation Demetrios were not hard-hearted brutes who thought the suffering involved in the detention and ill-treatment of prisoners didn't matter. They would agree that we must take account of that suffering and deprivation in our decisions about social policy. But they thought it should be balanced against the gains they were trying to achieve, or against the other suffering and deprivation that might result if the proposed policy was not adopted. We should be looking for the best overall result: the greatest net balance of good over evil, taking everything, including the suffering occasioned by our means, into account.

Indeed, utilitarians find it hard to imagine any other method of rational decision-making for such cases. Of course they are difficult, and we are pulled by our moral concerns in both directions. We don't want the suspects to be hurt; but we also don't want officials to stand idly by and let more people get blown up. We are going to feel bad whichever alternative is chosen. But if a choice has to be made, it seems crazy not to make it on the basis of the alternative which involves the least suffering in the long run. That, the utilitarians say, is fair. The trouble with the sort of commitment that we find in a document like the ECHR is that sometimes it requires us to choose the option which will lead to the *greater* amount of suffering overall. That extra suffering is real suffering too, for real people, and it is more suffering than necessary. What could possibly be the moral basis for that?

The distinction between acts and omissions

Before going on, it is worth mentioning one common response to the utilitarian argument. The dilemma we are discussing is the one that faced the security forces in Northern Ireland in August 1971: either (a) make use of the five techniques to obtain intelligence quickly from terrorist suspects, or (b) stand idly by while more explosions and sectarian assassinations are carried out. Both alternatives involve suffering that might have been avoided: under (a) there is the suffering of the suspects who have to endure the five techniques; while under (b) there is the suffering of those affected by terrorist outrages that might have been prevented if the five techniques had been used. The utilitarian argument compares the amount of suffering under each alternative, and choses the one that involves the least. But a common response is to say that the amounts of suffering here are not strictly comparable. If the government opts for alternative (a), it will actually be *inflicting* suffering on the suspects, whereas if it opts for alternative (b), the suffering that occurs will not be the result of any action by the government. The suffering occurring under alternative (b) will be a result of what the terrorists do if they are not prevented, and so the government is not responsible for it in the way that it is responsible for the suffering involved in the use of the five techniques. There is a difference, people say, between *doing something* and *letting something happen* – a difference between *action* and *omission*. And they accuse utilitarians of ignoring that morally relevant distinction.

The distinction between acts and omissions is often invoked when defenders of human rights face arguments from social utility. Utilitarians say that we have to take responsibility for *what happens* if we act in one way rather than another. Defenders of rights deny that and say that we are responsible not for everything that happens but only for the things *we do*. According to them, the idea behind human rights is that governments are prohibited from actively doing certain things to their citizens – torturing them, censoring them, and so on – and those prohibitions are not to be weighed against the possibility of preventing other bad things happening for which governments themselves are not responsible.[18]

That, as I said, is a common view of rights. Whether you find it persuasive will depend on what you think matters in morality. Suppose you are a conscientious RUC officer and you decide not to use the five techniques against the IRA suspects in your custody. You are convinced that some of these suspects have information about future attacks which you could prevent if you were to get the information by using the five techniques. But you refrain from doing that because it's immoral, and a few days later some more bombs go off with considerable injury and loss of life. What do you now say to yourself? I guess you have to say, 'Well that's too bad, but it was not my fault. I didn't detonate the bombs. To prevent them going off I would have had to have done something evil. My hands are clean of any wrong-doing in this whole filthy business'. If you think that what really matters in morality is that *you* should not do anything wrong and that suffering, however it comes into the world, should not be intentionally inflicted *by you*, then that will seem an adequate response. Your hands are clean and your moral integrity has not been compromised. The trouble is that this doesn't alter the fact that the bombs went off, innocent people were blown apart, and their loved ones are grieving. Surprisingly, perhaps, the fact that your hands are clean doesn't make any difference to that suffering. What might have made a difference to the suffering would have been your decision to use the five techniques to get information about the bombs before they went off. Since you avoided that decision in order to preserve your moral integrity, it's got to be the case that you think your moral integrity matters more in decisions like this than the suffering of others which your actions and compromises might have helped to prevent.[19]

The distinction between acts and omissions may make some sense in personal morality, where issues of conscience and integrity come to the fore. But it is hard to accept as an account of *political* morality. Though we want our politicians and officials to be good people, we don't want them to place greater weight on their own moral purity than on the welfare and suffering of those who are affected by their choices. That is partly because they are acting for all of us, not only on their own account. They have a responsibility to consider all the consequences of their decisions and to evaluate the difference that their choices make to the well-being of those committed to their care. They cannot simply say, 'We did not plant these bombs, so we are not responsible for preventing their detonation'. They have chosen to rule and to make decisions about the use of public power in a society where there are bad people and hard choices; having taken on that responsibility, they should not then be in the business of evading it in the interests of their own personal virtue. For all its nasty reputation, utilitarianism gives a somewhat more attractive account of the responsibilities of political office than the self-absorbed morality which distinguishes acts and omissions. So if human rights depends on the latter morality, they rest on rather unattractive foundations.[20]

Indirect utilitarianism

Is there any way of justifying human rights which does not rest on the acts/omissions distinction? There are some arguments that can be developed *within* the utilitarian approach.

Pursuing social utility is a complicated business, and involves delicate balancing and often imponderable calculations about the future. In making a decision, an official has to work out what the consequences of the various alternatives will be, and how far the goals of public policy will be promoted by the various choices available. Since the future is always uncertain, one is necessarily dealing with probabilities, and we all know that political decisions characteristically have consequences for human well-being that are simply unforeseeable at the time. Even if consequential calculations are possible, things can often go wrong. Officials may be blinded by prejudice or panic, and they may engage in wishful thinking or bias against a certain class of people. Under pressure to 'do something' in trying circumstances, a politician may produce a rationalization for a popular course of action without thinking through what its consequences really will be.

In some circumstances, the dangers of that sort of thing may be so great that it would be wiser simply to prohibit officials or politicians from relying on their own calculations about what the good of society requires. That is, it may be wiser on *utilitarian grounds* to prohibit them from making or trying to make utilitarian calculations. The general good may be better promoted by forcing them to follow some predetermined rule – some rule which will maximize utility in all but exceptional circumstances – than by letting them decide for themselves whether they are facing an exceptional case.

This approach is known as 'two-level' or 'indirect' utilitarianism.[21] Social utility remains our overall aim; but we think that aim may best be served in the fraught circumstances of human life by setting up principles about rights, and inculcating habits of absolute respect for them. Respecting those rights may sometimes lead us to overlook exceptional opportunities for advancing the general welfare (through the use of torture and so on). But we will still gain more utility overall if it leads us to avoid the costly mistakes that ignorance, panic, or bias might otherwise introduce into our moral and political decision-making. So it seems that a sophisticated utilitarian need not be an opponent of the introduction of right-based constraints.

This approach may apply particularly to policies that involve the *certain* infliction of suffering on some for the sake of the *possible* avoidance of suffering for others. That is exactly what was involved in the Northern Ireland case. If the five techniques are used, the suspects will certainly suffer the pain. *Maybe* that will be outweighed by the other suffering that we can avoid if we get the information out of them. But we don't *know* if we can get the information, or if we will be able to act on it in time, or what the longterm consequences of the policy will be. All we know for sure is that the suspects will suffer. Now the security forces in Northern Ireland are under very great stress and danger, and will often be tempted to lash out at those they suspect of being terrorists or to treat them as though their suffering mattered less than that of their own comrades or the civilians they are trying to protect. Under the peculiar pressures that they face, members of the security forces will sometimes be tempted to exaggerate the advantages and to underestimate the dangers of a policy of torturing suspects. So perhaps the general welfare will be better promoted by a comprehensive ban on torture in all circumstances than by allowing security officers to make decisions about what would serve the general good on a case-by-case basis.

You can probably work out similar arguments for many of the constraints laid down in a document like the ECHR. Maybe there are times when the suspension of freedom of the press and civil liberties is justified on utilitarian grounds. But we know that those are likely to be tense and dangerous circumstances, and we know also that those in power may be motivated by their resentment of political criticism as much as by any impartial consideration of the general good. We may think it wiser, then, on utilitarian grounds, to lay down rules prohibiting such people from making what purport to be utilitarian decisions about the suspension of these safeguards.

What's wrong with utilitarianism?

Yet some of our unease about utilitarianism is not merely about the reliability of official calculations of utility, but about the utilitarian calculus itself. As we saw, it claims to be a fair way of balancing individual interests against one another. But is it really fair?

One problem with the utilitarian approach to social decision-making is that it weighs and measures everything on exactly the same scale. In examining the costs and benefits of Operation Demetrios and the use of the five techniques, a utilitarian would have to balance the suffering of the suspects against a wide array of possible benefits ranging from the prevention of further injury and loss of life, through the lessening of inconvenience to ordinary inhabitants of the province because of an improvement in security, to the satisfaction of the wishes of those Protestant citizens and politicians who were crying out that 'Something must be done!'. All those would count as benefits in the great social calculus, and the question would be whether, added together, they amounted to enough to outweigh the costs that the use of the five techniques would involve.

Now one can understand the case for weighing injury and suffering that might be caused by an 'interrogation-in-depth' against the injury and suffering that might be thereby prevented. The two harms seem roughly commensurable, however difficult the decision to trade off one against the other might be. But should we be in the business of balancing the suffering and ill-treatment of suspects, on the one hand, against the mere political dissatisfaction of citizens, on the other? Are those two sorts of harm even in the same league?

Try another example. Imagine a society which is religiously homogenous except for one small but highly active dissident sect. The existence of that sect is an irritant to the majority faith; it makes the majority feel uncomfortable. The majority wish that the dissident sect would disappear or at least cease its irritating proselytism. So a political proposal is made and defended on utilitarian grounds: the sect is to be banned from any further activity in the society; they will not be allowed to worship or proselytize. When members of the sect hear about the proposal they complain about the harm they will suffer in no longer being able to worship God in their own way. Those who defend the proposal concede that, but they say it is outweighed in the social calculus by the pleasure and satisfaction gained by the overwhelming majority. Comfort for a hundred million, they say, is obviously worth securing if the cost is nothing more than the religious freedom of a tiny handful.

What has gone wrong here? The problem is that comfort and religious freedom are being weighed on the same scale, so that if the numbers of people involved are large enough on one side, the former will outweigh the latter. Our misgiving about utilitarianism and similar approaches to social policy is that we don't accept that they *should* be weighed on the same scale. There are some interests that individuals have that matter much more than others. The interest in life and the basic freedoms, for example, are more important than ordinary convenience or mundane satisfaction. Now, if that is treated as merely a difference in quantity – saying, for example, that *more satisfaction* is lost when a life is taken than when someone is deprived of comfort – then everything will depend on the numbers. One person's life will matter more than one person's comfort, but maybe not more than the comfort of ten thousand people. My feeling is that we want to say there is a *qualitative* difference here, and that you cannot express the value of a life or of some basic liberty in terms of any finite quantity of mundane satisfaction. If that is so, then we should treat issues of life, death, and basic freedom, for example, as issues that stand apart from, and have priority over, ordinary issues of utility. When any of those particularly important individual interests are at stake, we should look to them first, and only attend to matters of comfort, convenience and satisfaction once we have taken care of the more urgent considerations.[22]

I find that an attractive account of the priority accorded to individual rights. We call *rights* those interests which should not simply be thrown into the social calculus along with everything else. Our rights represent the interests that should be dealt with first, before the ordinary social calculus comes into play. When people disagree about what rights we have, we now know what they are arguing about. They are debating which interests should be left to the mercy of the ordinary social calculus and which should be given priority over it.

This view does not imply that rights are absolute. It leaves open the possibility that the rights of some may conflict with the rights of others, and that when that happens we shall have to sort it out, again using a balancing process. If it really seems that the only way to prevent death and injury for some is to inflict ill-treatment on others, then we will have to consider our choices very carefully to see how we can best respect all the morally important interests that are at stake. But the balancing of rights against one another is not be be confused with the balancing of rights against more mundane satisfactions. There are two levels of moral calculation involved, and respect for the specially important interests that may be at stake in these decisions requires that they be kept apart.[23]

Rights and democracy

Till now we have been considering the morality embodied in documents like the ECHR. We have said that politicians are likely to commit themselves to human rights only if they believe that there are limits on the costs that people should be expected to bear in the pursuit of social policy, and we have explored some of the grounds of that belief.

But the ECHR is not just a moral doctrine: it is also an institution that has a legal and political life of its own. There is the Convention itself, and there is the Commission, the Court, and the Council of Ministers: they make judgements and reports about alleged violations and people and governments respond to those judgements. It is true that the ECHR does not play the role in our legal and political system that, for example, the Bill of Rights plays in America. Still, as it happens, the British government does take notice of the reports of the Commission and the judgements of the Court, and it has invariably (though not always ungrudgingly) adjusted its policies and practices to take account of them.[24] It allows individual citizens to petition the court once domestic remedies are exhausted. It contributes to the cost of the ECHR system, and allows British judges to be appointed to the court. And increasingly, it makes policy and designs regulatory schemes using the ECHR as a background constraint. You could say that we have developed a convention in our constitution that we will defer to the ECHR. It is not a principle that can be vindicated in our courts, but, as we saw in Chapter four, that puts it in very good company so far as British constitutional law is concerned.[25]

If we were to enact a Bill of Rights in Britain or incorporate the ECHR more directly into our law, we would have to face another set of moral issues over and above the ones we have discussed in the previous sections. We would have to deal with questions about the relation between rights and democracy.

A Bill of Rights on the American model is a way of preventing the majority or their representatives from doing some of the things that they want to do. What is the justification for that? How can that be right if we believe in democracy and majority rule? Indeed the question arises even with the ECHR, for, as we have seen, the elected government of this country *does* feel it has to defer to the Convention or at least to the judgements of the court that interprets it. There was probably widespread popular support for a policy of interrogation-in-depth of IRA suspects. Still, the government felt it had to defer to the court rather than to the will of the people. So even without the explicit enactment of a Bill of Rights we seem already to be making compromises with democracy.

In essence the argument from democracy goes as follows. When the members of a society disagree about what ought to be done, what policies followed, what means pursued for what ends, there has got to be some way of resolving the disagreement or society will be paralysed. If one side cannot persuade the other, the fairest way seems to be to adopt the view that the majority favours. That way, everyone's views are counted equally, and what determines the outcome is not any doctrine of the innate superiority of one group of citizens over any other, but simply the preponderance of opinion among all those who are affected. Of course, pure majoritarianism may be impracticable in a large society facing complex issues, and maybe elite decision-making is unavoidable. Still, at the very least, fairness to everyone requires us to set up procedures (such as the election of representatives) which allow policy choices to be responsive to the majority view if there is one. The trouble with an institution like the ECHR is that it dictates decisions on grounds which are not sensitive to majority opinion. Policies are laid down or ruled out on the basis of whether they conform with the interpretation of some written principles of right rather than with the view of the people. And that, the argument concludes, is unfair to the people.

The argument assumes, of course, that even without the ECHR, British politics would be democratic and that there would still be genuine opportunities for accountability and for the expression of the popular will. As we saw in Chapter two, we may want to take issue with those assumptions. Maybe the argument from democracy isn't as strong in the real world as it is in political theory. Even so, the proper remedy is surely to repair and reform the democratic process itself rather than rely on rules about human rights. For all we know, taking decisions on the basis of those rules may make matters worse so far as democracy is concerned.

In the USA, people take the argument from democracy very seriously because the underlying values of the political culture are emphatically democratic, and it is difficult to reconcile those values with the Supreme Court's power to strike down enacted statutes without regard to their popular support. A state legislature may pass a bill, for example, prohibiting abortion, and that prohibition may remain on the statute books because legislators know that any attempt to repeal it would meet with vociferous opposition from a majority of their constituents. But if it is challenged in litigation, a court may rule it unconstitutional because it conflicts with women's individual rights to privacy.[26] And though that very argument about the right to privacy may have been canvassed among voters and legislators when the bill was originally passed, the courts will not pay any attention to the way the voters and legislators resolved the argument. Rather, the judges will impose their own opinion on the merits of the argument.

What makes defenders of democracy so angry about the enforcement of rights as constitutional *constraints* is that, in effect, the view of a few judges is being substituted for those of millions of citizens. Every political community has got to reach decisions on moral issues like abortion; but the problem with rights is that they stand in the way of that decision being reached by the collective determination of the people whose lives are ultimately going to be affected by the law. A Bill of Rights gives one side or the other what must sometimes seem like the unfair and autocratic advantage of having the judges on their side.

In Britain such issues are decided through the process of representative democracy, imperfect though it is. There is a continuing public debate on abortion, for example, and MPs seem sensitive both to the moral arguments and to the extent to which their constituents are persuaded by them. Legislation is passed and altered from time to time, and an MP's views on the matter will be a factor that constituents use in their decision about whether to vote for him or her. The process does not guarantee morally ideal results; it could certainly be improved; and it cannot satisfy everyone. But it represents an attempt by the community to articulate a collective decision on the issue, and, for all its imperfections, it is preferable (so the democratic argument goes) to the imposition of a solution by the small elite who would be involved in the drafting and interpretation of a constitution. That, I think, is what people are getting at when they say that a Bill of Rights, applied on the American model, would unacceptably undermine the sovereignty of Parliament. It is not that the House of Commons has an inherent dignity that must be upheld at all costs. The point is rather that what people do in that chamber and how they are influenced by their constituents should be cherished as our way of deciding hard moral issues together. It should not be cast aside in the name of an ideal of rights that will interfere with this way of expressing our will and our decisions as a community.

I have stated the argument from democracy as strongly as possible, for it is an argument that defenders of constitutional rights must take seriously and which they must be prepared to answer. People fought long and hard for democratic representation. They wanted the right to rule themselves and make decisions together about the content and structure of their laws. Though phrases like 'the tyranny of the majority' and 'the majority is not always right' trip easily off the tongue, and though there is certainly a lot of truth in them, still we had better be sure that we know exactly *why* we are prepared to brush aside the democratic process in cases where some of us think our moral intuitions would be vindicated by judges' enforcing a charter of rights, against the decision of a majority of our fellow-citizens.

In addressing this issue we need to remember one other thing. When people vote for policies or representatives they are not simply expressing their own preferences or anticipating their own satisfactions. (If they were, then rights against the majority would be justified roughly in the way in which we justify rights against general utility.) But that is far too crude a model of voting. Often when they vote (or lobby or put pressure on their representatives), individual citizens actually take human rights into account; they express their considered moral views about what the rights of the individual require. If we allow a judge's opinion about human rights to prevail, we have to face the fact that we will sometimes be allowing the judge's opinion to override the voters' opinions *about rights*, for the voters may have been expressing their judgement on the very thing the judge is making a decision about. Judges aren't the only ones capable of moral deliberation; and their legal training is certainly not a unique qualification for that task. Ordinary men and women and their representatives are capable of thinking (and voting) morally as well.

After all, people can disagree about rights, and disagree in good faith, without lapsing back into self-interested preferences. Though they are often expressed in simple slogans, human rights are not a simple matter. There are endless disputes about what counts as torture, whether pornography is free speech, what's required for a fair trial, which rights can be overridden in a public emergency, what counts as a public emergency, how conflicts of rights are to be resolved, and so on. Think about the issue of abortion. Do foetuses have rights and, if they do, how they do they weigh against a woman's right to control her own body? These are awfully difficult issues on which honest disagreement is more or less inevitable. When such disputes crop up, how are they to be decided? I don't think we should rule out the possibility of their being decided by democratic means; and if that happens, the democrat has got to be prepared to abide by the majority decision *about human rights* even when he thinks that the majority have made the wrong moral decision.

So, just because you believe in rights doesn't mean necessarily that you believe in constitutional constraints on democracy. A belief that rights are important doesn't entail a belief that a Bill of Rights is desirable. You may think that rights ought to be taken into account by citizens and representatives when they decide how to vote. But once the votes have been cast, society should act on the view that commands majority support. If we repudiate the judgement of the majority and substitute the judgement of a court, then that seems not only unfair to all the people who argued and voted but an insult to their capacity to weigh and consider moral arguments.[27]

Rights as part of democracy

When we considered the issue of rights versus utility, we examined the arguments of the 'indirect' utilitarians who believed there might be good pragmatic reasons within the utilitarian tradition for acting as though people had rights. Maybe there is a similar sort of defence for human rights to be found within the democratic tradition.

Democracy itself requires some human rights. We don't have a democracy unless people have the right to vote; and presumably it becomes a travesty if there is not also freedom of speech, freedom of the press, freedom of association, and freedom to organize and agitate. Without these, there certainly cannot be the sort of moral debates among the people that we envisaged in the previous section. To protect these rights, then, is to uphold democracy, not to undercut it. They are a way of preventing majoritarian democracy from undermining its own institutions.

But not all human rights are constitutive of democracy in this way, and the approach works less well with things like the right to religious freedom, the right to travel and emigrate, the right to marry, the right to privacy, and our old friend Article 3, the right not to be tortured. Maybe, though, it depends how generously you interpret the idea of democracy. It begs the question simply to equate democracy with respect for human rights – that's just wishing away the dilemma. But we may think that democracy means a little more than merely the formalities of voting. It means that all sides of all important issues are aired in public debate and that anyone affected by a policy or a policy proposal has a chance to bring their concern to the attention of their fellow citizens. It presupposes that people are in a position to participate in public debate, and that means they must have the time and the resources to do so. It means that representatives bear in mind the interests of their constituents when they make their decisions and that they are responsive to a variety of forms of political pressure. And it means that laws, policies, and political structures are at least open to change so that it is never institutionally hopeless for someone to propose a scheme of radical reform. So even if they are not constitutive of democracy in a formal sense, some of the other human rights may be necessary to ensure that all groups in society have a voice that will be heard in the democratic process, and the standing and power in the community that requires others to deal with them in the political process as equals.[28]

Similar points may be made about the role of courts in upholding constitutional constraints on the democratic process. We can, if we like, see courts as unrepresentative elites imposing their own convictions about human rights (or the convictions of those who, long ago, drafted the provisions that they are interpreting). But we can also see them as participants – indeed, leading participants – in national political debates. Sometimes their decisions force citizens to confront issues and concerns that they may not have been facing up to honestly or coherently. Though we talk glibly about democracy and the emergence of a majority view, we should remember that political debate among the people is not always something that simply *happens*. Sometimes, the impetus comes from the people themselves and arises out of their experience and concerns. But often what happens is that a subject is first raised by some small interest group or pressure group and only becomes a real issue for national political debate when the rest of the community is forced somehow to take notice of it. This may happen through skilful politicking, or as a result of symbolic protest or mass demonstrations which are difficult to ignore. That, for example, is how CND and other peace groups in Britain and Europe forced the issue of disarmament on to the national agenda. And in a system where there is something like a Bill of Rights, it may also happen through litigation. An issue which might otherwise have remained a marginal minority concern can be forced on the attention of society as a whole by being brought before a court and related to some human rights provision that enjoys widespread support, at least as an abstract proposition. The clearest case of this is the campaign in the 1950s and 1960s for civil rights and desegregation in the United States. Without a Bill of Rights, the issue of school desegregation might have remained an irritant of local politics in the South. By bringing it before the Supreme Court and by raising questions in that forum about whether segregation was compatible with the constitutional guarantee of 'equal protection', civil rights leaders were able to initiate a campaign and a debate that changed the face of racial politics in America.[29]

Are rights the price of democracy?

Though these arguments are available, it is unlikely in the end that we will be able to justify everything we want to say about human rights without stepping beyond the limits of democratic theory. That should not surprise us. There is no reason to think that everything we want to say about human rights has to be justified in the same theoretical terms.

Ultimately it may be important to concede that some human rights – again, Article 3 of the ECHR springs to mind – operate simply as constraints on democratic decision-making. They represent the outer limits on what we are prepared to see done to people merely because the majority say so, a ceiling on the costs we are prepared to impose on any individual or group merely because the majority desire to pursue a certain policy. There are good pragmatic reasons for that as well as the moral reasons we developed earlier.

Accepting the principle of majority rule involves a frightful risk for any individual or group. Politics is the sphere of power: it is where decisions are taken about the use of social force and the allocation of all the values society has under its control. To lose a political disagreement may be to see things you value disappearing; it may involve seeing your own well being and that of those you care about dramatically cut away, and in some countries it may be to expose youself to prison or death. Now if there is nothing you can do about it, then those dangers must simply be accepted stoically. But agreeing to majority rule means that, if you lose the debate, you accept the majority decision even though you believe you might have a chance of reversing or resisting it by force. Most people are probably willing to do that on many issues if only for the sake of peace and order. But maybe not on all issues. Maybe people will submit to majority rule only on condition that they are given guarantees that they will not be called upon to sacrifice certain very basic interests of theirs in the course of the democratic process.

It is pretty clear, for example, that something along these lines explains the prominence of religious liberty in most charters of human rights. People take their religious faith very seriously, and they know that in the past (would that it were *only* in the past!) dissident minorities have been required, on pain of penalties and disqualifications, to repudiate their beliefs and toe the orthodox line. Often this is something they have not been willing to put up with for the sake of social peace; where they have had a modicum of power, dissidents have fought bravely and to the death to be able to worship and profess what they believe in. It is understandable, then, that the development of modern democratic politics should be predicated on a guarantee that this interest – in religious practice – would be safeguarded. It is predicated, in other words, on a recognition that people would simply be unwilling to submit to any form of political decision-making that did not provide this as a baseline.

Modern doctrines of human rights can be seen partly as a generalization of that approach. Pragmatically, we want to ask: 'What guarantees must be given to keep the allegiance of all groups in society, to prevent secession and civil war?' And in moral and political philosophy, theorists ask themselves: 'What conditions would people insist on if they were designing a new social structure for a future life together?'[30] No-one believes of course that any actual society is ever set up and designed in the deliberate way envisaged in this 'social contract' fantasy. But it is a good question to ask none the less, because it forces us to scrutinize the price that various groups and individuals are forced to pay and the costs they are required to accept for the sake of our social policies and the maintenance of our social framework. We cannot start over and design a new society, but we can ask whether the price we are exacting from minority groups – blacks, mothers, the poor – is a price that they would have agreed to accept voluntarily as a condition of life in society. If the answer is 'no', then the justification for actually imposing that cost on them starts to look shaky. It is just our good fortune that we haven't had to secure their consent to the arrangements that we expect them to live with – it is our good fortune that we can sustain those arrangements by force or fraud or indoctrination – because if we had had to secure their consent, the social contract argument shows that we wouldn't have got it. And that must tell us something about the morality of our society.

Notes

1 *Ireland v. United Kingdom*, The European Court of Human Rights, Judgement of 18 January 1978, paragraph 98. My description of the techniques is taken from paragraphs 96–104 of this judgement, and also from paragraphs 46–105 of the Home Office 'Report of the enquiry into allegations against the security forces of physical brutality in Northern Ireland arising out of events on the 9th August, 1971' (*The Compton Report*) Cmnd. 4823. That the techniques were used and for the periods described was conceded by the British Government. Detainees also alleged that they were beaten and abused in other ways; these were not conceded, and it proved impossible to determine their truth.

2 It is worth noting that Operation Demetrios did not in fact diminish the violence; on the contrary it sparked a violent and riotous reaction in the Catholic community and an escalation of the IRA campaign. Between August and December 1971, another 146 people were killed in 729 explosions and 1,437 shooting incidents.

3 Quoted from an official British Government note included in the *Compton Report*, paragraph 46.

4 *Compton Report*, paragraphs 14 and 92–6.

5 The European Commission on Human Rights, the European Court of Human Rights, and the Council of Europe are a set of institutions quite

distinct from the courts, parliaments, and commissions of the European Community. Many more states are signatories to the ECHR than are members of the EC.

6 The term 'absolute' describes a rule or principle that has no exceptions and is intended to apply in all circumstances. Sometimes the term also means 'objective', but that is a different idea.

7 Though individual people have the right to complain to the Commission, only the Commission or one of the signatory states has the right to bring a case before the European Court. The Commission operates as a sort of investigating magistracy so far as the Court is concerned.

8 Not all European governments take this approach. After a decision of the Commission in 1969 that the government of Greece (the dictatorship installed in 1967) had been guilty of torture and ill-treatment of political detainees, Greece denounced the Convention and withdrew from the Council of Europe. (It was re-admitted, and it re-ratified the ECHR after the fall of the dictatorship in 1974.)

9 *Case of Ireland v. the United Kingdom*, paragraph 154.

10 *Case of Ireland v. the United Kingdom*, paragraph 154.

11 *Case of Ireland v. the United Kingdom*, paragraph 167.

12 This claim is controversial; my evidence is paragraphs 20–1 of the majority findings and paragraph 14(a) of the minority findings in the *Parker Report*. Of course, all we know is that the information was obtained; we do not know how much might have been obtained using more humane methods.

13 Ronald Dworkin, *Taking Rights Seriously* (London: Duckworth, 1977), p. 198.

14 If we believe in group rights, we will want to say the same about groups. For example, we may say that no ethnic group should have to suffer the extinction of its language as a necessary cost of wider social policy. See my article, 'Can Communal Goods be Human Rights?' *Archives européennes de sociologie*, 27 (1987).

15 Robert Nozick, *Anarchy, State and Utopia* (Oxford: Basil Blackwell, 1984), p. 33.

16 This is the Second Formulation of Kant's 'Categorical Imperative'. It is set out in his book, *Groundwork of the Metaphysic of Morals*, translated by H.J. Paton under the title *The Moral Law* (1785; London: Hutchinson University Library, 1961), pp. 95–6.

17 See for example Karl Marx, 'On the Jewish Question' (1843), in my collection *Nonsense Upon Stilts*: *Bentham, Burke and Marx on the Rights of Man* (London: Methuen, 1987), p. 146. On pp. 183–209 of that volume, I defend human rights against these charges; that argument is briefly summarized here.

18 Philosophers describe this as treating rights as 'side constraints' on action. The most famous recent proponent of this view of rights is Nozick in *Anarchy, State and Utopia*, pp. 28–51.

19 The distinction between acts and omissions is criticized at length in Jonathan Glover, *Causing Death and Saving Lives* (Harmondsworth:

Penguin Books, 1977), Ch. 7, and Ted Honderich, *Violence for Equality* (Harmondsworth: Penguin Books, 1980), Ch. 2.

20 My argument here echoes Max Weber in W. Gerth and C. Wright Mills (eds) *From Max Weber: Essays in Sociology* (London: Routledge & Kegan Paul, 1970), esp. pp. 114–28.

21 R.M. Hare is the best known defender of 'indirect' utilitarianism. See his article 'Ethical Theory and Utilitarianism' in A. Sen and B. Williams (eds) *Utilitarianism and Beyond* (Cambridge University Press, 1982), esp. pp. 30–8, and his book *Moral Thinking: Its Method, Levels and Point* (Oxford: Clarendon Press, 1981), Chs. 2, 3, and 9. Sometimes this approach is called 'rule-utilitarianism', but that is a mistake. (Rule-utilitarianism is a now discredited theory that urged us to follow the rules which *would* maximize utility *if* everyone were to follow them, whether everyone is in fact following them or not.)

22 To use some jargon made popular by John Rawls in *A Theory of Justice* (Oxford University Press, 1971), pp. 42–4, we give the urgent interests 'lexical priority' over the non-urgent ones. See also T.M. Scanlon, 'Rights, Goals and Fairness' in Jeremy Waldron (ed.) *Theories of Rights* (Oxford University Press, 1984).

23 Ronald Dworkin has developed a slightly different argument about the need to separate some interests from others in the utilitarian calculus. He worries that a utilitarian will try to satisfy not only preferences that people have for themselves, but also their preferences about how others should be treated. A racist, for example, not only wants certain benefits for herself; she also wants some benefits to be denied to blacks, and *that* preference – that blacks get less – counts as much in the utilitarian calculus as any other. A theory which allows that to happen looks very unattractive as a basis for political morality, for it leaves some people's welfare at the mercy of what others think of them. So, Dworkin argues, if we think that an individual interest is in danger of being outweighed in the social calculus by this sort of preference, we should give that interest special priority as a matter of right. (This argument is developed in Dworkin, *Taking Rights Seriously*, pp. 232–9 and 274–8, and in his article 'Rights as Trumps' in Waldron (ed.) *Theories of Rights*.)

24 Examples include reforms in mail censorship in prisons, in immigration procedures, and in committals to mental institutions.

25 Legally and politically, the ECHR occupies a position intermediate between that of the American Bill of Rights and a charter like the 1948 Universal Declaration of Human Rights (UDHR). Though the UDHR is associated with the institutional apparatus of the United Nations, it does not operate as a body of law nor is it as politically efficacious as the ECHR appears to be (except that, of course, the ECHR was inspired by the UDHR). The reality of the UDHR is ideological and political rather than legal: it provides a common discourse of rights and a rallying point for those involved in political campaigns.

26 The case is *Roe v. Wade* 410 US 113, decided by the American

Supreme Court in 1973, striking down prohibitions on abortion in the Texas Penal Code.

27 There is an expanded version of this argument in my article 'Rights and Majorities' in J.R. Pennock and J.W. Chapman (eds) *NOMOS XXXII: Majorities and Minorities* (New York University Press, 1988).

28 This approach has been developed at length, for American constitutional law, in John Hart Ely, *Democracy and Distrust: A Theory of Judicial Review* (Cambridge, Mass.: Harvard University Press, 1980).

29 I am grateful to Susan Sterett for emphasizing to me the role courts play in the initiation and enhancement of democratic debate.

30 The most powerful modern work in this genre is John Rawls, *A Theory of Justice* (Oxford University Press, 1971). There is a good overview of Rawls's approach in pp. 3–22 of that book.

Chapter six

Judges

The 'Fares Fair' case

'Within six months of winning the election, Labour will cut fares on London Transport buses and tubes by an average of 25%.' The Labour Party made that commitment in its manifesto for the 1981 elections to the Greater London Council (GLC). It won the election and within six months bus and tube fares were reduced as promised. The move necessitated an increase in the rates (i.e. property taxes) levied on the London boroughs, and one of those boroughs, Bromley (a Conservative controlled council), brought an action in the High Court to challenge the decision. The GLC did not take the challenge very seriously, and were not surprised when the High Court judge rejected the Bromley application.

A few weeks later, the Bromley council appealed, and three judges sitting in the Court of Appeal reversed the original decision and upheld the Bromley challenge. The judges condemned the fare reduction as 'a crude abuse of power', and they quashed the supplementary rate that the GLC had levied on the London boroughs to pay for it.[1] The GLC appealed to the House of Lords, the highest court in the land, but to no avail.

The Law Lords held unanimously that the GLC was bound by a statute requiring it to 'promote the provision of integrated, efficient *and economic* transport facilities and services in Greater London', and they interpreted this to mean that the bus and tube system must be run according to 'ordinary business principles' of cost-effectiveness. The Labour council, they said, was not entitled to lower the fares and increase the deficit of London Transport in order to promote their general social policy, and they were certainly not entitled simply to shift a large percentage of the cost of travel in London from commuters to ratepayers.

The fact that the policy had been announced in advance and had secured majority support, carried little weight with the courts.

According to the Law Lords and the judges in the Court of Appeal, members of the GLC should not have treated themselves as 'irrevocably bound to carry out pre-announced policies contained in election manifestos', particularly when it became apparent that central government would penalize the move by witholding some of the normal subsidy that it made to bodies like the GLC. So, though the voters had supported it in their thousands, the fare reduction was reversed, the supplementary rate quashed, and the policy frustrated, by the order of five judges.

It is fair to say that the GLC and their lawyers were taken aback by the Court of Appeal and House of Lords decisions – 'shell-shocked' was the term one lawyer used. The council officers said things like 'an Alice-in-Wonderland construction of the 1969 Act', and 'I can't understand how it was possible for the Law Lords to read the Act the way they did'. As they began dismantling the new fares structure, they found themselves acting so cautiously in response to the House of Lords interpretation that other London boroughs started threatening them with lawsuits for acting too slowly! They had to take every step with lawyers at their elbow, moving in consultation with and on advice from counsel. (Indeed one of the lasting impacts of the decision has been to give lawyers much greater power in the day-to-day politics of committee decisions at the local level.) Eventually they came up with a new, more modest fares plan, and humbly submitted it to the courts for approval. It was approved.[2]

More than anything else, the Labour councillors were flabbergasted by the Law Lords' intrusion into a decision so clearly legitimated by electoral democracy:

For generations in local government we understood that if you put something in your manifesto and got elected, you got on and did it. We cherished the belief that people believe in democratic government. If you got a popular vote you could do it.[3]

As they saw it, the electorate had been given a choice: to subsidize London Transport in the interests of social and environmental policy or to persist with the existing fare structure. The electorate had made their choice, and councillors couldn't understand why the judges – who knew almost nothing about the detailed policy issues involved – would want to overturn their decision. Council solicitors were at a loss to explain the vehement unanimity of the Lords' decision: 'There is *always* room for argument where there is discretionary power.' The only thing they could see was that the courts were indulging in a gut-level reaction to Labour policy, to the beginning of some apprehended revolutionary socialist challenge.

Concern was also expressed in the House of Commons about the political character of the judges' intervention. But it was met with a familiar response:

> *Mr Lyon* (Labour): Does the Prime Minister recognize the danger of the judges arrogating to themselves political decisions? Although it may be one thing to say that the council has exceeded its statutory power, it is quite another thing to say that, even if it had the statutory power, it acted unreasonably in balancing the interest of ratepayers and fare-paying passengers? In such circumstances, the judges were making political decisions and not judicial decisions.
>
> *Mrs Thatcher*: I wholly reject that. Judges give decisions on the law and on the evidence before them. They do so totally impartially.[4]

Once again, we see a conflict between 'neutral' and 'partisan' conceptions of the law. The GLC acknowledged that their reforms were partisan in character and the only sense they could make of the judges' decision was that it was a partisan intervention from the other side. And the difference was clear to them: the GLC had an electoral mandate to implement partisan decisions, whereas the judges had nothing of the sort. For Mrs Thatcher, however, the judges' decision was the neutral invocation of a value that transcended party politics – something called *'the law'*. One of the things I want to do in this chapter is to relate the contrast between the two models specifically to decision-making by judges. What is a 'judicial' decision? What does it mean to make a decision 'on the law'? Is that different from a 'political' decision? If so, how?

Judges and political power

No-one can doubt that the decision of the House of Lords represented a political defeat for the Labour leaders of the GLC and a victory for the Conservative councillors of Bromley. Whatever we think about the way judges make their decisions, the *effects* of their decisions are undoubtedly political. But does that make the *judges* political?

Some commentators have noted that the great advances in judicial review in the 1960s and 1970s came almost entirely at the expense of Labour policies, and that judicial reluctance to review the decisions of the executive is most likely to be decisive in cases where the executive has a Conservative cast to it.[5] That is probably an exaggeration: Conservative administrations have suffered occasional setbacks at the hands of the courts also. But certainly when people complain about the political bias of the judiciary, those complaints tend to come from the Left. Observers on the Left see judges as symbolic representatives of the traditional side of the British conservativism. With the ceremony of their office, their horsehair wigs, and their too-readily exercised power to lash out at anyone who makes fun of their pomposity, they stand for all that is most ancient and corrupt in the British establishment – 'class-ridden vandals in ermine', as one Labour councillor described them.[6] Inherently suspicious of any change in the way things are done in this country, they will resist the innovations of socialist policy to the extent that they can, and protect the arbitrariness of Tory power from almost any challenge. We may think that view scandalous and simplistic. But undeniably it is held by a large number of people who are disillusioned with the British judiciary.

Unfortunately it is hard to evaluate the claim that judges act politically, when the term 'political' is as ambiguous as it is. There are at least six different senses of the term that might be relevant in this context.

(i) 'Political' may mean nothing more than *part of the political system*. In this sense, it is obvious that courts are political institutions and judges play a political role. They are part of the system of politics in this country, because they are part of the overall apparatus by which we are governed.

(ii) 'Political' may mean *their decisions make a difference to the allocation of power, liberty, and resources in society*. Someone once defined the great issue of politics as 'who gets what when and how'.[7] Again it is undeniable that judges' decisions are political in this sense. As a result of the decision in the GLC case, commuters paid more for their transport in London than they would otherwise have done, and ratepayers paid less in taxes. The GLC's Labour voters were frustrated in their wishes, and the Bromley councillors got what they wanted. That is simply another way of saying that courts are part of the political system. They are decision-centres in a great organization that determines the conditions of life in this country, and their decisions make a difference.

(iii) 'Political' may mean *involved directly in political interaction with others*. This is a more subtle sense of politics. 'Politics' can refer not only to the great processes of society, but also to face-to-face interactions among small groups of people. We talk about the politics of the committee room, the politics of a family, or the politics of a government department, meaning the way people struggle for influence, persuade one another, or make threats and offers of various sorts to get their way. There is no reason why we shouldn't talk about the politics of the judiciary, in the same sense. In an appellate court, there are usually several judges sitting on each panel, and they will attempt to influence one another, as well as the barristers and parties who appear before them. There are also questions like the influence which the Lord Chancellor has on the rest of the judiciary (promotion, appointment to particular panels, etc.) as well as the interactions between courts at different levels and between judges and non-judicial actors, such as academics, practising lawyers, politicians, and so on. Once again, judicial behaviour is clearly 'political' in this sense.[8]

(iv) 'Political' may mean *'biased towards one side or another in a partisan dispute'*. That was the allegation made by many Labour supporters in the 'Fares Fair' case. They thought, as we have seen, that judges were influenced by the mood of the press, by a red scare, by inherent antipathy to socialist policies. The bias may or may not have been conscious, and it may or may not have been articulate. But – so the allegation goes – judges' class background disposes them to respond more favourably to some arguments than others, or to side more readily when they can with some causes rather than others. Even if they try to be 'neutral' and 'impartial', they can't help being influenced by their background and by the conservative ethos of their office. And usually, it is alleged, they don't even try. This claim is more controversial.

(v) 'Political' may mean *'consciously motivated by ideological or moral beliefs'*. This is more specific: it claims not only that judges are politically biased, but that they deliberately use political premises in their decision-making. Judges would be political in this sense if, in their decisions, they decided to take a stand in favour of things like individual liberty, Christian values, *laissez-faire*, or social democracy. If that were the case, their actions would be based on political values just as much as those of a statesman. Like all politicians, they would be motivated by some vision of how society should be organized. The only difference would be that judges have to organize their decision-making around statutes they did not make and precedents of previous courts; they would be more constrained in the realization of their vision than elected politicians are. But in their interpretation of the law, they would be displaying their own values, their own ideology, their own policy aims, and their own principles.

(vi) 'Political' may mean *'motivated by ambition or the desire to stay in office'*. This is the most sordid sense of the term. For example, many of Richard Nixon's actions in the course of the Watergate affair were political in this sense, rather than sense (v).

Often, when ministers are accused of making political decisions, what is meant is that they are acting to increase their chances of re-election, or protect their reputation, or promote the fortunes of their friends. Now judges in this country don't have to worry about the electoral process, but they may have to worry about promotion, particularly in the early phases of their judicial careers. A more disturbing possibility is that judges may be motivated to aid and abet the political position of those who do have to face an electorate. Often when people say that judges are 'political', they imply that judges are simply trying to protect the government (usually a Conservative government) from political and electoral embarrassment.

As I have indicated, it seems obvious that judges and their decisions are 'political' in at least senses (i), (ii), and (iii). The controversy centres around 'politics' in senses (iv), (v), and (vi). Are our judges biased? Are they trying to impose their own values? Are they concerned for their own political position or maybe that of their friends?

In the exchange between Alex Lyon MP and Mrs Thatcher which I quoted earlier, it seemed that 'political' was being used (on both sides) as a negative term. 'Political' is what judges ought not to be. Lyon said that judges were being political and therefore not doing their job. Mrs Thatcher said the judges were *not* being political and were therefore doing their job perfectly well.

But the view that 'political' should always be a negative term when applied to judges is an over-simplification. 'Political' in sense (vi) is clearly a sordid and negative epithet; nobody wants our judges to be influenced by considerations like that. But some of the other senses are not negative at all. Senses (i) and (ii) simply tell us that judges are part of the overall political process and that their actions have political repurcussions. If judges *weren't* political in these senses, there would be no point paying their salaries. What about the other meanings? Is sense (iii) negative – the sense in which judges play politics with one another? It depends partly on what you want to say about (iv) and (v), and partly on your overall image of judicial office. Some people think that a judge ought to be a wise and lofty individual dipping into leather-bound books for the wisdom of the common law and not stooping to play politics with his brethren. But most of us think that interaction is inevitable and desirable – and on the whole what matters is the *quality* of 'intra-judicial politics' (for example, is he arguing or bullying?) rather than the mere existence of these interactions.

That leaves (iv) and (v). The neutral model of law is so dominant, and we are so accustomed to associate *impartiality* with judicial office, that we are alarmed if anyone suggests that political or ideological bias might be a healthy thing. But 'impartiality' primarily means impartiality between the parties – not being influenced by fear or favour on either side. It doesn't necessarily follow that the judge should be a political neuter – emasculated of all values and principled commitments. Offhand it is hard to see how he could – for a judge must surely hold at least the values associated with the rule of law, and as we saw in Chapters two and three, those are bound up with a particular outlook on politics, society, and freedom. One of the things we will see as we go on through this chapter is that it is impossible for a judge to comprehend the various constraints of his office without some commitment to the values that sustain them. Deference to statute law, the importance of precedent, justice, equity, fairness, certainty, rectitude, the public interest – these are values which judges ought to be drawing on all the time. Moreover a judge is often required to balance these values against one another when they conflict. Surely the responsible thing to do is to think through such possible conflicts in advance and develop a general sense about which values should give way to which others in various circumstances. But if a judge does that, then he is already embarking on the very enterprise that political ideologists are engaged in – the enterprise of trying to make sense of the social and political world in a way that will help guide decisions that have to be taken.

In many areas – politics, society and law – where value-commitments are unavoidable, the thing to do is not to try to hide them, but to be as *explicit* about them as possible. Maybe if judges have developed particular theories of morals, politics, and society they should say so up front, and incorporate them explicitly into their decision-making. Later in the chapter, we shall see that the best theories of judicial decision-making insist that this is exactly what they should do. But that is a matter of *normative* jurisprudence – saying what judges *ought* to do, rather than *descriptive* jurisprudence – saying what in fact they *do* do. Controversies rage about whether judges in Britain do in fact act politically in either sense (iv) or sense (v). My hunch is that they do, in both senses. But I am going to argue that at any rate judges *ought* to be political in sense (v) and not in sense (iv). If they are biased towards a political consideration, they ought to incorporate it into the substance and wording of their judgements. If they are uncomfortable about doing that, that is probably a good indication that they should re-examine their bias and see whether it is an appropriate consideration for them to be influenced by.

Our conclusions, so far, are quite striking. The decisions of most judges are political in senses (i) to (v) at least and, arguably in the case of some judges, in sense (vi) as well. They *ought to be* political (or at least there is nothing wrong with their being political) in senses (i), (ii), (iii), and (v). But then there's a puzzle. If all this is true, why has anyone ever thought it sensible to maintain that our judges are neutral, that they either stand or ought to stand above considerations of politics? Why does Mrs Thatcher, for example, 'wholly reject' the view that judges make political decisions?

To answer this question, I shall examine in some detail the attractions and shortcomings of something I shall call 'the traditional view of judging'.

The traditional view

People sometimes tell a story about the role of judges which is analogous to the story traditionally told about the role of civil servants in politics. The job of a civil servant, the story goes, is not to make policy but to implement the policy made by elected politicians. A civil servant should be the neutral 'transmission belt' for policies decided upon by those who have been democratically elected to choose them. Similarly with judges, on the traditional story. The job of a judge is to apply existing law to the particular cases that are brought before him. It is not for him to make new law or to impose his own moral or political preferences on the parties unfortunate enough to fall into his power, for he is neither elected to do that nor accountable to an electorate for the preferences he holds. The law is made by the people's representatives in Parliament, and the judge's job is to find out what that law is and apply it to the facts that the litigants bring to his courtroom.

That is the view held by many non-lawyers and many politicians. It is also the view espoused, at least in print, by many judges, and for a long time it was the standard accepted doctrine in jurisprudence. Today, however, when legal theorists outline the traditional view, they do so merely in order to deride it (just as students of public administration sneer at the traditional view of civil servants). This conception of judging, the theorists say, is technically naive and politically disingenuous. Now they are undoubtedly right about that, and I shall explain why in a moment. But the traditional view is based on a number of legitimate anxieties and, before dismissing it, it may be worth saying something about what those anxieties are.

An unaccountable elite

The anxieties start to arise as soon as we ask, 'Who are our judges? Where do they come from?'. With very few exceptions judges are barristers who have practised at the bar for more than twenty years and have been appointed by the Queen on the advice of the Lord Chancellor (in the case of High Court appointments) or the Prime Minister together with the Lord Chancellor (in the case of appellate appointments). To have been a successful barrister, one must have been educated at a university and have survived the first few years of 'pupillage' at the bar. J.A.G. Griffiths suggests that, for most people, survival during those years requires access to a private income; and the statistics of judicial appointments indicate that the overwhelming majority of judges are products of public school and Oxbridge education and come from families in the upper, professional, or upper-middle classes which are capable of supporting their careers. (Between 1820 and 1870, the percentage of senior judges from lower-middle or working class backgrounds was 14·1; between 1951 and 1968, it was 9·3.) Apart from background, the requirement of successful practice leads also to a certain sort of socialization: for the twenty years or so before appointment (usually after age 50), a judge will have been engaged in a successful practice in London – effectively as a self-employed professional – earning, as Griffith puts it, a 'very considerable' income. Unless somebody has slipped up in the Lord Chancellor's office, the judge will not be known for his unconventional political opinions. Though there are a handful of women judges on the Circuits and in the High Court, there has never been a woman in the Court of Appeal, and no woman has ever sat as a judge in the House of Lords. In gender, education, background, socialization, and lifestyle, judges are about as unrepresentative an elite group as it is possible to imagine.[9]

Nevertheless, we entrust a certain amount of power to them and, as we have seen, some of their decisions have a considerable impact in politics. When they make a decision, they can call immediately on the full force of the state to back it up. To defy their decision may be to risk the unlimited sanctions associated with contempt of court.[10]

What checks are there on this power? Can judges be held accountable for the way they exercise it? The answer is 'Yes – but only by other judges in a higher appellate court'. Once a decision has been made at the level of the House of Lords, then that is where the process stops. Outside the charmed circle of the judiciary, there is no check and no review. Parliament can change the law, of course, but as we saw in the Clay Cross case, there may be the greatest reluctance to alter retrospectively the direct impact of a judicial decision. As a group, our judges are accountable to nobody. Indeed, we have gone to extraordinary lengths to ensure that this shall be so.

One of the great issues at stake during the upheavals of the seventeenth century was the independence of the judiciary from the influence of the Crown. The great jurist Sir Edward Coke was dismissed by James I and VI for presuming to challenge the king's right to interfere in court proceedings where he conceived royal interests to be threatened; under the later Stuarts, judges held office only as long as they retained the favour of the king. With the overthrow of the Stuarts, the basis of the office was reconstituted, and since the Act of Settlement of 1701 the position seems to have been that judges' commissions are held *quamdiu se bene gesserit* (for as long as they behave themselves) and they can be removed only by a motion passed in both Houses of Parliament. Until 1959, good behaviour guaranteed a job for life; however, judges appointed since then must retire at age 75. Bad behaviour is usually understood to mean neglect of judicial duties or conviction for a serious criminal offence; but only one judge has ever been removed on this basis (Sir Jonah Barrington in 1830). In the present state of things, it is quite inconceivable that Parliament would entertain a motion to remove (or even censure) a judge because they disagreed with his decisions.

In addition, the following points should be noted: no-one can sue a judge for anything he says and does in the discharge of his office; Parliamentary Standing Orders require MPs to refrain from casting aspersions on a judge's conduct; there is nothing in the British political process remotely corresponding to the American procedure whereby Presidential nominees to the Supreme Court are first scrutinized by a congressional committee and the appointment voted on by the full Senate; even during the parliamentary appropriations for judges' salaries, there is no opportunity for MPs to question the pattern or tendency of their decisions; and, until relatively recently, any imputation to a judge of bias or incompetence by a member of the public was liable to be punished as contempt.

No doubt it is good that judges are protected from direct governmental pressure. It is interesting, however, that, although they may be independent in constitutional theory, English judges have acquired a reputation second to none in the free world for subservience to the government and the executive. In the wartime case of *Liversedge v. Anderson*, Lord Atkin voiced the following concern about the decision by a majority of his brethren in the House of Lords that the Home Secretary was not required to give reasons to justify the detention of a citizen:

> I view with apprehension the attitude of judges who on a mere question of construction when face to face with claims involving the liberty of the subject show themselves more executive minded than the executive. . . . I protest, even if I do it alone, against a strained construction put on words with the effect of giving an uncontrolled power of imprisonment to the minister. It has always been one of the pillars of freedom, one of the principles of liberty for which on recent authority we are now fighting, that the judges are no respecters of persons and stand between the subject and any attempted encroachments on his liberty by the executive, alert to see that any coercive action is justified in law. In this case I have listened to arguments which might have been addressed acceptably to the Court of King's Bench in the time of Charles I.[11]

The view that English judges are 'more executive minded than the executive' has had ample support in more recent times. Lord Denning, regarded as one of the more colourful and innovative of British jurists, is famous for his dismissal of an action alleging police brutality against the six men accused of the Birmingham Pub Bombings:

> Just consider the course of events if this action were to go to trial. . . . If the six men fail, it will mean that much time and money and worry will have been expended by many people for no good purpose. If the six men win, it will mean that the police were guilty of perjury, that they were guilty of violence and threats, that the confessions were involuntary and were improperly admitted in evidence: and that the convictions were erroneous. That would mean that the Home Secretary would have either to recommend they be pardoned or he would have to remit the case to the Court of Appeal under section 17 of the Criminal Appeal Act 1968. This is such an appalling vista that every sensible person in the land would say: It cannot be right that these actions should go any further. They should be struck out.[12]

In the case of Clive Ponting, the civil servant accused of passing details of the government's cover-up of the circumstances in which the Argentine vessel *General Belgrano* was torpedoed to a member of the Commons select Committee on defence, Ponting argued that he had a duty to act as he did 'in the interests of the state' (a defence laid down in the Official Secrets Act). Mr Justice

McCowan directed the jury that 'interests of the state' meant nothing more or less than 'the policies of the government then in power'. (The jury had the good sense to ignore this direction and to acquit Ponting.)[13] I could multiply examples from the numerous cases where British courts have provided safeguards for individual rights that fall far short of those guaranteed by the ECHR.[14]

In other words, protecting judges from executive pressure seems to have the effect of insulating them from any accountability to the people or their representatives in Parliament for their apparent willingness to embrace the interests of the executive whenever they have the opportunity.

So far we have talked about the lack of any official accountability. But are there some less formal ways in which judges may be sensitive to the prevailing moods and beliefs of the community? The answer, of course, is bound to be 'Yes', if we acknowledge that judges read newspapers and raise families in this society the same as anyone else. They are not cloistered away from public opinion, and despite their comic affectations of ignorance ('Who or what are "the Rolling Stones"?'), they are as much in tune with the times as any other group of rich and educated men in London.

Are they at least informal representatives of a consensus within the legal community? Once again, the answer is mostly negative. British conventions of deference make it almost impossible for a Law Lord ever to hear direct criticism of his decisions by members of the Bar or members of the academic legal community. Recent interviews have revealed that some pay no attention to written criticism and find it difficult to engage in lively intellectual exchanges with scholars or barristers. Unlike their counterparts on the American appellate bench, they do not have budding law professors as their clerks, nor are they ever recruited from the ranks of the academic profession. There is not anything remotely resembling the exchange between bar, bench, and law school that there is in the American system.[15]

The concern about accountability is therefore a valid one. If judges cannot be held accountable for their decisions, and if they are insulated from the pressures of public opinion and other forms of criticism, then surely it is undesirable that we should entrust any decisions of great political moment to them. When the Conservative councillors of Bromley disagree with Labour councillors on the GLC over the setting of bus and tube fares, do we really want the issue resolved by *judges*? Shouldn't it be settled rather by some sort of electoral contest ultimately involving the ratepayers and commuters affected? These are the questions we should bear in mind as we examine the legal theorist's dismissal of the traditional view that the judge's role is simply to apply the law, not to legislate or make policy.

I should mention one other argument in favour of the that view. To regard the judge as a mere 'transmission belt' for the will of Parliament is to adopt an image of the law that involves clarity, certainty, and predictability. In Chapter three, we saw the importance of people knowing where they stand in the law, so that they can make plans, enter into stable arrangements with others, and know what they can count on in social and economic life. So long as legal decisions are determined by the clear provisions of parliamentary statutes, these requirements of certainty and the rule of law seem to be satisfied. But if the law is to be determined by the whim of the judge in his courtroom, then people don't know where they stand until he has made his decision.

Quite apart from anything else, there is an element of disrespect and insult in the idea of laws being made up by the judges as they go along. The great eighteenth-century critic of English law, Jeremy Bentham, called the decisions of judges 'dog law':

> When your dog does anything you want to break him of, you wait till he does it, and then beat him for it. This is the way you make laws for your dog: and this is the way judges make law for you and me. They won't tell a man beforehand what it is *he should not do* ... they lie by till he has done something which they say he should not *have done*, and then they hang him for it.[16]

Another image he uses is even more lurid:

> Multitudes are thus doomed to inevitable ruin, for the crime of not knowing a judge's opinion, some ten or twenty years before the question had ever entered his head. This confusion and injustice is of the very essence of what in England is called the *common law* – that manyheaded monster which, not capable of thinking of anything till after it has happened, nor then rationally, pretends to have predetermined everything. Nebuchadnezzar put men to death for not finding a meaning for his dreams: but the dreams were at least dreamt first, and duly noted. English judges put men to death very coolly for not having been able to interpret their dreams, and that before they were so much as dreamt.[17]

Why judges have to make a contribution

I shall move on now to discuss some of the reasons why theorists remain sceptical about the traditional view, despite the legitimate concerns that underlie it.

The reasons for scepticism can be summed up as follows. First of all, the 'application' of a law to a particular case is never a mechanical matter. Words are often vague, facts must be framed, and the whole business is impossible without an active process of interpretation.

Second, and historically, much of our law is and always has been *judge-made*; this is what we mean by *the common law*. Much of our private law has this character and, in addition, apart from actual doctrine, the ethos of the common law permeates the entirety of our legal system and our culture of lawyering.

Third, and a little less tangibly, in our system the judges have been left to define their own role and the role of the courts generally in the political system more or less as they please. The courts have rebuffed any legislative attempt to rule them out of the administrative process, for example. On their own initiative and their own authority, they have insisted on the right to review decisions of any public body even when Parliament has said those decisions are not to be reviewed.[18] And they seem to be able to get away with it: that is, people take notice of and obey their decisions even when Parliament has tried to exclude them.[19] Similarly, the courts have insisted on defining their own attitude towards the interpretation of statutes. They say they will take a very narrow view of any statute that encroaches on common law rights or judge-made law. In addition, they remain entirely in control of their own *modus operandi*. In 1966 the House of Lords simply announced that it would no longer be bound by its own previous decisions; neither Parliament nor any other agency of government gave them the authority to do this. Our judges simply define their own role in the name of the rule of law.

The interpretation of statutes

The other two points I mentioned – statutory interpretation and the common law – require a more extended discussion. I shall begin with the interpretation of Acts of Parliament.

Think back to the GLC case. The Conservatives thought the transfer of funds from ratepayers to commuters involved in the new fares policy was wrong and undesirable. They claimed it was something the GLC was not entitled to do, and that was the basis on which they complained to the court. Now in Britain the powers of local authorities are defined entirely by statute, and there is an assumption that if a power has not been granted to a local authority by Parliament then it is not a power the authority is entitled to exercise. The judges' job, then, was to find out what powers Parliament had granted the GLC and to determine whether or not the new fares/rates package fell within the ambit of those powers.

When he opens the statute book at the appropriate page, a judge is confronted with a text – that is, a succession of words, a legal formula. In the 'Fares Fair' case, section 1 of the Transport (London) Act read as follows:

It shall be the general duty of the Greater London Council ... to develop policies, and to encourage, organise and, where appropriate, carry out measures which will promote the provision of integrated, efficient, and economic transport facilities and services in Greater London.

Under this general rubric, other sections of the statute empowered the GLC to make grants and issue policy directions to London Transport and to make up any deficits that its services might incur. The GLC had directed London Transport to lower its fares by 25% and it proposed to make a grant out of general revenue to cover the shortfall that would result. This is the action that was challenged. The courts had to decide whether that was a measure which would 'promote ... efficient and economic transport facilities and services'.

There was no dispute about the facts. Both sides conceded that revenue would fall (and that the GLC might also lose a portion of its block grant from the central government) and that property taxes would rise. The Bromley council (LBC) agreed that more passengers might use the services, that commuters might move from cars to buses and tubes, that the roads might be less congested and polluted. There was no dispute in court about any of that.

The two sides disagreed simply about the meaning of the words. The GLC said 'economic' meant 'cost-effective': in other words, giving good value for money. Good value might, on their account, cover any of the policy goals that transport services could promote: movement of passengers, reduction of pollution and congestion, maybe even social redistribution. The Bromley LBC, on the other hand, said that 'economic' meant 'breaking even': covering the expenses of its operation out of the fares charged to the passengers. That looks like a purely 'semantic' dispute – an argument about words – but in fact it makes all the difference. The only way we or our Parliament can legislate is to use words. But we want to use those words to apply to things, to actions, and to situations in the real world. The term 'semantics' is often misunderstood, as though it was merely verbal quibbling. In fact, semantics is about the relation of words to things, and the semantics of legislation is about the difference that our laws are going to make to real things and real actions. So don't let anybody tell you that legal semantics is a sterile issue. Until we find some way of governing our society without using words, we will always face this task of having to agree some way of relating the words that have been used to the situations we face.

In recent American jurisprudence, people have tried to develop an analogy between the interpretation of statutes (or, particularly, the interpretation of the 1787 Constitution) and the interpretation of literary works like *David Copperfield* or *Hamlet*. Some have wanted to suggest that judges and lawyers have the same freedom in construing statutes and the constitution as literary critics have in construing the work of Shakespeare. Just as a critic can decide that *Hamlet* is a Freudian play (though that category would have meant nothing to the author), so a judge can decide that the Fourteenth Amendment prohibits discrimination against gays, though that idea would have been anathema to the framers. We shall see shortly that the idea of framers' intent is indeed of very limited use in statutory interpretation.

But, for the rest, the literary analogy is misconceived and overblown. To interpret a novel and to apply a statute to the world are quite different enterprises. Statutes are explicitly normative, and the question is how we are to comply with the norms; novels are not. Though a novel may be didactic or intended to change our view of things, intepreting it as such is a very diffuse enterprise which involves establishing all sorts of hunches about connections in the culture and so on. Now we can do that too with statutes and with constitutions if we like. But doing that is doing something apart from or in addition to the application of its normative provisions. These are two different things you can do with a statute. So the first of them cannot possibly provide a useful analogy for the second. Also, we don't hang, imprison, or bankrupt people on the basis of literary interpretation; for that rather obvious reason, we can permit a degree of intellectual indiscipline and self-indulgence in literary circles that would be morally irresponsible in the law.

In problem cases like the meaning of 'economic' in the Transport (London) Act, the way a judge relates the words of a statute to the world is going to be determined in large part by his sense of why these *particular* words matter: why *these* are the words we should be focusing on. The obvious answer suggested by what we have said already is that these are the words that came from the legislature: these words *are* the agreed and formulated expression of the legislative will. The judges are to take these particular words seriously because the representatives of the people whose lives are to be governed by the law decided that they are the words that should matter.

Perhaps, then, if a judge is unsure about what a statute means, he should refer the matter back to Parliament and ask the MPs what they had in mind. The suggestion is not quite as daft as it sounds; Bentham proposed something similar (though in relation to a *code* of laws that would be formulated in a systematic way rather than in relation to the half-hearted agglomeration of particular statutes that made up the law, in his day as in ours). But it *is* daft: legislation usually outlives the Parliament that enacted it; Parliament in any case has enough pressure on its time without having to solve the problems of judges; different MPs may have had different views of the legislation; MPs may have forgotten what they intended or, worse still, may never have had any idea themselves how to answer the judge's question; indeed, they may have left the phrasing deliberately vague so that someone else could fill in the gaps.

Though that is all obvious, what is not always seen is that the very same reasons cast a large question-mark over an approach which judges *do* take to legislation: namely, they ask *themselves* what Parliament intended, or, more generally, they ask *themselves* what the purpose of the legislation is. Why is this a problem? The statute talks about 'economic transport services'. It is probable that in voting for this form of words, some of the MPs thought they meant 'cost-effective' (the GLC's interpretation), some of them thought meant 'breaking even' (the Bromley interpretation), some of them thought they meant something else, some of them hadn't really given any thought to the matter, and one or two were just wandering through the lobbies in their usual alcoholic haze. Such are the states of mind of our lawmakers: which of them are to be taken to represent the *intention* or the *purpose* of the Act? Suppose the minister who sponsored the bill said he hoped that the transport authorities would construe their responsibilities widely rather than narrowly; suppose some of her colleagues were disturbed by that sentiment but voted for the bill anyway because what the minister said was not in the wording of its provisions; suppose the committee that considered the bill after its Second Reading took a slightly different approach: again, whose intentions are to count in determining *the* purpose of the statute?[20]

The underlying point is simple. When you have any organization, like a Parliament, made up of a large number of people, there has got to be some way of deciding what counts as *its* actions rather than merely the actions of its individual members. We have solved that problem in a very formal way: something counts as an *act* of Parliament if it appears on the record as a form of words having been voted through in the appropriate way. Apart from that formality, we have no way of telling what the acts of Parliament are or what count as 'its' intentions. Though our judges may want to defer to Parliament, *this* – the written statute – is all they have to defer to. They have got to make the best they can of that.

Bearing all this in mind, let's go back to our problem. The Law Lords were stuck with the word 'economic' in the Transport (London) Act. There were two conflicting interpretations of it; how were they to decide? I am going to quote at length from the speech of Lord Scarman, addressing that difficulty, because it will give us a flavour of the sort of thing judges say:

As a matter of English usage, the term 'economic' (as also the noun 'economy') has several meanings. They include both that for which the appellants contend and that for which Bromley contend. It is a very useful word: chameleon-like, taking its colour from its surroundings. Even in the statute now being considered, the adjective 'economic' where used in s 1(1) may have a wider meaning than the noun 'economy' which is to be found in s 5(1).[21] . . . I, therefore, refuse to consider the question of the meaning of 'economic' in s 1(1) (or, indeed, the meaning of 'economy' in s 5(1)) as capable of being determined by reference to a dictionary. The dictionary may tell us the several meanings the word can have but the word will always take its specific meaning (or meanings) from its surroundings, ie in this case from the Act read as a whole. But while the Act must be read as a whole, it is not to be construed in isolation from the duties of the GLC as a local authority having the power (by precept) to raise a rate. As soon as the Act is considered in this context, a vital feature emerges. The GLC owes not only a duty to the travelling public of Greater London but also a duty to the ratepayers from whose resources any deficit must largely be met. Understandably the appellants have emphasised the first, and Bromley the second. But they co-exist. . . . 'Economic' in s 1 must, therefore, be construed widely enough to embrace both duties. Accordingly, I conclude that in s 1(1) of the Act 'economic' covers not only the requirement that transport services be cost-effective but also the requirement that they be provided so as to avoid or diminish the burden on the ratepayers so far as it is practicable to do so.[22]

There are several important things going on here. First there is Lord Scarman's dismissal of the dictionary as an aid to interpretation. The ordinary meaning of 'economic' is no help in resolving the conflict. Second, there is the importance put on statutory context: what does the rest of the statute tell you about the way this key term might be applied? Third, Lord Scarman brings in a consideration that is certainly not explicit in the statute, but which is something he thinks should affect its interpretation: the duty that the GLC owes to its ratepayers.

The point about dictionary definitions and ordinary meanings is important. Obviously, if the courts are going to defer to Acts of Parliament, they have to take the words at face value. But theories of 'literal' interpretation are of limited use in this area. A case is unlikely to be before a judge if there is no disagreement about the law (otherwise why would people on both sides pay their lawyers to bring the action?), and so judges are unlikely to hear many cases where the meaning of the words is literally beyond dispute. This is obvious enough with words like 'economic' which can connote a variety of different and conflicting standards. But even apparently concrete terms can lead to semantic disagreements. Suppose a statute says 'No vehicles are allowed in the park'. We all know that this prohibits the driving of cars and trucks in the area. But does it prohibit bicycles or horse-drawn buggies? Does it prohibit the erection of a war memorial in the form of an armoured car on a plinth?

No dictionary is going to answer those questions. And 'legislative intent' won't help either, for the reasons already considered. The categories we use are inevitably open-textured: there *is* no hard and fast answer to the question of whether a bicycle is a vehicle. We can try and pin things down using more and more precise terms and specifications. (For example, the meaning of 'park' in our imaginary statute may be specified by the area shaded green on a map in the Town Hall.) But if legislation is not to lose its general character altogether, if it is to involve anything more sophisticated than merely *pointing* at particular people, particular things, and particular deeds, the 'open-texture' of general categories will be unavoidable.[23]

We saw, in the extract from Lord Scarman's speech, that other provisions in the statute may help us to pin down the meaning of a problematic expression. The Law Lords thought, for example, in the case of the Transport (London) Act that the provision in a later section about the need to avoid deficits cast some light on the meaning of 'economic'. Similarly, in our imaginary statute about vehicles, provisions for towing and parking facilities outside the grounds of the park might indicate that the prohibition on vehicles should be taken to cover large car-like objects rather than things like skate-boards. But again there is nothing hard-and-fast about this. In making what he can of the text in front of him, the judge will obviously want to interpret it as a unity, so that its different provisions are coherent and are not construed in a way that makes them cut across one another.

The same desire for a coherent interpretation may lead the judge also to look beyond the particular statute to other legal provisions. The law, after all, is not just a set of independent edicts; it is supposed to hang together as a system. Great emphasis has been put on this aspect of interpretation in Ronald Dworkin's recent work. Dworkin argues that, in approaching a case, the job of the judge is to develop a theory about how the particular measure he is dealing with fits with the rest of the law as a whole. If there are two possible interpretations of 'economic' or 'vehicle' (or whatever the term is) the judge should favour the one that allows the provision to sit most comfortably with the spirit of the rest of the law and with the principles and ideals of law and legality in general. He should do this, not for any mechanical reason, but because a body of law which is coherent and unified is, just for that reason, a body of law more entitled to the respect and allegiance of its citizens. Having a coherent scheme to fit particular laws into means that the law as a whole provides a frame of reference for political argument, something that people share in common as a backdrop to their social life.[24]

The remarks in Lord Scarman's speech about the GLC's duty to its ratepayers can be read in this light. The Transport (London) Act does not say anything about ratepayers, but other statutes do and there is a general sense in English law that local authorities have this responsibility. Interpreting 'economic' so that section 1 of the Act fits comfortably with the general law on local body responsibilities is obviously going to be a somewhat different matter from interpreting it in isolation.

Once we see how this works, a number of other points about statutory interpretation fall into place. One of the so-called 'canons of interpretation' that judges invoke from time to time is the rule that penal statutes (i.e. laws that establish offences and provide punishments) should be construed narrowly and in favour of the citizen. Another rule, gaining popularity among the judges, is that statutes should be interpreted as far as possible in a way that makes them compatible with the principles of the ECHR. Both can be seen as ways of fitting particular statutes comfortably into the wider principles and traditions of the legal system. Without such requirements of 'fit' our law might be nothing more than an assemblage of miscellaneous, loosely connected and sometimes mutually incoherent propositions.

A lot of ink has been spilled on the topic of 'hard cases'. Easy cases are cases where there is no dispute about what the law says or how it applies to a particular set of facts. Hard cases are supposed to be ones in which there is a dispute about what the statute says and the courts have to decide how to resolve it. I don't think there is any bright line between the two. Even in cases where the meaning of the statute is undisputed, the courts may decide that the results of applying it would be absurd or unreasonable, and plump for a different, less obvious interpretation. (This is sometimes even referred to as 'the Golden Rule' of interpretation.)[25] Judges differ about when this should be done, and obviously there are no cues in the statute to guide them. Those who do it often claim they are using what semanticists call 'a principle of charity' in interpretation: Parliament couldn't possibly have meant that – they must have meant something else. But you can only push that line so far. In the end it comes down to a question of political principle: how far are the judges prepared to defer to the acts of the legislature and how far are they prepared to strike out on the basis of their own sense of fairness and reasonableness? That is not a question that can be answered by any theory of meaning or interpretation.

When courts take an initiative of their own in cases like this, preferring their own sense of justice to the literal words of the legislature, or deciding a hard case one way rather than another, are they taking on a legislative function themselves? Are we then in a situation where our judges are *making law*?

The answer is 'Yes', particularly because of the way the doctrine of precedent works. A judge (in an appellate court, for example) who decides that a bicycle is a 'vehicle' for the purposes of the statute we imagined is making a decision about a particular case: he will be making the evaluative judgement that the statute looks best in the context of the rest of the law when it is read in this way. But judges who come after him particularly in the lower courts will regard him as having *established* the general proposition that (all) bicycles are vehicles for the purposes of this Act (and others like it). (We will discuss the doctrine of precedent shortly.) Certainly, at the level of the immediate case, the judge is applying a legal proposition which, if not entirely new, was by no means obvious to the parties concerned (or the person who rode the bicycle into the park) before he made his decision. Jurists may argue till the end of time about whether the judge is *making* or *finding* law; but there is absolutely no doubt that some of the reasons for being troubled about retrospective legislation (which we discussed in Chapter Three) apply to such decisions.

If judges are making law in such cases, should they behave like law-makers? Some scholars have suggested that judges should decide hard cases on policy grounds – weighing social consequences, choosing the best option for the future, in the way we expect a legislator to do. H.L.A. Hart, for example, thinks it an advantage of the open-texture of legal language that it leaves room for the flexible adaptation of policy in this way.[26]

Others, however, have expressed doubts about whether judges are the appropriate officials to engage in policy-based legislation, even interstitially in hard cases.[27] There are obvious reasons for caution: judges have neither the competence nor the accountability to deal adequately with considerations of policy; and the adversarial environment of the courtroom may not be the best forum for addressing the needs of society as a whole.[28] It seems to me that, particularly in situations like the 'Fare's Fair' case, the judges should always refrain from assuming the burden of policy discretion when there is some agency available which is more competent to exercise it and more accountable to the people affected. Certainly, if the issue of interpretation that the court faces is the extent of the power of a competent and accountable policy-maker like the GLC, there should be a presumption (analagous to the presumption in favour of the citizen in penal statutes) against any interpretation that requires policy-making by the courts.

Having said that, there is no escaping the fact that sometimes – indeed often – courts must make decisions that no-one else can or will make, and that those decisions will represent important choices for the community. Even if their main responsibility is to interpret the law in such a way that it fits comfortably into a coherent whole, still what counts as a comfortable fit will inevitably require value-judgements by the judge concerned. When they have a choice, judges should shy away from judgements of policy and social choice based on issues of fact of which they are ignorant or issues of value for which they are unaccountable. But they don't always have a choice, and the values and ideology of the bench therefore still have the capacity to decisively alter the flavour of public policy in this country.

Common law

So far we have talked about the interpretation of statutes. But it is not always recognized that a large part of our law is not statutory at all: it is judge-made from start to finish. The law of contracts (the enforcement of agreements, bargains, and debts), for example, and the law of torts or delict (who can sue whom for things like defamation or negligence) are still largely judge-made. Historically, the principles, rules and doctrines of these areas of law grew up in the courts, rather than in Parliament; and many of the most important developments – for example, the development of negligence as a tort – involved initiatives by judges that have profoundly affected the circumstances of life in this country.

It is true that in many of these areas, statutes have been passed, and occasionally Parliament has attempted to embody whole areas of common law in statutory form. But that by no means establishes any clear subordination of common law or judge-made law to the law made in Parliament. For one thing, when Parliament tries to make law in these areas, the legislators often see themselves as subservient to the categories, principles, and doctrines of the common law. They see themselves as trying to embody common law in statutory form, rather than as trying genuinely to *make* law on their own account.

Some theorists argue that Parliament is still sovereign over the common law because it *could* abolish any body of common law if it wanted to. The decisions of a judge – even the immemorial decisions of generations of judges – can be wiped out by the decision of the 630-odd Members of Parliament. But actually, it's not as simple as that. The judges have indicated that they would be very cautious about implementing any statute purporting to abolish a common law rule: such a statute would always be given the narrowest possible effect. Moreover, as we have just seen, once legislation has been passed, Parliament in effect loses control of its words: the judges take them over and start on the process of interpreting them and shaping our understanding of them so that they fit comfortably into the rest of the law. Since all existing law will have already undergone that process of accommodation, a statute can lose its flavour very easily – particularly its innovative flavour – in its passage from Westminster to the Strand. I suppose (if we want to press the point) Parliament could at a stroke abolish and replace whole blocks of common law thus radically altering the background legal context that judges have to play with. But our legal culture is so dominated by common law modes of thought and so structured by its categories that this would be a revolutionary move. It might happen for all that, but I don't think it tells us anything interesting about the sovereignty of Parliament in the day-to-day workings of our political system as it actually exists.

The common law is something that defies easy analysis. If you wanted to give a rough and ready definition it would be this: 'common law' refers to the way judges decide and have decided the cases that come before them in areas of activity not governed by Acts of Parliament. I say 'decide *and have decided*' because the most striking thing about the common law is the way it is built up as a system of precedents. A modern judge, expounding what he takes to be some rule or principle of common law, will usually refer explicitly to a line of cases where that principle or something like it has been invoked; and often that line of precedents will go back one or two hundred years. The practice of justifying present decisions on the basis of past decisions in this way is very old too; there is evidence of it as early as the thirteenth century, though its importance was greatly enhanced with the availability of written reports of judgements since the sixteenth century.[29]

Precedent

Why this practice of always looking over one's shoulder? Why is older better? Why shouldn't modern judges – who presumably know as much as their predecessors and more – make decisions for themselves instead of being constrained by the immemorial prejudices of judges long since dead and rotten? If a mistake has been made in the past, why is that a reason to carry on repeating it for the future? What is the justification for the curious principle of *stare decisis* (let the decision stand)?

The issue is not just one of vertical authority within the hierarchy of courts (with lower courts deferring to the past decisions of higher ones). Our judges regard themselves as bound by previous decisions made at the *same* level, and sometimes they are influenced by past decisions reached at a *lower* level. Thus, for example, the Court of Appeal regards itself as bound by its own previous decisions (even decisions made decades or centuries ago); and the House of Lords sometimes defers to the decisions of courts below it, like the Queen's Bench or the Court of Appeal.

The House of Lords is in a very interesting position with regard to *stare decisis*. In 1966, it issued an announcement saying that in future it would no longer regard itself as bound in all cases by its own previous decisions. Though the Law Lords said they continued to regard precedent 'as an indispensable foundation', they would depart from it in particular cases where it seemed right to do so or when the constraint of precedent seemed to be hindering what they referred to as 'the proper development of the law'.[30] In effect, the announcement was an invitation to barristers to offer arguments in court, if they thought it appropriate, showing why one of their Lordships' previous rulings should be rejected. The way in which the Law Lords have dealt with such arguments since 1966 provides a revealing insight into judicial attitudes towards *stare decisis*.

If we ask why courts should follow precedent, we are implying that there is an alternative. How would they decide cases if there were no precedents? Remember that in common law we are dealing with areas that are not covered by statute. Two possibilities suggest themselves, though they really amount to the same thing. The courts could simply decide the cases that came before them in the way that seemed right. One person is injured by another, and sues for damages. The court could simply ask itself the *moral* question: should the second person compensate the first? If the answer is yes, they would award damages to the plaintiff. If the answer to the moral question was no, they would let the defendant go free. (The word 'moral' of course is used very widely here: it refers to the whole array of evaluative, principled, and policy considerations that enter into our discussions about what *ought* to be done in society.)

However, people sometimes get nervous about moral adjudication and they opt for a second approach. On the second approach, we say that if Parliament has not provided a rule of liability, then the defendant should not be held liable by the moralistic decision of a judge. If the laws are silent, judges should keep quiet too, and the liberty of the subject should prevail. The plaintiff has no right to damages against the person who injured her unless Parliament has specifically provided one.[31]

In fact, the second approach is no different from the first. Both involve an appeal to moral principle. In the second approach, we say that people ought to be free, from restrictions and from damages, unless a statute explicitly binds them. That is a presumption in favour of freedom (to go about one's business without responsibility for the harm and injury one causes). But we could equally well have a background presumption that you must pay damages for the harm you inflict unless a statute provides otherwise. So even when the law is silent, the judge has to choose which is the background principle, which is the 'default' position. And in the absence of any guidance from the legislature, that is undeniably a judgement of value.

If there were no doctrine of precedent, then, judges would have to decide cases on moral grounds. To the extent that they ignore or overrule (or wriggle their way around) precedents, the judges *are* deciding cases on moral grounds (in the broad sense of 'moral' I mentioned a moment ago).

Now how does respect for precedent fit into that process? Is it a part of moral thinking? Or is it a result of nervousness, a deference to the past because one is uneasy about making moral decisions of one's own?

One reason for deferring to the past is conservatism (with a small 'c'). We can think of a line of past decisions as a collective achievement by generations of judges building on and adapting each other's work. Compared with that achievement, one's own efforts to think through a moral issue seem puny and idiosyncratic. In the words of Edmund Burke:

> We know that *we* have made no discoveries; and we think that no discoveries are to be made, in morality; nor many in the great principles of government, nor in the ideas of liberty, which were understood long before we were born, altogether as well as they will be after the grave has heaped its mould upon our presumption, and the silent tomb shall have imposed its law on our pert loquacity. . . . Instead of casting away all our old prejudices, we cherish them to a considerable degree, and . . . the longer they have lasted and the more generally they have prevailed, the more we cherish them. We are afraid to put men to live and trade each on his private stock of reason; because we suspect that this stock in each man is small, and that individuals would do better to avail themselves of the general bank and capital of nations, and of ages.[32]

The conservative argument, of course, has its difficulties. If the conditions of modern life are changing, we have a responsibility to think through for ourselves how our principles and values should be adapted to those conditions; it surely cannot be wise to go blindly on applying moral ideas which make sense only in relation to conditions that no longer exist.

Notice too that the Burkean argument falls to the ground if every generation of judges blindly follows the decisions of its predecessor. For then, we are all of us bound by the decision of the first in the line. But he is an individual with a 'private stock of reason' no larger than our own; why should we follow him rather than trust our own judgement? The argument works only if, at each step in the process, the precedent has been adapted or altered slightly, previous adaptations tested and reconsidered, new lines of development sketched out and so on. Only then can we talk seriously about an accumulating body of wisdom (as opposed to mere blind repetition). But if this is so, *we* in turn have a responsibility to future generations to play *our* part in that process. If we *blindly* follow the precedents we inherit, we will be exploiting the heritage of the past without contributing our bit to the heritage of the future. Fortunately – as we shall see – the practice of using particular cases as precedents for other particular cases means that there is bound to be some adaptation in the process anyway. All the same, it is worth noting that the Burkean argument cannot support a *rigid* doctrine of *stare decisis*.

Other more persuasive arguments, however, have to do with the role precedent plays as a moral factor in its own right. One is about fairness and consistency. If someone last week did not have to pay damages for her carelessness, it seems unfair that someone this week, having done exactly the same thing, should be held liable to pay by a court. No-one is in favour of absolute equality, but equal treatment in equal circumstances seems a desirable ideal, and that principle will be violated if judges are allowed to change their minds about what's right and wrong from case to case. By itself, though, this argument is weak. Certainly, morality requires consistency: if we think something is the right answer for one type of case, we commit ourselves to the view that it is right for other cases of that type also, unless there is a relevant difference. But precedent requires more than that: it requires that even if we now think the earlier decision is mistaken, we must *still* keep on applying it to all similar cases. And that – when you think about it – is absurd.

A much more powerful argument in favour of precedent is the value of certainty: the importance of people being able to predict what the judges will decide. It goes back to a theme we have stressed many times. People need to know what they can count on, what they can expect from the state (both in the way of help and in the way of interference) so they can make medium- and long-term plans for their lives. If judges are deciding each case afresh on moral grounds, then the only way to predict their decisions will be to acquire information about the values, principles, and ideology of the judges. And even that is going to be useful to the citizen only once he comes to court and knows who is going to hear his case.[33] Most people want the sort of knowledge about the law that will keep them out of the courtroom.

The need for certainty is itself a moral factor: when we are considering the values at stake and the rights and wrongs of a particular case, one of the things we should consider is the moral significance of the fact that people will be trying to rely on their knowledge of the law for the future. We should give some weight in our decision-making to the importance of making that possible. This, of course, does not argue in favour of an absolutely rigid doctrine of precedent. The need for certainty, after all, is only one factor among several – to be weighed, for example, against the demands of justice in a particular case.

Moreover, we should remember that the sort of predictability that enables people to make plans is not necessarily the fastidious consistency of the lawyer's notion of precedent. The doctrine of *stare decisis*, as lawyers use it, is not necessarily guided throughout by any regard for certainty in society at large. It requires that a previous decision be followed unless its facts can be 'distinguished' (that is, shown to be relevantly different) from the facts of the case at hand. At best, such a distinction will be based on lawyers' and judges' views about what facts ought to make a moral difference. At worst, it will be based on their sense of what they can get away with in the cause of innovation and revision without abandoning the *form* of precedent based reasoning. On neither account will the 'distinctions' that are made correspond necessarily to what an ordinary person or her legal advisers would expect. It is wishful thinking to believe that ordinary expectations are contoured to moral differences, and certainly entirely un-reasonable to think that ordinary expectations are based on any cynical understanding of how precedents will be manipulated by judges. So, although the need for certainty is important, its cogency *as a justification of the English doctrine of precedent* has probably been exaggerated.[34]

Connected with the value of certainty is the importance of the reliance that people have already placed on their expectations about the law. Certainty is a value that faces both ways: it makes demands on how we decide for the future, but it also generates demands from the past. If someone has been led to believe that, say, street vending will not be prosecuted or that a contract for the sale of encyclopaedias will be enforced, it seems unfair for the courts to turn round and defeat those expectations. Of course, if these expectations were based on the person's own ill-informed hunches or on bad legal advice, the courts owe her nothing. People must accept responsibility for the reliance they have placed on their own mistakes. But if the law itself has induced these expectations, and if the person has taken risks or made investments on the basis of them, then fairness seems to require that the law should refrain from defeating the expectations that it induced.

Admittedly, that argument only works if there is already a background presumption of *stare decisis*. If people believe that the courts will do anything they like, then they are foolish to place any reliance on past decisions. But the idea of precedent is so deeply entrenched in our legal culture that it is impossible to dissuade people from forming expectations of this kind, particularly because they line up with the views people will have about equality of treatment, consistency, and the like.

I have said that the importance of certainty is only one moral factor among others and that it doesn't necessarily support the English doctrine of *stare decisis* in all its arcane detail. Lawyers sometimes distinguish between a 'rigid' doctrine of precedent and a 'relaxed' one. On the 'rigid' doctrine, earlier cases of co-ordinate or superior courts are to be followed in all circumstances. On the relaxed doctrine, they are to be given some influence (which they might not have been accorded were the matter being decided afresh). We've seen that the second is probably the most that can be argued for. But in any case, the distinction is an artificial one. Even on the most 'rigid' doctrine of precedent, there is nothing mechanical about 'following' an earlier decision. The American jurist, Benjamin Cardozo once conjured up an image of *stare decisis* in which:

> Judges march . . . to pitiless conclusions under the prod of a remorseless logic which is upposed to leave them no alternative. They deplore the sacrificial rite. They perform it none the less, with averted gaze, convinced as they plunge the knife that they obey the bidding of their office. The victim is offered up to the gods of jurisprudence on the altar of regularity.[35]

But, as every law student knows, there is nothing remorseless about the inference from the conclusion of one particular case to the conclusion of another, for the facts are always different.

Suppose that, in one case, Mrs Jones was run down by Mr Smith's truck on a pedestrian crossing in a hailstorm; and that, in the next case, Mr Brown was knocked over on a sunny day by Granville, the delivery boy, on his shop bicycle. If a court held in the first case that Mr Smith must pay Mrs Jones damages for his negligence, to what conclusion is it driven remorselessly by the logic of precedent in the second case?

The answer that lawyers are taught is that one must look to the judgement of the court, and to the reasoning that led the judge to decide in favour of Mrs Jones (the *ratio decidendi*, to use the Latin tag). That is the reasoning which is to applied pitilessly to all subsequent cases. But the judge's speech is likely to contain all sorts of things: disquisitions on pedestrian crossings, road surfaces and braking systems, observations on the character of Mrs Jones and Mr Smith, discussions of previous cases on quite different material, animadversions on the weather and the frequency of hailstorms, and, over the course of several pages, maybe half a dozen different statements of the principle of tort liability for negligence. There is nothing mechanical about 'following' such reasoning, particularly if the business of precedent is modified anyway by the doctrine that relevantly different cases may be treated differently.

Another way of putting this is to say that principles of common law are never formulated explicitly as *rules* to be followed. Even if they were, our discussion of statutory interpretation ought to have convinced us that there would be nothing remorseless or mechanical about their application. But they never are. People come up with various statements of principle from time to time: they say things like 'people are liable for the reasonably foreseeable consequences of their carelessness' and 'everyone owes a duty of care to his neighbour.' There is nothing canonical about any of these formulas: unlike the provisions of a statute, there is no authoritative text or form of words which *is* the rule. They are just familiar slogans, quotations from famous judges, reformulations of what they might have meant, and so on.

Since this is so, precedent should perhaps be regarded as a matter of style as much as a constraint on the substance of judicial decision-making. On the rigid doctrine, judges make all their moves with reference to, and with the support of, quotations and snippets from previous decisions. They will be uncomfortable with any move that cannot be given that support, and they will cite that in itself as a reason for not making it. On the relaxed doctrine, judges will sometimes prepared to make a move in their decision-making that does not have this sort of support; they will feel less embarrassed striking out explicitly in a new direction than having to grope about for a past decision to justify every move they have to make.[36] But on both accounts, it is inevitable that judges must engage their own sense of values and the priorities of public morality as they move from one decision to another.

Politics again

I hope I have said enough to establish that the idea of 'neutral' or 'value-free' decision-making by judges is a non-starter. Whether they are interpreting statutes or following the principles of common law, judges are inevitably deploying their own values and political beliefs.

That, however, does not mean that the judge's values are the only ones that prevail in the courtroom. The point is more subtle than that. The judge's job *is* to follow the value-decisions made by Parliament (and by his predecessors on the bench); to that extent, the 'transmission-belt' theory which we discussed earlier is correct. The point is that following and applying someone else's values is not something that can be done in a 'neutral' or a 'value-free' way. Even the most democratically minded judiciary, even the judge who is most deferential to the legislature, is going to have to face an interpretive task. So, while the language that Parliament or his predecessors use will certainly make a difference to the parameters of his decision-making, the decision he faces will still be one that requires moral sensitivity and judgement. And even acknowledging those parameters, it will be a decision that honest and democratic people can disagree about.

I said earlier that it is desirable for judges to articulate the values and moral concerns that underlie the decisions that they make. It is inevitable that those values and concerns will affect and partly determine their decision, and I suggested that they ought to be explicit about it. They ought to be *transparently* political.

The reason for this is that the controversial decisions that judges make *matter* to society, and since they matter for moral reasons, we ought to be able to identify and discuss the moral basis on which they have been made. We have conceded many times in this book that democracy in Britain is imperfect. But if there is anything to the democratic idea it has got to involve an enterprise of public debate in which the members of the community deliberate among themselves about the conditions under which life is to be lived in this country. If decisions are being taken by those in power, we want to know the reasons, so we can evaluate them and see whether we want to rely on reasons like that for the future. It is an insult to our capacity for self-government to try and hide the reasons for political decision-making behind smokescreens of legal mystery. As we saw at the end of Chapter five, the courts can perform a useful function in a democracy of initiating and orchestrating public debate, but they can do that only if they are open about the terms in which that debate is conducted.

Notes

1 The phrase is taken from the judgement of Lord Justice Watkins in the Court of Appeal: *Bromley London Borough Council v. Greater London Council and another* [1982] 1 All ER 129, at 150. (This report also contains the decision of the House of Lords.)

2 *R. v. London Transport Executive, ex parte GLC* [1983] 2 All ER 262.

3 The councillors' reactions are quoted from Lee Bridges and others, *Legality and Local Politics* (Aldershot, Hants: Avebury, 1987), pp. 63 ff.

4 *Hansard*: House of Commons Debates, Volume 12 (1982), col. 418. The exchange was quoted in Carol Harlow and Richard Rawlings, *Law and Administration* (London: Weidenfeld & Nicholson, 1984), pp. 334–5.

5 J.A.G. Griffith, *The Politics of the Judiciary* (Manchester University Press, 1977), p. 210.

6 Bridges, *Legality and Local Politics*, p. 93.

7 Harold Lasswell, *Politics: Who Gets What, When, How* (New York: Meridian Books, 1958).

8 There is an excellent description of politics (in this sense) at the

highest level of the judiciary in Alan Paterson, *The Law Lords* (London: Macmillan, 1982).

9 The points in this paragraph are all taken from Griffith, *Politics of the Judiciary*, Ch. 1.

10 See the discussion at the beginning of Chapter seven.

11 *Liversedge v. Anderson* [1941] AC 244.

12 *McIlkenny and others v. Chief Constable of the West Midlands* [1980] 1 QB 323.

13 See Clive Ponting, *The Right to Know: the Inside Story of the Belgrano Affair* (London: Sphere Books, 1985), pp. 190–1.

14 There is an excellent review in Antony Lester, 'The Constitution: Decline and Renewal' in J. Jowell and D. Oliver (eds) *The Changing Constitution* (Oxford: Clarendon Press, 1985).

15 Alan Paterson, *The Law Lords*, Ch. 1.

16 This passage from Bentham is quoted by Gerald Postema, *Bentham and the Common Law Tradition* (Oxford: Clarendon Press, 1986), p. 277.

17 *The Works of Jeremy Bentham*, edited by John Bowring, Volume IV, p. 315.

18 E.g. *Anisminic Ltd. v. Foreign Compensation Commission* [1969] 2 AC 147, where the House of Lords overruled a decision of the defendant Commission even though the statute which established the agency stated explicitly that 'the determination by the commission of any application made to them under this Act shall not be called in question in any court of law'.

19 Similarly, in America it was the initiative of Chief Justice Marshall in the landmark case of *Marbury v. Madison* that established the principle that the Supreme Court could review and strike down legislation as unconstitutional. There is nothing explicit in the 1787 Constitution to this effect.

20 The argument against appealing to legislators' intentions is hammered home by Ronald Dworkin in *Law's Empire* (London: Fontana, 1986), Ch. 9.

21 Section 5(1) provided that the London Transport Executive should exercise its functions 'with due regard to efficiency, economy, and safety of operation, to provide or secure the provision of such public passenger transport services as best meet the needs for the time being of Greater London'. Obviously there is a lot here that cries out for interpretation also: for example, does 'needs' only include transport needs, or can it include social and environmental needs as well?

22 *Bromley LBC v. GLC* [1982] 1 All ER 174.

23 The term 'open texture' is used in H.L.A. Hart's discussion of this issue in *The Concept of Law* (Oxford: Clarendon Press, 1961), pp. 120–32.

24 Ronald Dworkin, *Law's Empire*.

25 For an accessible discussion of this and other 'rules' of statutory interpretation, see J.W. Harris, *Legal Philosophies* (London: Butterworths, 1980), Ch. 12.

26 H.L.A. Hart, *Essays in Jurisprudence and Philosophy* (Oxford: Clarendon Press, 1983), pp. 269–71.

27 The best-known view is that of Dworkin. In his early work, *Taking Rights Seriously* (London: Duckworth, 1977), Dworkin argued that judges should decide cases on grounds of principle rather than policy. But that distinction is not an easy one. The argument in his latest book, *Law's Empire* (London: Fontana, 1986), is that judges have no right to take new policy initiatives of their own; at most, it is their job to participate in and contribute to a conversation with the rest of the community about the policies that the community has already agreed to (pp. 340–1).

28 There is an excellent discussion in Lon Fuller, 'The Forms and Limits of Adjudication', *Harvard Law Review*, 92 (1978).

29 There is a full discussion in C.K. Allen, *Law in the Making* (Oxford University Press, 1958), Chapter III.

30 The Law Lords' announcement is worth quoting in full:

> Their lordships regard the use of precedent as an indispensable foundation upon which to decide what is the law and its applicability to individual cases. It provides at least some degree of certainty upon which individuals can rely in the orderly conduct of their affairs, as well as a basis for the orderly development of the law. Their lordships nevertheless recognise that too rigid adherence to precedent may lead to injustice in a particular case and also unduly restrict the proper development of the law. They propose therefore to modify their present practice and, while treating former decisions of this House as normally binding, to depart from a previous decision when it appears right to do so. In this connection they will bear in mind the danger of disturbing retrospectively the basis on which contracts, settlements of property and fiscal arrangements have been entered into and also the especial need for certainty as to the criminal law. This announcement is not intended to affect the use of precedent elsewhere than in this House. [1966] WLR 1234.

There is an excellent discussion of the background of the practice statement and of the way the Law Lords have viewed it in Paterson, *The Law Lords*, Ch. 6.

31 This was held in an American case, *Union Pacific Railway v. Cappier* in 1903 (the reference is 66 Kan. 649). Mr Cappier was run down by a train while trespassing on the tracks and the railway employees who saw that he had been hurt failed to stop promptly and attend to his injuries. When his widow sued the railway, the Supreme Court of Kansas held that there was no legal duty to give aid to an injured trespasser and so dismissed her claim. (I am grateful to Michael Moore for the example.)

32 Edmund Burke, *Reflections on the Revolution in France* (1790; Harmondsworth: Penguin Books, 1969), pp. 182–3.

33 Political scientists do this of course, producing both formal models to predict judicial behaviour, and informal categories like 'liberal' and 'conservative' to guide rough-and-ready prognostications about the

view that a particular judge will take. All the same, as Lord Gardiner remarked in an interview: 'Nothing is worse when people go to a solicitor [for advice], and he says, "I cannot tell you what the answer is. It entirely depends which judge we get." ' (Paterson, *The Law Lords*, p. 125.)

34 'It is notorious that where an existing decision is disapproved but cannot be overruled, courts tend to distinguish it on inadequate grounds. . . . But this is bound to lead to uncertainty for no one can say in advance whether in a particular case the court will or will not feel bound to follow the old unsatisfactory decision. On balance it seems to me that overruling such a decision will promote and not impair the certainty of the law.' (Lord Reid in *Jones v. Secretary of State for Social Services* [1972] AC 966.)

35 Benjamin Cardozo, *The Growth of the Law* (New Haven, Conn.: Yale University Press, 1924), p. 66.

36 Before the 1966 Practice Statement, Lord Reid had said in the course of a decision: 'My Lords, it is very unsatisfactory to have to grope for a decision in this way, but the need to do so arises from the fact that this House has debarred itself from ever reconsidering any of its own decisions. It matters not how difficult it is to find the *ratio decidendi* of a previous case; that *ratio* must be found.' (*Nash v. Tamplin* [1952] AC 250; quoted in Paterson, *The Law Lords*, p. 147.)

Chapter seven

Breaking the law

Taylor v. NUM

In the great miners' strike of 1984–5, the National Union of Mineworkers (NUM) sought to close down every pit and every colliery in the country. The strike was not for higher wages or better conditions; the miners went on strike to challenge the government's policy of ending production at pits which, in the opinion of the state-owned National Coal Board, were not contributing sufficiently to the profitability of the industry. With the overwhelming support of rank-and-file membership in the affected areas, the union leaders, Arthur Scargill and Mick McGahey, proclaimed a national work stoppage in opposition to the closure of 'uneconomic' pits and called on all the members of the NUM and all associated trade unions not to cross the picket lines that they set up. The strike went on for over a year before the NUM admitted defeat, and it was the occasion of much hardship to the miners, much difficulty and embarrassment to the government, and considerable conflict, innumerable arrests and injuries on the picket lines, and actually one or two deaths. Though support for the strike remained solid in some coalfields throughout the dispute, there was opposition in other areas, and by the middle of 1984 informal groups of 'working miners' were emerging. The activities of these groups played a large part in the eventual defeat of the NUM.

Trade Unions depend heavily on discipline and organization, and every union has its rule book, with procedures for action and decision-making. Rule 43 of the the NUM Rule Book states:

> A national strike shall only be entered upon as a result of a ballot vote of the members taken in pursuance of a resolution of Conference, and a strike shall not be declared unless 55 per cent. of those voting in the ballot vote in favour of such a strike.

No national ballot was ever held, either immediately before or during the course of the 1984-5 dispute. Both NUM members and outsiders criticized the union leaders for that failure. But Arthur Scargill, the NUM president, had reason to be wary of national ballots. More radical in his approach than many of his members, he had been rebuffed in his call for a strike to oppose pit closures in 1983. So the 1984-5 stoppage proceeded instead on the basis of a resolution by the national executive committee backed by regional ballots in many areas.

In September 1984, two members of a working miners' group, Robert Taylor and Ken Foulstone, went to the High Court in London, seeking a declaration that the stoppage was 'unlawful' so long as a national ballot was not held. 'Unlawful' here did not mean 'criminal'; it meant failing to comply with the union's rules. But Taylor and Foulstone also asked for injunctions to restrain the union in their area (Yorkshire) from acting as though the strike *were* official.

In court, Mr Justice Nicholls rejected the NUM argument that Rule 43 did not apply since the stoppage was not 'a national strike' but a concerted series of regional actions. He issued the declaration and the injunctions that the working miners wanted. The NUM now faced a court order forbidding it from instructing its members not to work and not to cross picket lines, and forbidding disciplinary action by the union against any miners who went back to work. (Similar cases were also mounted, and similar injunctions issued, in Wales, Derbyshire, and other areas.)

The union responded defiantly. Arthur Scargill declared:

> I am going to say this, and quite clearly: that any miner in this union who crosses a picket line in defiance of our union's instructions runs the risk of being disciplined under our rules. And there is no high court judge going to take away the democratic right to deal with internal matters. We are an independent democratic union.

Hearing this, Taylor and Foulstone went back to the court seeking a judgement that Scargill's speech amounted to contempt. The judge gave Scargill five days to consider his position before coming into court to show why he and the NUM should not be punished for their defiance. Scargill's response was:

> If the choice is to spend a term in Pentonville or any other prison or to live by the imprisonment of my mind for betraying my class, the choice is that I stand by my class and my union.

The strike continued to be treated as official by the NUM leadership.

When Scargill did not appear in court on the appointed day, he was fined £1,000 and the union was fined £200,000. Mr Justice Nicholls commented:

> A great and powerful union with a large membership has decided to regard itself as above the law. . . . If orders of the court are set at nought in this way – openly and repeatedly defied by such a body with impunity – where is the rule of law?

The union refused to pay (though Scargill was saved from prison when an anonymous 'well-wisher' paid his fine). Taylor and Foulstone then pressed for the seizure (the legal term is 'sequestration') of the NUM's assets. Still Scargill's response was defiant: 'It has not penetrated the minds of this government or the judiciary that you cannot sequester an idea or imprison a belief.' A month later, the court appointed an Official Receiver to handle the NUM's property and affairs. The court held that the union's trustees (Scargill and McGahey) were 'not fit and proper people to be in charge of other people's money' since their intent was obviously 'to continue serious and deliberate contempts of orders which place the funds they hold for the union in jeopardy'. Arthur Scargill retorted that the choice for the union was to be in contempt of court or in contempt of its members and traditions.

It seems that by defying the law the NUM lost more than money, it lost a great deal of public support. The *Daily Mirror* said:

> Mr Arthur Scargill and the miners' executive have broken the law and must face the consequences. It is not a Tory law. It is an English law. It does not mean submitting to a Tory government but to parliamentary government.

The Labour Party leaders called on the NUM to obey the law, apparently feeling that enthusiasm for Scargill's defiance could not possibly improve their own electoral chances. Even other trade unions fell back when Scargill pleaded for support in the face of sequestration. Breaking the law and defying the courts was further than any of these left-leaning organizations were prepared to go.[1]

The case of the NUM and its defiance of the High Court raise many of the issues we considered in Chapter two. Is the law a neutral arbiter above party politics and factions in industrial conflict? Or is the law itself a reflection of certain partisan values, and so a legitimate target for resistance by those who reject those values? In Chapter two, we used the Clay Cross case to address those questions in general terms. In this chapter, we are going to confront the moral issue of obedience and defiance more directly.

Framing the moral issue

We all know that if you break the law, you may suffer a penalty. In the case of an ordinary provision, it is a penalty on the scale set down by the statute. In the case of defiance of a court order (contempt of court), the penalties are potentially unlimited. These penalties are laid down for a number of reasons, but prominent among them is the attempt to *deter* people from breaking the law, to give them a self-interested reason for obedience which they can weigh in the balance against whatever reasons they may have for disobedience. A penalty is likely to deter someone if the harm the person suffers through punishment exceeds the benefit they could gain from breaking the law – though of course we also have to discount deterrence by the probability that the law-breaker will not be found out or will not be convicted if he is. (Those who are tempted to smoke marijuana, for example, may have no real expectation of being caught, so the deterrent effect of the penalties is almost zero.)

That makes it look as though our legislators expect us to engage in a cost-benefit analysis when we approach a particular law. Why then do they and the public talk about breaking the law as though it were some gigantic *moral* failing rather than merely an idiosyncratic calculation of personal advantage? Maybe the law-breaker has a legal duty which she is violating, and a legal liability to penalties as a result of her breach. But why is it also said that he has violated a moral obligation and should be subject to moral penalties? To put it bluntly: why do we say to people that it is *wrong* as well as illegal to break the law? If they know what the penalty is, and are prepared to take the risk of being caught, what does morality have to do with it?

We must start by realizing that there are two different types of moral argument about law-breaking: (1) moral arguments about the content of the law and (2) moral arguments about legality itself. We need to consider them separately.

(1) Moral arguments about the content of the law

Often the law prohibits things that are morally wrong, and commands actions that are morally right. If I contemplate breaking the law against murder, drug peddling, or drunken driving, I am contemplating doing something wrong. But that is not because *law-breaking* is wrong; it is because killing, drug peddling, and drunken driving are wrong, considered quite apart from their legal consequences. In all these cases the moral duty ought to override whatever personal temptations I have. I may think it in my interest to drive home drunk and worth the risk of being caught; but the danger I pose to other people matters more than the inconvenience to me of walking.

(2) Arguments about legality itself

In other cases, we say that it is wrong to do what a law prohibits not because (or not merely because) what the law prohibits is wrong, but because we think the illegality or the unlawfulness is itself a factor. These are the cases where we say, for example, that people ought to obey the law because legality is necessary for order, or because laws are passed with majority support, or because society will break down if some institution doesn't have the final say, or because they have consented to be bound by it, or because we need to have some settled framework for action and the law provides one. If we find reasons like those persuasive, we do so not because of anything intrinsic to the actions that the law is commanding or forbidding, not because of the content of the law, but because of the importance attached to law and the passage of law as political values, either in general or in this particular area.

We often appeal to these political or legalistic reasons in cases where there is disagreement about the independent moral justification of the legal rule. For example, someone who feels very strongly that marijuana smoking is depraved and wrong will recognize a reason of type (1) for obeying the Misuse of Drugs Act. But most users don't believe that: they believe the weed is harmless and certainly not immoral. To convince them that they are doing something wrong, then, you will have to appeal to reasons of type (2) – reasons about legality as such or the way the law was made.

We will also have to appeal to reasons of type (2) in cases where the content of the law folds back into the legal system itself. In the case of *Taylor v. NUM*, Arthur Scargill's offence was contempt of court: he defied the explicit order of a judge. At that stage, the reasons for holding that he was doing something wrong probably didn't have much to do with the wisdom or morality of the judge's original order. Reasonable people may disagree about the moral justifiability of calling a strike 'official' when its members haven't voted. But the reasons for holding that defiance and contempt are wrong are likely to be based on the idea that in the last resort the authority of the courts has to be upheld: there's got to be *someone* who has the last word in dispute situations or there will never be a possibility of solving any of them. (Later we will consider whether that argument holds water.)

For the rest of the chapter I shall concentrate on the second type of moral reason. I don't want to say that moral reasons of type (1) – independent reasons concerning the content of the law – are uninteresting or inevitably subjective. Often, as in the case of murder, they provide the most powerful reasons for refraining from the actions which – as it happens – the law also forbids. Even when we move into areas where the independent moral reasons are controversial – like dope-smoking, abortion, or calling a strike without a ballot – there may still be some objective truth of the matter. But in these cases, it is inevitable that the further question will be raised, namely: 'Never mind about the moral rights and wrongs of the action which the law requires or prohibits. Leave that aside for the moment. Does the fact that it is *the law* provide a moral argument for obedience?' In what follows, I will discuss in some detail some of the arguments that are used to show that, in this sense, we have a moral duty to obey the law.

Political obligation

Theorists call this the problem of political obligation: it is the problem of determining what we *owe* to the state in which we live. In fact, however, political obligation is a somewhat wider issue than this problem of whether it is ever right to break the law. Compliance with the law is only one of the things the modern state asks of us. It also asks us sometimes to volunteer for its defence; it asks us to participate in its democratic, judicial (jury service), and administrative procedures; it asks us to provide information of various sorts; and generally to give its officials our co-operation and support. Sometimes these things are required by law; often they are not. And even when they are, the law requires them because legislators believe that we have these (moral) obligations to the state, not the other way round.

It may also be worth mentioning at this early stage that, even with regard to its laws, compliance is not the only thing the state asks of us as citizens. The state also asks that if we *do* feel morally compelled to break the law, we should do so in a certain way; this is seen as part of our political obligation as well. That's what the term '*civil* disobedience' is supposed to express when it is used properly (though often it is used carelessly to mean any case of disobedience undertaken for moral reasons). 'Civil disobedience' means disobedience which somehow still preserves the spirit of citizenship, and it usually refers to deliberate and public acts of law-breaking undertaken peacefully and symbolically to communicate some important moral point to one's fellow-citizens. It is disobedience which still respects the idea of legal order as far as possible. One of the objections to the NUM episode was that Scargill and the other union officials were not only disobeying a legal order but doing so in a way that evinced contempt and indifference so far as the rule of law was concerned.[2]

'The law-makers know best'

When an individual breaks the law, she seems to be setting herself and her own judgement above that of society and its legislators: 'The law can't tell me anything. I will use my own judgement to decide what I should and shouldn't do.' If that is what she is saying, society's response may be: 'No – you must defer to the collective wisdom of the law, because it embodies more experience, more knowledge of how the world works, and a better opinion of right and wrong, than you are ever likely to come up with on your own.'

The American philosopher Robert Paul Wolff has provided a famous defence for the individualist position. He argued that each person had not only a right but a duty to decide for herself what to do, and that no-one should decide to do something (or not to do something) merely because someone else has told her to. We all have a moral duty to take responsibility for our actions, Wolff argued, and 'taking responsibility means making the final decisions about what one should do'. An autonomous and responsible person has a duty to weigh up the reasons for and against various actions herself, for in the end *she* is going to have to accept responsibility for what she does and for its consequences. Sometimes – as we have seen – there will be independent moral reasons for doing what the law says: if so, it is her job as a moral agent to weigh those reasons, indeed to weigh all the relevant facts about the actions she is contemplating. But, Wolff went on, the fact that something is commanded by law is not itself a morally relevant fact. On the contrary, it is a good indication that someone is trying to abrogate his responsibility and short-circuit his own effort to weigh up the reasons. The person who says 'Do it because it's the law' is like someone who says 'Do it because I say so'. Obedience, Wolff says, is not just a matter of doing what someone tells you to do: 'It is a matter of doing what he tells you to do *because he tells you to do it.*' It means he's trying to replace your moral reasoning with his own, and that is something no responsible agent should tolerate.[3]

How are we to respond to this argument? The first thing to say is that if it is ever the case that the legislature really *does* know best, then we ought to defer to its judgement. For all the highminded things Wolff says about autonomy and responsibility, it cannot be the responsible thing to trust one's own judgement in circumstances where one knows one's judgement is unreliable. The problem is, of course, to be able to recognize those circumstances, and distinguish them from cases where the legislature is no better placed – perhaps worse placed – than we are.

Here's a simple example. I am driving on an unfamiliar road, and I see there is a solid centre line to indicate that overtaking is prohibited. I look ahead and I seem to have good visibility. Should I trust my own judgement and pass the car in front or should I defer to the authorities? Maybe I should defer to their rule. They know the shape and camber of the road better than I do, for they built it and they are familiar with its hidden dips and curves.

Now here's a more complicated case. I am a clerk in the Ministry of Defence and I come across a secret memorandum which *I* think the public ought to know about. Section 2 of the Official Secrets Act prohibits me from divulging *any* information I have come across in the course of my work, though I cannot see how any harm could come from publication.[4] But of course the government knows much more about the exigencies of national security than I do. There may be a reason unknown to me why this information should be kept secret: if divulged it may be the last piece in a jigsaw that gives an enemy access to a whole network of our agents. Should I defer to them as I did in the earlier case?

The reason the secrets case is not so straightforward is that, although governments sometimes conceal information from us for legitimate reasons of national security, we know for certain that they also sometimes conceal information from us for reasons of political advantage (in the sordid sixth sense of 'political' that we distinguished in Chapter six). They conceal it to avoid embarrassment or to mislead the public about their achievements or intentions. Often when they do this, they pretend it's a matter of national security even though it's not. So if the citizen simply accepts the government's say-so that this is a national security issue on which the government knows best, she is being gullible. Simple trust in this area is stupid.

Instead, the rational thing to do is to try and estimate the probability that the government has a legitimate reason for keeping the information secret. One must balance that against the likelihood that they are in fact committing the wicked act of deceiving the public that votes, pays for, and suffers under their policies. That is a desperately difficult thing for an ordinary citizen to do, and it is a massive indictment of the governments we have had that their abuses make such calculations necessary. Sometimes the citizen will know more or less for sure that the government is engaged in a cover-up. Clive Ponting was in this situation in his divulgence of information about the sinking of the Argentine ship, *The General Belgrano*.[5] In such a case, it is a cynical abuse of the language of political obligation to say that he should have deferred to the authorities. But in other cases it will be more difficult, and honest people may differ.

National security is an area where, in the nature of things, the information the government relies on cannot be made available to the public. In other areas, however, the information on which the law is based may be widely and publicly available. Take the law against marijuana use, for example. In the scientific literature, there are lots of studies and articles claiming to show that marijuana is relatively harmless (in comparison, say, to legal drugs like caffeine, tobacco, and alcohol). And there are also lots of studies around which claim the opposite – that marijuana use is intrinsically harmful and can lead to the use of more dangerous drugs. Now all this information is in the public realm and can be read by any literate person. The government does not have any special information of its own on the matter which it cannot divulge to the people.

It may decide for paternalistic reasons that, since a lot of potential users won't bother to read the literature, it will impose its own judgement anyway and use penalties to dissuade them from using the drug. But if someone has read the literature and understood it, there is no basis whatever for saying to *him*: 'Still, the legislature knows best.' He already knows all that the legislators could know on the issue. If he forms a judgement different from theirs, then we will have to give him some other reason for obeying the law if we want him to comply with it.

One final point under this heading. A little later we will consider the view that people ought to obey the law because it is democratic. But *that* argument cuts across the argument from superior knowledge. Often a legislator's support for a law is based not on her own judgement (or on any specialist advice) but on her quite understandable deference to the views of her constituents. If so, then a citizen who is urged to obey the law is being asked to defer, not to the greater knowledge that may be accumulated at Westminster or Whitehall, but in effect to the views of her fellow voters who ultimately influence the legislators and who may be no better informed on the issue than she is.

Law and order

A criticism often made against those who break the law in a political setting is that their actions are likely to lead to a more general breakdown of order in society.

In many cases of law-breaking, this is simply far-fetched. Breaking the law is something most of us have done at some stage, and many of us do much of the time. Check down this list: exceeding the speed limit; crossing against the lights; driving with more than the allowable level of alcohol in one's bloodstream; smoking marijuana; failing to declare income to the Inland Revenue; concealing dutiable goods through customs; stealing a newspaper; writing graffiti on a wall; revealing secret information; even hitting somebody. I doubt there is a single reader who can honestly say he has not performed one or more of these actions in the past twelve months. Millions of these acts are performed every year. And though they are all *against the law*, the sky does not fall, anarchy and disorder do not erupt, civilization as we know it does not collapse. The community seems to be able to absorb a considerable amount of ordinary law-breaking without any serious decline in social order.[6]

Of course, if you define 'order' as simply the situation in which everyone obeys the law then, trivially, order is diminished by every violation. The point is that an enormous amount of that can take place without any significant deterioration in the conditions under which most people live their lives, plan their affairs, and safeguard their personal security.

But though it is far-fetched in some cases, the spectre of a breakdown in social order should be taken seriously in others. During the months of the miners' strike, for instance, there *was* very serious disorder in Britain. Mass picketing produced volatile and bad-tempered confrontations, as groups of workers struggled to dissuade 'scabs' from breaking the strike and in some cases prevent supplies from entering a factory, and as groups of police struggled to keep roadways open and pickets under control. There was disagreement about the legality of both the picketing and the measures that the police took to limit it. But, quite apart from that, on *any* definition of 'disorder', there was very serious trouble. Police officers batoned picketers and bystanders indiscriminately. Some picketers formed 'hit gangs' to beat up miners who were working. (In some cases their actions were homicidal.) Each side tried to provoke the other to violence. The cavalry charges and batoning at Orgreave, the fire-bombing of police stations in South Yorkshire, the killing of David White whose taxi was carrying working miners, the random attacks by police squads – all this indicated a situation in which two large and organized groups of young people (one of them the group charged with the duty of upholding public order) clashed violently for a period of months up and down the length of the country in a physical struggle governed by fewer and fewer restraints.

In those circumstances, no-one of any stature or influence in the dispute could say confidently that his defiance of a court order would have no impact on law and order. That Arthur Scargill continued to call the strike 'official' – the action for which he was held in contempt – probably had little impact. But that this well-known figure went on television to say that the law counted for nothing in a struggle between classes may well have exacerbated the disorder and made it more likely that people would put their normal inhibitions aside. No clear path of cause and effect can be established: perhaps there would have been the same violence anyway; perhaps the dignity of Scargill's rhetoric made things better than they would otherwise have been. But it was clearly a situation which *could* get worse, and in which the impact of individual actions could not be calculated. It was therefore a situation in which some degree of caution and responsibility was called for. It is true that Scargill did not incite or condone violence. But argument about law and order imposes a broader requirement. It holds that people have a moral obligation to consider the effects of what they do in relation to the law, and not to be reckless about how it may lead others to think and behave.

The argument depends, of course, on the recognition by the law-breaker that the disorder he occasions is undesirable. That cannot always be taken for granted. For some radical trade unionists, order may mean 'bourgeois order' (the smooth continuation of economic oppression), and the anarchy and *dis*order we are worried about may be for them the honest and open reality of class struggle. They may think it a good thing that Scargill's defiance aroused the proletariat from its passivity and drove it into conscious struggle with the agents of the state. I think they are wrong about that: if there were more space I would undertake to show that freedom from fear and violent conflict are things that *everyone* has a reason to want. But the controversy shows that public order is not necessarily a neutral idea.

Democracy: 'There's got to be a rule'

Many readers will be irritated that I have not yet considered the most *obvious* argument against law-breaking – the argument that the law has been enacted by Parliament, and so breaking it amounts to a rejection of parliamentary democracy. The idea is that a majority of the people or their representatives have a right to decide these things, and everyone has an obligation to abide by the majority decision. Otherwise they are being undemocratic. I will consider this argument in the next section. But first I want to consider an important assumption that lies behind it.

We don't let majorities (or their representatives) decide everything for us. We let them decide only in cases *where it is important for there to be a collective decision.* It is important to have a collective decision about the basic rate of income tax: we can't have some people paying one rate, others paying another rate, as the spirit moves them. So we elect representatives and they assemble in Parliament to make a single decision on behalf of society. But lots of the things that happen in society don't require a collective decision. We don't make collective decisions as a society about religion; we leave it up to each individual to decide. We don't make collective decisions about population policy; that's left to individual families to decide. Since a decision of the whole society is not required in cases like these, the principle of majority-rules and parliamentary democracy are utterly out of place.

Often it is controversial whether a matter is appropriate for social decision or not. Those who like smoking marijuana think that that issue has nothing to do with society. And in the miners' case, the NUM officials insisted that society as a whole did not need to involve itself through the medium of the law in the internal organization of the union. When the judge held that the union should not call the strike 'official' because the decision to go on strike was at odds with the terms of its own rule-book, Arthur Scargill's response was: 'There is no high court judge going to take away our democratic right to deal with internal matters. We are an independent democratic union.' What he was saying is that the NUM is an independent body that can deal perfectly well with its own rule-book, thank you very much. It doesn't need the supervision of the state or the interference of the courts. It's not a matter of defying the majority of British people who have voted for the law-makers and who support the courts. The majority has no business meddling with private matters, and so it has no right to be obeyed in this sort of case.[7]

That was the NUM argument. However, the judgement in *Taylor v. NUM* rested on a general principle of administrative law – that if a private or quasi-private organization (like a trade union) can act in a way which affects the interests and livelihood of its members, then the courts *will* interfere to see that it abides by its own rules. In a closed shop, union discipline may mean that a person never works again at her chosen trade. That is a serious matter; and the fact that the union is not a state organization simply indicates that not all power in society is state power. The courts have taken the attitude that they may interfere to ensure that any power of this kind is exercised fairly and responsibly. The 'rule-book' principle doesn't just apply to trade unions: it applies to political parties expelling members, to the Rugby Football Union blacklisting people because they play Rugby League, and so on. Society assumes a jurisdiction here because of the nature of the power and the seriousness of the interests involved.

In a way we are up against the same issues that arose in the case of rights. When people disagree about the proper limits of majority rule, how are those disagreements to be resolved? Perhaps, in the end, they too have to be resolved by majority decision (though in America, as we have seen, such issues are generally left to the Supreme Court). At any rate, it is worth noting that they are separate from the issue of what the law on the matter ought to be. The fact that the majority holds a particular view on, say, what the official religion should be *if* there is to be a state religion, doesn't mean that the majority is in favour of there being a state religion. And in terms of moral justification, quite different considerations will be relevant to these questions.

In general, then, we should be bound by the majority only in cases where a social decision is necessary and desirable. In cases where a social decision is unnecessary or undesirable, the will of the majority has no moral force. This means that if you want to make out a democratic argument against breaking the law, you have got to preface it with an account of why the area of law in question is one that society ought to be dealing with. Otherwise the majority you invoke are just a mob of interfering busybodies.

Let's suppose now that that first hurdle has been passed. How does the argument about political obligation in a democracy proceed?

How democratic are our laws?

Often, when people break the law for political or conscientious reasons, the first thing they do is to question its democratic credentials. If the law *were* democratic, they say, there might be a case for obeying it. But in fact the law is a travesty of democracy, or in fact it has now forfeited whatever democratic support it originally had. Though we think of Britain as a democracy, we have seen already (in Chapter two) how tenuous the link is between the will of the people and the law that is actually enforced.

I mentioned there the obvious points that laws are seldom ratified by referenda, and that there are serious questions about how representative our legislators are, given the processes by which they are chosen. Although there is some evidence that many who voted Conservative in 1979 did so because they wanted tighter control of trade unions, still that falls far short of establishing a democratic *mandate* for the Employment Act 1980, let alone for the particular details about secondary picketing that became the crux of the law-breaking issue. The most that can be said about that law is that it emerged as a result of the rather indirect and pragmatic system of electoral government that we have in this country. And if we think there is a moral case for not breaking it, we should be careful not to rest that case on presuppositions about democracy that are unrealistic in the British context.

A second thing to note is that the opportunities for public debate on particular measures are often very limited. The classic case is the Official Secrets Act, which has been involved in some of the most celebrated cases of political disobedience in recent years. The 1911 Act which introduced the infamous Section 2 into British Law went through all its stages in forty minutes, and section 2 was not discussed at all. The change in the law had not been debated in any election campaign and the Under Secretary of State for War simply told the House of Commons that 'none of his Majesty's loyal subjects run the least risk whatever of having their liberties infringed in any degree or particular whatever' by the new measure.[8]

The Official Secrets Act also illustrates a third point. Statutes remain on the books long after popular support for them (assuming they originally had some support) has faded away. We are still bound by the Official Secrets Act, though all parties have called for its reform. The earliest statute still in force in England is dated 1236.[9] Clearly, any argument from democracy is not going to work equally well for all our laws.

The final point is the most important. It is very seldom that we are ever dealing with a situation of direct and straightforward disobedience of the acknowledged terms of a statutory prohibition passed by a democratic parliament. As philosophers we use this simple term 'breaking the law'; but as students of the real world of British politics we should note that this covers an enormous variety of situations.

A messy example will illustrate. The Employment Act 1980 establishes that it is unlawful for a worker to picket except at her own place of work; that is, it makes 'secondary picketing' unlawful. But 'unlawful' does not mean criminal. It means 'not protected by the general immunity for trade unions against being sued in tort for interference with contractual relations'. If someone engages in secondary picketing, she clearly renders herself open to a civil action for damages. But does that mean she is defying the majority and acting undemocratically? Suppose that an employer gets a judge to issues an injunction against secondary picketers to restrain them from from committing the tort mentioned above. They defy the injunction; that is, they disobey the judge. The judge is not an elected representative. Is their disobedience an affront to democracy? The complications do not stop there. The Department of Employment issued a Code of Practice under the 1980 Act suggesting that no more than six pickets should be present at any one place. There was nothing about that in the Act, and no-one voted for the DOE officials. Is a picketer being undemocratic if she ignores the guidelines? Again, on his own initiative a police inspector orders a gateway cleared of pickets because he thinks a breach of the peace is imminent. Whether it is imminent or not is a matter of opinion, and the pickets disagree with him. Are they flouting the law? Are they being undemocratic?

I am not mentioning all these possibilities to confuse the reader, but to drive home the point that in cases where law-breaking becomes politically important, there is very seldom a neatly defined democratic issue at stake. Any argument we want to give about why it is wrong (or perhaps right) to break the law must be sensitive to the variety of ways in which democratic considerations may apply.

Why should the majority rule?

Having said all that, let's consider the democratic argument on its strongest ground, to see if there's anything to it. Suppose there is clear majority support for a measure. Why should a minority obey when they disagree with the majority decision? If we can't find a plausible argument in this case, we are certainly not going to find an argument strong enough to carry us through the mess and complexity of the cases just mentioned.

There are three connected answers in the literature on democratic obligation – one based on *outcomes*, one based on *fairness*, and one based on *consent*.

Outcomes

One reason for abiding by the decision on some issue is that it is the *morally best* decision. Now, most of us accept the view that the majority is not always right, so we are unlikely to be convinced that this is a reason for submitting to majority rule. Still perhaps we should briefly consider the view that the majority is *more likely* to get it right, if only to see what is wrong with it.

Utilitarians believe that what is right in politics is the promotion of the greatest happiness of the greatest number.[10] If you believe this, and if you believe that people are authorities on their own happiness, then you may have some reason to think that the alternative supported by the majority is better, on utilitarian grounds, than the alternative supported by the minority. The majority know where their true happiness lies and they are voting for it. It is a pity that the minority will have to suffer (for *their* true happiness lies with the other measure); but at least the doctrine of majority rules minimizes the amount of suffering in the world. The minority's obligation, therefore, to defer to the majority decision is simply their utilitarian duty to join in the maximization of human happiness.

But even at its best, this argument is full of implausible assumptions. It works, first, only if you accept the utilitarian theory about what's right and wrong, and, as we saw in Chapter Five, many people don't. Second, it rests on the assumption that voters can tell reliably in advance whether a given law will make them happy or unhappy in the future. Third, it relies on the assumption that people vote for or against particular measures on the basis of pure self-interest; if people start voting on the basis of what they think will make their neighbours happy, the argument as it stands simply falls apart. Fourth, it ignores the fact that a given law may affect different people to a differential degree. If we can only vote 'yea' or 'nay', we cannot possibly express *how much* happiness or unhappiness the law will cause us. The vote of a person with a very mild preference at stake counts equally in the majoritarian calculation with the vote of a person whose happiness may be drastically affected by the measure. If a law causes hideous suffering to a minority while making each member of the majority marginally better off, who can possibly say that the majority decision is necessarily the best one? And why on earth should the minority defer to the others in such a case? So the coincidence between utilitarianism and majoritarianism is likely to be rather shaky.

Apart from the utilitarian argument, the only other reason for thinking that the majority is probably right has to do with the dynamics of argument. When a proposal is first mooted, some people will be for it and others against it. At this stage the distribution is random; there's no reason to think that the side that happens to have the largest number of supporters is right. But suppose a debate now ensues, and people on both sides try to convince their opponents with arguments. If the issue is one where rational argument is possible, and if the people involved in the debate are, on the whole, susceptible to rational argument, then we would expect that at the end of the debate the more rationally defensible position would be the one commanding the greater support. Both are big 'if's, of course. In many political disagreements, the criteria of a good argument are as much in dispute as the issues themselves. And the argument assumes that people are, on the whole, not stupid or obtuse, that they will vote with their brains not their stomachs, and so on. That may not be a sensible assumption. But the argument is at least worth considering.

Fairness

If majority voting does not guarantee the best outcome, still it might itself be the fairest procedure. When people disagree about an issue where it is important for them to reach a decision, it seems natural to go with the wishes of the majority. But as a matter of fact, it is very difficult to say *why* this is the case.

It is not hard to show that majority-rule is a *fair* procedure. If it is important for society to reach a decision, and there is disagreement about what that decision should be, then majority-rule has the advantage that it takes everyone's view into account, that it treats all views equally, and that it satisfies elementary constraints of rationality (such as implying that if one person is in favour of a proposal and no-one is against, then the proposal should be adopted).

But it is more difficult to show that majority-rule should prevail over some other procedure, such as tossing a coin between two supported proposals or letting the disputants settle the matter by combat. The philosopher John Locke suggested that 'it is necessary the Body should move that way whither the most force carries it, which is the consent of the majority'.[11] But that makes voting sound like a surrogate for fighting – which it clearly isn't – and it would in any case reduce the minority's obligation to nothing more moral than the principle of 'might is right'. I think we have to face the fact that it is difficult to produce a philosophical proof of the fairness of majority-rule based on first principles. It is one of those things that strikes us as fair, and there is not much more to say about it than that.

Consent

If I say I will do something, and people rely on my undertaking, then it is morally wrong for me later to go back on my word. That is the basis of the moral obligation to keep one's promises. Political theorists have tried to apply similar reasoning to voting. If I vote in a referendum, or in some other process of decision-making, I am implicitly saying to my fellow voters, 'You can count on me to abide by the outcome.' That is how they will interpret my action, and they will rely on my implicit undertaking in their decision to vote themselves. After all, there would be no point in their voting if they thought the vote wasn't going to *settle* anything. So, by voting, the argument goes, I have tacitly consented to the outcome, and that tacit consent is tantamount to an agreement to be bound.

It is no good objecting that the voter didn't *say* she would abide by the outcome. We all know there are such things as implicit promises, and we know that people often rely on them. When they do, the person whose conduct led to the reliance has a moral duty to follow through on the impression she gave. An Australian philosopher, Peter Singer, cites a good example:

> A group of people may go out for a few drinks. One member of the group buys the first round of drinks for everyone, then the second member does the same, and so on in turn. If, after most members of the group have done this, one member, who has accepted drinks paid for by the others, refuses to buy anyone else a drink, he will be thought to have behaved badly. One could say that he has an obligation to buy the others a drink. The obligation does not arise from actually consenting to buy drinks, for the man may never have agreed to do so, either expressly or to himself. He may even have intended all along to have a few drinks at the expense of other people. Yet by acting in a particular way, one may become involved in an obligation to which it is no defence to say: 'I never consented.'[12]

However, if this works as an analogy for political obligation, then we have got to accept the possibility that individuals or minority groups might want to opt out. If the man who wouldn't buy his round had told his friends at the beginning, 'Look, I'm not going to pay for anyone else's drinks, but if you still want to pay for mine, that's OK with me', he wouldn't be doing anything wrong. The important thing about implicit undertakings is not to give a false impression on which others may rely. But if the man makes his position clear from the outset, his friends can hardly then turn round and complain that they were relying on him to stand his round. By analogous reasoning, it ought to be possible for a person to announce to his fellow-citizens as he votes: 'Don't be under any illusions. I am going to vote in this referendum but I have no intention of abiding by the outcome if it is not the one that I vote for. You have been warned.' If this announcement is made sufficiently clearly and publicly in advance, we can hardly say that his voting indicates consent and that we were counting on her compliance.

By the same argument, it would seem that someone who doesn't vote in the referendum – the abstainer – has no obligation to abide by the outcome. *She* has not given a false impression about her willingness to comply: indeed she has not given any impression at all, and may be acting just as she would have acted if the matter hadn't arisen.

Often people do strike one or other of these attitudes to voting. Revolutionary communists may think that voting is a sham and that it commits them morally to nothing. They participate, if they do, only as a tactical ploy – because for the time being, till the revolution comes, this is the only way they can have any impact on politics. If their position is well-known, their fellow citizens can hardly complain that they were misled. Similarly, it is common for radical groups to call for an election to be boycotted, precisely so as to deprive it of any legitimacy. If a substantial sector of the population refuses to vote, they may say, then the election settles nothing and no-one is bound by the result.

If pressed, most people believe that even those who abstain from voting (quietly or vociferously) have a moral obligation to accept the result – at least in a society like ours. Maybe this is just wishful thinking; they have this prejudice and they wish there were a moral argument to justify it. Let's see what they would have to show. To establish the position that even *non*-voters are obliged to obey, they would have to show, not only that voting is a fair procedure, but that its fairness is in some sense *compelling*. As well as showing that voting gives rise to an obligation, they would have to show that we have a duty or an obligation to take part in the procedure and that this is sufficient to generate, in turn, an obligation to abide by the result even if, for some reason, we decide to abstain. How could they argue for that?

Our background social duty

Remember our starting point. Before any of these arguments about democracy get underway, we first have to show that the issue under consideration is one on which society *needs* a decision. What does this mean? What do we mean when we say that society needs a decision on some issue?

One thing we mean is that people may be harmed, and life in society may deteriorate (people's prospects may diminish, injustice may increase arbitrarily, confusion may reign, expectations may flounder, etc.) if we do not reach a decision. People who live in our society ought to care about that, even if they are not among the ones who will suffer if a social decision is not reached on this matter. They should therefore do what they can to make a social decision possible. I shall call this their 'background social duty'. We could argue about *why* people have this duty. The reasons partly involve the altruistic content of morality: we ought to *care* about others, at least to some extent, and do what is in our power, when it is not too onerous, to make life bearable for them. This is a general duty we owe to all mankind, but it applies particularly to those whose fate is affected by our behaviour in the way members of our political community are. We and our fellow-citizens find ourselves bound together in a framework that offers us the possibility of making life bearable for one another. We should not spurn that opportunity without some very good reason.

Other reasons may be less straightforwardly altruistic, appealing instead to the debt of gratitude and reciprocity we owe to those in the community who are already helping to make life bearable for us. Some are even reasons of self-interest: there are certain ways in which all can benefit from social co-operation only if everyone is assured that all or most of their fellow citizens will join in the co-operative scheme. For these reasons – and there is much, much more that could be said along these lines – it does not seem unreasonable to postulate a background duty of social co-operation incumbent on everyone.

The duty is to join with others in reasonable schemes of co-operation to ameliorate the conditions of life for all. Often, however, there is persistent disagreement about what the scheme of social co-operation ought to be. When this happens, there has got to be a procedure for reaching a decision despite that disagreement. Democratic voting is one such procedure, and it is a fair one. But voting *itself* doesn't solve the social problem; voting answers the need for a social decision only if the outcome of the vote actually settles the matter. And that can happen only if people generally accept and abide by the outcome.

Someone who takes part in such a decision procedure indicates to her fellow citizens that they can count on her to do that. She gives an impression that they can rely on her, and this is the basis of the familiar argument that voting is like a promise. But what I have referred to as the background social duty dictates that people *ought to be able* to rely on others to do this anyway. People have a right to expect that others will join with them in fair procedures oriented to the solution of genuine problems in society.

Announcing loudly that you are abstaining, or that your vote is just a cynical strategy which shouldn't be taken to bind you, dispels any illusion others may be under that they *can* rely on you. But it doesn't refute the moral point that they *ought to have been able* to rely on you. And that will be the basis of their moral reproach when you break the law.

I find this argument plausible and attractive, not least because it seems more flexible, more open to exceptions, more open to distinctions of degree, than the traditional arguments about obligation and consent.[13]

The argument is attractive inasmuch as it makes *realistic* use of the ideas of democracy and consent – ideas so often deployed artificially in discussions of political obligation. It does embody the traditional idea that the person who votes in an election or referendum makes some sort of commitment to her fellow voters. But it does not rest the duty to obey exclusively on that idea. Instead it draws attention to the moral reasons that exist for making this commitment in the first place. In that way, the consensual act of voting, if that's what it is, occupies a less contingent and less arbitrary role in the determination of what the citizen morally ought to do.

The argument also has the attraction of not portraying the duty to obey as an all-or-nothing affair. It is a duty that might plausibly apply in some cases but not in others. If the area in which the law purports to bind us is not an area where social regulation is necessary or desirable, then the argument has little force. But if it is an area – like, for example, picketing or traffic control – where the conditions of life are likely to deteriorate markedly unless there is general acceptance of some conventions and restraints, then the argument has considerable force. In other words, it is an argument which is sensitive to the possibility of disagreement on these matters: it clarifies rather than conceals the moral considerations that might make someone of good will and honest judgement think that a particular law had no claim on her.

By the same token, it is also an argument which varies the moral importance attached to obedience and disobedience. That a social decision should be reached, even in the face of disagreement, may matter more in some cases than in others. The importance of others' being able to rely on you to help make that decision possible may then vary accordingly. This is important because often the considerations which motivate us to break the law are also moral considerations. Arthur Scargill, for example, had reasons of altruism and solidarity, not just reasons of self-interest, for defying the law. Our obligation to obey the law is not the only moral obligation we have have. If our obligations conflict, it is important to have some way of thinking about their relative importance, and the present argument provides a helpful measure of what may be at stake when an individual is wondering whether it is right to break the law.[14]

Above all the argument seems to fit well with our general theme of trying to find ways of thinking about law, not as something that stands above us, but as something which can be regarded as *ours*, something we have constructed together to make social life bearable and better. Of course there are going to be cases where that image of law is simply incredible. Many of the laws we face were made neither by us nor for us. For those cases, the advantage of the argument is that it helps us to gauge the woefulness of the shortfall between the rhetoric of those who insist we must always obey and the reality that deprives their rhetoric of any substantial moral force.

Notes

1 I have drawn freely from Alex Callinicos and Mike Simons, *The Great Strike: the Miners' Strike of 1984-5 and its Lessons* (London: Socialist Worker Publications, 1985) and K.D. Ewing, 'The Strike, the Courts and the Rule-Books', *Industrial Law Journal*, 14 (1985), pp. 160–75. (Mr Justice Nicholls' decision is reported in *Taylor v. NUM (Yorkshire Area)* [1985] IRLR 445.)

2 There is an excellent discussion of civil disobedience in John Rawls, *A Theory of Justice* (Oxford University Press, 1971), pp. 350–91. Rawls correctly infers that the requirement to disobey *civilly* applies only in a society which is not radically unjust.

3 R.P. Wolff, *In Defense of Anarchism* (New York: Harper Torchbooks, 1976), especially pp. 3–19.

4 The case I have in mind is that of Sarah Tisdall who was prosecuted and jailed in 1984 for leaking a memo to the *Guardian* about how the MOD proposed to conceal the arrival of cruise missiles from the public.

5 See Clive Ponting, *The Right to Know* (London: Sphere Books, 1985).

6 See, for example, Stuart Hall, *Policing the Crisis: Mugging the State, and Law and Order* (London: Macmillan, 1978).

7 The situation is messy because the case also concerned majoritarian decision-making *within* the union. Scargill's point was that the majority of British people have no right to insist that the decision to strike be taken by a majority of coal miners rather than by the executive or by the regions (any more than the nation has a right to insist that clubs or families govern themselves democratically).

8 There is a good account in Ponting, *The Right to Know*, Ch. 1.

9 The Statute of Merton (20 Hen 3) concerning commons of pasture and 'special bastardy'.

10 There is a discussion of utilitarianism in Chapter five.

11 John Locke, *Two Treatises of Government* (1689; Cambridge University Press, 1960), Second Treatise, section 96.

12 Peter Singer, *Democracy and Disobedience* (Oxford University Press, 1974), p. 49.

13 In his book, *Moral Principles and Political Obligations* (Princeton, N.J.: Princeton University Press, 1979), A. John Simmonds suggests that arguments like these prove too much: they seem to generate a duty to support any reasonable scheme of social co-operation in the world not just the one in our own country. But in fact I think we *do* have a duty to support (or at least not undermine) the laws and institutions of other countries if they are reasonably just; and the obligation we have in our own country is not *sui generis* but simply in the circumstances an acute application of this.

14 There is an excellent discussion in Michael Walzer, 'The Obligation to Disobey' in his book *Obligations: Essays on Disobedience, War and Citizenship* (Cambridge, Mass.: Harvard University Press, 1970).

Chapter eight

The legal framework

Bleak House

'The raw afternoon is rawest, and the dense fog is densest, and the
muddy streets are muddiest, near that leaden-headed old obstruction,
appropriate ornament for a leaden-headed old corporation: Temple
Bar. And hard by Temple Bar, in Lincoln's Inn Hall, at the very
heart of the fog, sits the Lord High Chancellor in his High Court of
Chancery.

'Never can there come fog too thick, never can there come mud
and mire too deep, to assort with the groping and floundering
condition which this High Court of Chancery, most pestilent of
hoary sinners, holds, this day, in the sight of heaven and earth.

'On such an afternoon, if ever, the Lord Chancellor ought to be
sitting here – as here he is – with a foggy glory round his head, softly
fenced in with crimson cloth and curtains, addressed by a large
advocate with great whiskers, a little voice, and an interminable
brief, and outwardly directing his contemplation to the lantern in the
roof, where he can see nothing but fog. On such an afternoon, some
score of members of the High Court of Chancery bar ought to be –
as here they are – mistily engaged in one of the ten thousand stages
of an endless cause, tripping one another up on slippery precedents,
groping knee-deep in technicalities, running their goat-hair and
horse-hair warded heads against walls of words, and making a
pretence of equity with serious faces, as players might. On such an
afternoon, the various solicitors in the cause, some two or three of
whom inherited it from their fathers, who made a fortune by it, ought
to be – as are they not? – ranged in a line, in a long matted well (but
you might look in vain for truth at the bottom of it), between the
registrar's red table and the silk gowns, with bills, cross-bills,
answers, rejoinders, injunctions, affidavits, issues, references to
masters, masters' reports, mountains of costly nonsense, piled before
them. Well may the court be dim, with wasting candles here and

there; well may the fog hang heavy in it, as if it would never get out; well may the stained glass windows lose their colour, and admit no light of day into the place; well may the uninitiated from the streets, who peep in through the glass panes in the door, be deterred from entrance from its owlish aspect, and by the drawl languidly echoing to the roof from the padded dais where the Lord High Chancellor looks into the lantern that has no light in it, and where the attendant wigs are all stuck in a fog-bank! This is the Court of Chancery; which has its decaying houses and its blighted lands in every shire; which has its worn-out lunatic in every madhouse, and its dead in every churchyard; which has its ruined suitor, with his slipshod heels and threadbare dress, borrowing and begging through the round of every man's acquaintance; which gives to monied might, the means abundantly of wearying out the right; which so exhausts finances, patience, courage, hope; so overthrows the brain and breaks the heart; that there is not an honourable man among its practitioners who would not give – who does not often give – the warning, "Suffer any wrong that can be done you, rather than come here!" '[1]

Pomp and ceremony

The opening pages of Charles Dickens' *Bleak House* provide a somewhat different perspective on the law from the one we have taken so far. We have discussed the rule of law, the wisdom of qualifying power with restraints of legality, the way law can operate as a sensitive framework for the pursuit of social policy, the resolution of disputes, the obligation to obey, and above all the ideal of the law as our own. Yet here in Dickens' prose is the legal system in all its majestic *reality*. Wigs, ribbons, and paper. Forms, precedents, and procedures. Delay, technicality, monopoly, mystery. Power, pomposity, money. Bewilderment, frustration, lunacy, decay, and despair.

It is true that things have changed a little since Dickens' days (due in part, I think, to his criticisms and those of others like him). The Court of Chancery is no longer able to drag out cases like his fictional example of *Jarndyce v. Jarndyce*, enmiring them in technicalities for generations.[2] It is ironic, incidentally, that the Court of *Chancery* could be described in this way, for in its inception in the fifteenth century the jurisdiction of the Lord Chancellor was set up precisely to offer relief to those litigants who could find no justice in the rigid forms and convoluted technicalities of the courts of common law. Inevitably, I suppose, over the centuries, institutions set up to offer this sort of relief themselves become as ossified and technical as those they were meant to supplement. At any rate, it is true things have changed a little for the better. But the kinds of abuse that Dickens highlights are echoed in many of the concerns that are still expressed about our legal system.

Much of the humbug that Dickens described – and indeed, much that survives today – is peculiarly and exquisitely *English* in character, and most of it could be thrown overboard with little real loss to the law itself or the public interest. An obvious example is the costume and ceremonial of our courts – the fur and ermine of medieval gowns, 'the paraphenalia of horsehair wigs',[3] the processions, the prayers, and so on. Clearly all this is supposed to have some salutary effect upon the public.[4] The idea (to the extent that there is one) is presumably to encourage respect and order through bewilderment and unfamiliarity, to use theatrical technique to impress a solemnity upon those who have the misfortune to come into a courtroom, and to distract attention away from the human being on the bench or at the bar towards the symbolism of the role that he occupies. If any of these aims succeeds, it is because the public are somehow gulled by the paraphernalia into thinking that the law of their land is not *their* law, that its ways are not *their* ways, and that it is necessary for it to be administered by a special priesthood of initiates as remote from ordinary mortals as royalty or the papacy.

We have already discussed, in Chapter six, the cult of reverence for the judges of our higher courts that seems to preclude any open criticism within the legal profession of their decision-making and to dampen debate about judicial role and judicial behaviour among politicians and the public at large. The view that the judges must somehow be beyond the reach of political debate in order to preserve their legendary stance 'above' politics is, as we have seen, unacceptable. For all that it might once have been necessary to sustain judicial independence, its main effect now is to render judges even less accountable on matters of social importance and even less a part of the public debate to which their speeches might otherwise contribute.

The organization of the legal profession is equally wonderful. Though lawyers are always free to specialize as they please, no other advanced common law system preserves the rigid demarcation between the professions of barrister and solicitor that we find in this country. Someone who wants to bring a case before a court must not only consult and pay for the services of a solicitor, but the solicitor must then brief, and the client must pay for, the further services of counsel to actually present the case in court. In some jurisdictions – Australia and New Zealand, for example – a notional distinction between the two functions of legal advisor and courtroom representative is preserved, but a single individual may occupy both roles and a solicitor may brief herself in her capacity as barrister. In others, like the United States, even the notional distinction has been abandoned. Yet in Britain we continue to put up with what David Pannick has called 'restrictive practices that would bring envious tears to the eyes of the toughest trade union official'.[5] It is only with the utmost difficulty and in the teeth of the most trenchant opposition that solicitors have won the right to appear in court on uncontested matters or to secure any possibility of appointment to the higher ranks of the judiciary.

These issues of ceremony, reverence, and privilege could be addressed by fairly straightforward reforms, as they have been in other countries which do not make such a fetish of the spectacle of tradition. But some of the other misgivings evoked by the imagery of *Bleak House* cannot be dealt with so easily.

Rules, legalism, and injustice

The worries most people have about the law, and the reasons most people 'dread a lawsuit beyond almost anything else short of sickness and of death',[6] concern things like the obscurity of legal language, the technicality of legal forms, the delays that seem to be built into legal procedures, and above all a lingering unease, which is hard to pin down but remains remarkably resilient, that the law does not always offer, and maybe in the nature of things cannot offer, the ordinary person what she has been brought up to expect from it – justice.

Unlike the pomposity of wigs and so on, these concerns are not peculiar to the United Kingdom. Many scholars entertain the possibility that they might be endemic to the idea of law itself. It is true that progress can and has been made on all these fronts. Recent Lord Chancellors have made strenuous efforts to reduce delays, by appointing more judges, extending the sitting times of courts, cracking down on time-wasting by counsel, and trying to reduce the time that defendants in criminal cases spend waiting on remand before their cases are heard. There have also been efforts to reduce the formality in certain areas of the law – replacing the atmosphere of the courtroom with that of the conciliation table in matrimonial disputes, for example – and to diminish the technicality of documents. But the reforms have not been comprehensive, and, as I have said, many believe this is because the problems raise issues that go to the heart of law and legality as such, and cannot be dealt with simply by changing the rules or procedures.

The problems I have mentioned – obscurity, technicality, delay, and the lingering sense of injustice – are obviously bound up with one another. Ask a solicitor why legal language is so obscure, and he will say it is designed to forestall an array of technical problems that the ordinary person might not think of and with which ordinary language is not designed to cope. Ask what these problems are and he may mention ways in which people have tried to squeeze through the 'loopholes' in the technicalities of some legal formulation. Ask about delays and one is likely to get the same sort of answer: the steps in a legal process take so long because each one has to be scrutinized and checked in a way that defies belief so far as ordinary decision-making is concerned. It is easy to regale the nervous client (who sees the delay – and the bill! – extending more or less indefinitely) with stories of the catastrophes that have befallen those who cut corners or tried to pursue such transactions on their own. The trouble is those catastrophes often seem themselves to stem from legal procedures. A person tries to do her own conveyancing and she ends up catastrophically entangled in the snares of ancient leaseholds, estates, and easements. One does not get the impression that lawyers and legal language protect us from dangers that exist independently of the legal framework (in the way vaccines protect us from independently existing diseases). Instead, it seems, we need barristers, solicitors, and the legal apparatus to protect us from *other* barristers and solicitors manipulating the same apparatus. I am sure that impression is sometimes unfair, and that it arises only because we tend to underestimate the independent potential for things to go wrong in social relations, and because we blame the law itself for any difficulty that happens to be framed in legal terms. I am equally sure, however, that it is a very widespread impression.[7]

Above all, these factors of formality, technicality, and delay contribute to the widespread sense that there is a woeful but perhaps inevitable gap between law and justice.

Justice

I have not said a great deal about the idea of *justice* in this book. Like many concepts in legal and political theory, it has both a wider and a narrower meaning.

In the narrower meaning, we say that justice is done when the rules of law (whatever they happen to be) are applied fairly, impartially, and correctly to the cases that arise.[8] In criminal law, justice is done when those who have committed the offences that the law defines are duly convicted and punished, and when those who have not are acquitted. In the law of contracts, justice is done

when people are made to do what they agreed to do, according to
the principles of contract law, or when they are made to compensate
those who suffered loss as a result of relying on their agreement.
And so on. Obviously, in this narrow sense, justice is going to be
relative to the rules of each society.

The wider sense of 'justice' goes beyond the terms of the rules
of law and asks whether the legally prescribed result is itself really
right. Is it *right*, for example, that a person should be punished for
possessing marijuana? We know it is the law, but is the law itself
good? Is it right that a person living in rented accomodation should
acquire security of tenure after a certain period? We know the law,
as it stands, gives her this security, but *should* it do so? Wouldn't it
be a *fairer* or a *better* law if it enabled landlords and tenants to
strike their own bargains in this regard? As the terminology
indicates, these are evaluative, normative, indeed moralistic questions. They are questions not about what the legal result is, but
about what the legal result *ought to be*. Justice, in this wide sense,
is a moralistic standard which judges and lawyers – to the extent
that they have a choice – are supposed to be striving to emulate;
and it is a standard we use to assess the fruits of their efforts.

There is certainly no space here to discuss the provenance of this
standard. Justice is now one of the most talked about topics in
political philosophy.[9] For some, justice is embodied in the word of
God; for others, it is simply a reflection of our deepest human
concerns and commitments. For some, justice is a standard we
construct, asking ourselves how we would go about designing a
society to live in if we had a choice and what the results of those
rules would be for the choices that we actually face in the law.[10]
For others, justice is a standard implicit in the social meanings that
we already live by, and therefore something that may differ fom
culture to culture.[11]

But no matter what the background theory, people use the idea of
justice to summon up what they regard as the ultimate standard by
which laws and legal decisions are to be assessed. Moreover, it is
thought of as a compelling standard, not just a matter of aspiration.
It's not simply that we would – in our philosophical moods –
rather like our laws to be just. The point is that without justice, law
lacks any moral quality at all. It is not a moral luxury or an
indulgence. The standard of justice is a *sine qua non* of legal
morality. If we have the slightest interest at all in distinguishing
good laws from bad laws, then we should turn first to consider the
standards of justice.[12]

It is not as easy to say what those standards actually entail.
Everything from here on is controversial. We may say that justice

concerns the way the most important benefits and burdens are distributed in social life. Some people are rich and live in luxury; many are reasonably well-off; others, however, live in poverty, disease, and misery. Justice is a way of evaluating those differences, or perhaps a way of evaluating how they came about. Similarly, some people in society are rewarded and esteemed; many live their lives with a satisfactory modicum of freedom and self-respect; but there are others who are penalized, condemned, and sometimes even killed. Justice is supposed to provide a fundamental standard for assessing that too. The differences in question are not trivial: for the people concerned they matter as much as anything on earth matters. Life and death, sickness and health, ambition and despair – these are the consequences of the distinctions with which justice is concerned.

The other fundamental point about justice is that it is seen as a set of *equal* standards, even though it may not in itself ordain economic equality. The same standards apply in the same way to everyone. Since all of us are human beings, we have to ensure that the claims of our humanity are properly respected. Are people getting what they deserve or what is due to them? Are radical differences in happiness and misery in our society being based on arbitrary distinctions (like race, for example, or gender) or is there some reason appropriate to the awfulness of the distinction? Do we have a social framework which takes proper account of the claims that can be made on behalf of every human person? These are the questions of justice.

I said there was a lingering sense of a woeful but perhaps inevitable gap between law and justice. Most of those who have this sense are not political philosophers or specialists on the theories of justice that abound in the literature today. They don't spend their days reading *Philosophy and Public Affairs*. They simply have an intuitive feeling that many people are being 'exploited' or 'screwed' or 'done out of what is rightfully theirs' in our society, and that the institutions of the legal system – the courts, the solicitors, the statutes, and the jargon – tend on the whole to make matters worse, not better.

One possible explanation is the one we considered at the beginning of the book. Maybe the legal system is simply the tool of the dominant class, a tool which it uses as a means of duping and exploiting and feeding on the rest. The reason why there is a gap between justice and law is because law is being manipulated, consciously or unconsciously, in the interests of some groups and against the interests of others. Law is a partisan enterprise through and through, and those with a sense of injustice are those on side of the losers. There is no reason to believe this is false, certainly not in Britain in the late 1980s. But still, it is not the whole story.

Many believe a law/justice gap would remain even after the best efforts were made to eradicate exploitation, even after the revolution (if there were to be one). Maybe this is the product of a deep pessimism about human politics: there will always be exploiters and exploitees, and self-styled radical or revolutionary liberators are ultimately nothing but a changing of the guard. A deeper explanation, however, is that it is the legal enterprise itself that will always appear to fall short of our standards, no matter how righteous the motives of our jurists and legislators.

Laws and words

I said in Chapter six that there was no getting away from words and their meanings in the law. Modern law is, in large part, an enterprise of subjecting human conduct to formulated verbal rules. We take the diversity of interactions and relationships, and we try to indicate what is acceptable and unacceptable, or what behaviour is to lead to what consequences, or who is to get what, when and how, using rules which describe actions and situations succinctly in terms of their discernable features.

Now one difficulty with this is well-known, and we discussed it in the chapter on judges. If a rule picks out some feature of an action and makes it legally significant (e.g. 'Anyone driving a vehicle in the park is liable to a fine not exceeding £100'), difficulty will arise where we are unsure whether a given action in the real world actually has that feature or (and it often amounts to the same thing) what the meaning of the specified feature really is. For example, does riding a skateboard count as 'driving a vehicle', does 'vehicle' include 'bicycle', and so on? But as well as these difficulties of definition, there are also deeper difficulties about the very idea of pinning down what is acceptable or unacceptable, desirable or undesirable, in verbal terms.

A verbal formulation will usually focus our attention on a very small number of the characteristics that an action or situation may possess. Once we have ascertained that a vehicle was involved and that it was being driven in the park, then that is it, so far as the rule we have imagined is concerned. The aims or motives of the driver are not referred to, nor are her skill and experience, even though both might be relevant to a moral assessment of whether she should be punished for what she did. Of course, we could have a more complicated rule referring to these features of the situation as well. But there would always be room for complaints about other omissions. What about what other people were doing? Was the park empty or crowded? And so on. There is no reason to think that any manageable rule would be able to specify *all* the features of a situation that might be relevant to its moral assessment.[13]

The verbal specification of a rule may not be the best way to capture what is moral. After a long time searching for the magic formula that would sum up the essence of morality – the magic rules that would pin down all the morally relevant considerations – philosophers are once again toying with the idea that moral decision-making may be a necessarily 'intuitive' and relatively inarticulate business.[14] Indeed, the idea that formulated definitions and verbal rules might be inappropriate for expressing moral insights is not exactly new:

> But he, desiring to justify himself, said to Jesus. 'And who is my neighbour?' Jesus replied, 'A man was going down from Jerusalem to Jericho and he fell among robbers, who stripped him and beat him, and departed, leaving him half dead. Now by chance a priest was going down that road; and when he saw him he passed by on the other side. So likewise a Levite, when he came to the place and saw him, passed by on the other side. But a Samaritan, as he journeyed, came to where he was; and when he saw him, he had compassion, and went to him and bound up his wounds . . . Which of these three, do you think, proved neighbour to the man who fell among the robbers?' He said, 'The one who showed mercy on him.' And Jesus said to him, 'Go and do likewise.'[15]

Christ, asked for a definition, tells a story, and we come away with the sense that a good man will understand what it is to 'do likewise' without having to formulate a rule to tell him which cases are like, and which cases are unlike, the case of the good Samaritan. Indeed Christ's challenge to 'the Law' of his time was precisely the suggestion that morally we can learn more from an 'intuitive' understanding of a parable than from the recitation of a formula. If this is so, then inevitably any formulated rule will seem unsatisfactory to our moral sensibility; it will always seem like an attempt to pin down in words what should be left at the implicit level of insight and judgement.

If the 'parable' image captures anything about our moral sense, then it helps explain the persistence of a gap between law and justice. Even the best-made rule is always going to fall short of our *sense* of right and wrong, if that sense operates as an unarticulated disposition rather than as a formulated body of principle.

It is true that law doesn't always have to comprise a set of rigid verbal rules. Sometimes instead of saying 'X must do A in a situation of type B', a legal provision will say something vaguer and more open-ended such as 'X must behave *reasonably*' or 'X must strike a *proper balance* between considerations A and B'. Moreover, as we saw in our discussion in Chapter six, the doctrine of precedent in common law operates much more in the manner of 'Go and do likewise' than through the extrapolation and interpretation of formulaic rules.

The trouble is that in law there is a constant pressure to formulate things verbally – to lay down rules and make principles explicit – a pressure which simply doesn't exist to anything like the same extent in the arena of moral debate. The pressure arises partly out of the desire for predictability. People want to know, in advance, the basis on which their actions will be judged and dealt with by the state, and they are in fact willing to sacrifice moral subtlety for certainty in many cases, particularly in areas where they suspect that the unformulated sensibility of those who wield state power may not operate in a way that coincides reliably with their own.

This is particularly so in those areas of law where it is important for someone to make it understood that she is intending to bring about a particular legal consequence. We need a formulated rule laying down exactly the conditions for making a valid will, for example – not because those conditions in themselves capture anything important about the morality of the transaction, but because it is important for a testator to be able to signal explicitly to the world what is to count as her disposing of her property and what is not. She needs a way of marking out those expressions of her desires which are to be taken seriously and given legal effect after her death. The somewhat ritualistic and in themselves perhaps meaningless requirements of form and attestation fit that bill exactly.

Law and political deliberation

In addition to all this, we need to remember the connection between law and *politics*, and how that affects this business of formulation.

In one of its meanings, 'politics' refers to the way in which the members of a community or their representatives can come together to talk about and reach agreement on the conditions for ordering their lives.[16] To do that, they need to be able to recognize what they are talking about, and what it is that is being proposed or discussed. It always seems a little pedantic that something like 'the Rules of Public Meetings' or 'the Standing Orders of Parliament' commit us in our discussions to things like the formulation of a *motion* and lay down quite rigid rules for its proposition and amendment. That sometimes seems unduly formal and obsessive. Its virtue is that it allows a variety of people with a diversity of perspective, insight, and experience to build a framework for their lives together and to share some assurance that it is a *common* framework they are building. This is true of legislators, who need to share a sense that they are debating the same measure, even though they come from a diversity of backgrounds. And it is true also of citizens, if they are to be able to participate in political deliberation, put pressure on their legislators, and hold them accountable in public for their actions. The words of a common language provide a sort of co-ordination point for what might otherwise be a hopeless maze of crossed purposes and mutual confusion.

In a relatively homogenous society it would be possible, I suppose, for a social framework to be maintained in terms of customs and shared understandings that were implicit rather than formulated, understood rather than articulated, constitutive of people's social consciousness rather than posited externally as something they might or might not accept. A number of writers associated with what is called 'the new communitarianism' have recently suggested that modern society lost a lot when it moved away from these relatively implicit modes of understanding and organization.[17] Our sense of the persistent gap between law and justice, I am suggesting, is part of that cost. But society gained a lot as well. It meant that we could begin to live and organize ourselves together in society even with people who did not share our cultural and ethnic background, our customs, or very many of our social understandings. By being able to posit the rules of social order explicitly, we could consider them as something independent of ourselves and intelligible and debatable apart from our particular preconceptions. No doubt there are limits to this. We could not participate in a social order, explicit or implicit, with beings with whom we shared no understandings at all. But with formulated, articulate law, we can go a long way.

Adversarial individualism

I have mentioned several times the belief, shared by many radicals, that law is not a 'neutral' mode of social organization (whatever that means), but a tool for facilitating the exploitation of some members of society by others. In Chapter two, I alluded to the Marxist claim that this is not merely an incidental fact about who happened to control the state. Some Marxist writers believe that the very *form* of modern legality is bourgeois and capitalist through and through: it is a form, they say, that could never be used *except* for class domination. It follows that a genuinely socialist society might have to eschew the forms and structures of law altogether.

In the hands of some Marxists, like Lenin, this argument simply reduces to triviality. If law is *defined* as part of the state and if the state is *nothing but* an instrument of class oppression, then, as a matter of definition, the way a society organizes itself once class oppression has been done away with will not be called 'law'.[18]

But other writers in this tradition have tried to argue for more interesting conclusions. Modern law, they say, is adversarial and individualistic. It takes as its primary subject matter the individual legal person with his (the masculine form is used advisedly) property and his rights, and its underlying purpose is to recognize and protect that individual, and facilitate the exchange and transfer of property in the capitalist market. The Soviet jurist E.B. Pashukanis is now the best known exponent of this view (though he perished in obscurity in the 1930s, ironically after Stalin found it politic to proclaim a belief in socialist legality after all!). According to Pashukanis, 'law' should not be defined simply as a system of norms or as the authoritative imposition of social order. Law is a particular mode of social order in which individuals are raised to the level of abstract subjects and invested with rights and the ability to dispose of them to one another at will. It is a mode of social order which treats all objects as interchangeable commodities rather than as useful resources and which defines owners simply as the occasions of this interchangeability rather than as flesh-and-blood men and women with human needs and interests:

> The legal subject is thus an abstract owner of commodities raised to the heavens. His will in the legal sense has its real basis in the desire to alienate through acquisition and profit through alienating. For this desire to be fulfilled, it is absolutely necessary that the wishes of commodity owners meet each other halfway. This relationship is expressed in legal terms as a contract or an agreement concluded between autonomous wills. Hence the contract is a concept central to law.[19]

For Pashukanis, all legal obligations are relative to the rights of some abstract individual. There are, as it were, no free-floating obligations, or requirements simply laid down by the state, or imposed in the interests of society. The state is conceived only as a guarantor of individual exchange and of the environment necessary for it to take place. Law is a chain of legal relations between purportedly self-sufficient individuals.

These points probably seem more vivid and plausible in the context of the civil law tradition – the tradition with which Russian and most continental socialists were most familiar – than in the traditions of Anglo-American common law. The latter have tended to develop piecemeal, case by case and statute by statute, without detailed exploration of their underlying assumptions. In civilian systems, by contrast, law tends to be set out systematically in treatises that begin explicitly with the notion of a legal person and of the rights and obligations that that subject might have.[20]

If we accept this view, there is no question of proletarian *law* for a communist society. However the society of the future is ordered, it will not present people as self-sufficient atoms, related only by rights and obligations, nor will it try to abstract from the reality of human dependence and co-operation in economic life.

There is wide agreement now that Pashukanis's understanding of law is a little narrow to cover what most people mean by the term. There is a lot of law that is pure regulation and framework, and that cannot be explained in terms of perfect correlativity between obligations and the rights of atomistic individuals. If he is to avoid the triviality of Lenin's argument, he must be claiming that what is destined to 'wither away' with the capitalist economy is the individualistic law of the abstract subject, rather than law or legal order as such.[21]

Certainly, there is something in the Pashukanis analysis which resonates with some of the concerns about law that we have been exploring. What strikes us about Dickens' courtroom is partly the unreality of the proceedings – the abstraction whereby flesh-and-blood people become 'parties' and their most intimate family relationships are represented in a nightmare of rights, obligations, writs, demurrers, and rejoinders that appear impossibly ethereal compared with the reality of life. But it is also partly the fact that this set of abstractions has got itself allied with the force of the state, so that real people actually go mad, or are imprisoned or ruined because of what happens in this fairy-tale world of wigs and concepts and equivalences.

Allied with this is a more mundane sense that the law somehow makes adversaries where there need be no antagonism or leads to the protraction of disputes which, if left to themselves, could be settled over a glass of wine between people of good-will. The legal system is always presented to us by our rulers as a guarantor of social harmony. But in effect it is often divisive, setting people at odds with one another, and defining them in ways which place emphasis upon the potential for conflict with the interests of others, similarly defined. And surely, people will think, there is enough self-centred conflict in the world, without the legal system trying to exacerbate it.[22]

The impression that results – a system of social order that can divide us rather than bring us together – is not entirely inaccurate. But it is misleading to associate this simply with the requirements of capitalism as an economic system, and a mistake to regard it as an unmitigated evil. For a better assessment we need to consider the place law occupies – the place it can occupy and the place it has to occupy – in our lives.

Getting along with law

Would it be possible or desirable, as Dickens' practitioners at Chancery suggest, for a person simply to *avoid* the legal system – to suffer any wrong, put up with any injustice, rather than bring her case before a court of law? More broadly, is the legalistic way of resolving disputes and achieving social order – the way that involves verbal rules, procedural formality and adversarial confrontation – something we can ignore if we like and steer clear of, either individually or as a society?

As individuals we do this to a certain extent. We can make lives for ourselves and enter into relationships with others on our own terms, or on the basis of implicit trust and friendship. If our interests clash with those of someone else, we can either let her have her way, or try to reach some accommodation informally, through negotiation rather than through recourse to the legal system. Even in the basic structures of interpersonal respect, we can – as I argued in Chapter Seven – think of ourselves as simply following the requirements of morality when we refrain from murder, drunken driving, etc. rather than as conforming slavishly to the externally imposed dictates of the criminal law. In all of this, our actions may *coincide* with what would be legally expected, but that can happen even though we pay little attention to the formality of law itself. An anarchist need not flout the law; he's just someone who doesn't think that law in itself provides him with any reason for action.

Still this takes us only so far. One way of looking at the legal framework is to see it as a 'fall-back' position, something on which we and others know we can rely if other aspects of our social relations begin to crumble. Consider, for example, the position of someone who agrees to let another person live in her house. The two may be friends, and it may simply strike them as a good idea that the house be used in this way. They may not think it necessary to draw up a formal lease or anything like that, for each trusts in the other to respect her interests and to act fairly and responsibly. And then something may happen, something unexpected. Perhaps mortgage rates shoot up, and the owner feels she has to ask for a higher contribution from the occupier. Perhaps the occupier falls ill, and it seems wrong for the owner to ask her to leave the house when the agreed period comes to an end. We all know that even the most friendly arrangements may come to grief over unexpected contingencies like these.

One hopes that the parties would be able to talk their way through the problem without going to law. But if friendship and trust start to weaken, each person will wonder what she and the other can insist upon as a last resort and in the absence of any good will. And here the existence of a legal framework, governing the relations of landlord and tenant, or licensor and licencee, impinges on the situation unavoidably.

I am not saying that people *have* to organize their relations in the terms laid down by the law. For example, although under certain conditions, the law in England gives a tenant security of tenure and fixes her rent at a certain level, there is nothing to stop a tenant from agreeing in friendship to pay a higher rent or to leave at the end of a certain term and nothing to stop her from carrying out the agreement. The agreement may be unenforceable, but that does not mean the parties cannot or are not allowed to live up to it! Still, a friendly agreement made against the background of a law that provides security of tenure etc. is a different matter from a friendly agreement made against some other legal background. So long as friendship is fragile and exposed to the contingency of circumstance, there is always the question 'What happens if...?' at the back of each person's mind, and the answer to that affects at least a part of the basis of the relationship, because it determines what each of the friends knows she can count on, in the end, no matter what.

It may seem that this is an unduly pessimistic and suspicious mood in which to approach an arrangement conceived in mutual trust. In fact it is quite liberating. It means that we can enter into co-operation with other people in ways that expose our interests to certain risks without having to have any absolute cast-iron assurance of their friendship and goodwill. I can make use of a friend's house, but I can also enter into a similar arrangement with someone who is a stranger, someone I have just met, someone I have no independent reason to trust. If both of us are conscious of a background set of assumptions on which we can fall back if necessary, then we can deal with one another up front in a reasonably relaxed manner, which we could never do if our face-to-face assessment of the other's character (and strength) were all we had to go on.

Think of the extent to which the quality of our lives depends on our being able to deal and co-operate confidently with strangers (transactions like using a credit card to order a theatre ticket). Adam Smith began his work on economics by noting that in modern society, each person 'stands at all times in need of the co-operation and assistance of great multitudes, while his whole life is scarce sufficient to gain the friendship of a few persons'.[23] Smith used this point to highlight the role of reciprocal self-interest in human economy, but it can be used also to bring out the importance of the impersonal framework of law, whether self-interest is involved or not. If there is no law or if we are determined to have nothing to do with whatever law there is, then we cut down our ability to co-operate with others to that meagre set of relations where either our trust in others or our confidence in ourselves is sufficiently strong to mitigate the possibility that things may go wrong between us.

Law is not the only fall-back position. People sometimes wheel and deal outside the legal framework, knowing that there is no tribunal that will enforce their agreements or define the terms of their relationship. They sell drugs and sex, and they rely on their own weapons and whatever scanty goodwill and credit can be rustled up out of nothing on the street. Or they enter into legally undefined relations like surrogate motherhood and hope that nothing will go wrong, having no idea what will emerge from the tangle of affections, physical possession, adjacent law, and their own determination, if they do. The upshot of these arrangements may seem arbitrary and brutal, dependent on contingencies that have little to do with justice or morality. A world without law is a world in which *that* – together with whatever trust we can establish with our intimates – is the sole basis of human co-operation. One does not have to be a partisan of capitalism to see the limitations in that scenario.[24]

Of course, for all we have said, the law itself may be little better. The history of most legal systems is replete with instances of people who thought they could rely on the law and ended up at the mercy of those who were stronger or more powerful, because it was they who had written the rules. To say that the law tells us what we can count on in the last resort is not to say that this is necessarily very much. A tenant cast out into the snow by her landlord may find when she goes to court that the only difference is she is now cast out into the snow with a barrister's bill to pay. The law in Britain – and that means the framework that tells people what they can count on at the end of the day – has been and remains biased towards the rich and powerful in many areas. It is still used – as it was in Dickens' time – as a way of breaking the body and the spirit of those whose exploitation it facilitates.

And yet – there is this to be said for the legal enterprise. Unlike the fall-back that is determined by the sheer strength of the parties, by class struggle or individual resolve, the law is something that can be made an object of discussion and collective decision. We can decide, for example, as a community that we are not prepared any longer to lend our force to a situation in which a landlord can get rid of a tenant as she pleases. We can call for a change, we can discuss it, agitate, get our representatives to vote for it. We can redefine the legal framework, and set up a new array of positions, as the arrangement that people may fall back on.

Granted, there will be resistance and difficulty in implementing it; the fact that something is *the law* doesn't mean that it happens by magic; and the fact that we think it should happen doesn't mean it will become the law. But it is worth persisting in the enterprise, worth trying bit by bit to enhance the extent to which, as a people, we preside openly over the explicit terms of our association with one another. For all its dusty paraphenalia, and for all its openess to abuse, mystery, and exploitation, the law is something we should strive to claim and construct and insist on as our own.

Notes

1   Charles Dickens, *Bleak House* (1853; New York: Signet Classics, 1964), pp. 18–19.

2   Dickens was adamant in his Preface to the book that *Jarndyce v. Jarndyce* was not an unfair example: 'At the present moment there is a suit before the court which was commenced nearly twenty years ago, in which from thirty to forty counsel have been known to appear at one time, in which costs have been incurred to the amount of seventy thousand pounds, which is *a friendly suit*, and which is (I am assured) no nearer to its termination now than when it was begun.' (Preface to *Bleak House*, p. viii.)

3   Anthony Trollope, quoted in David Pannick, *Judges* (Oxford University Press, 1987), p. 143.

4   It is worth noting that the Law Lords – the highest court in the land – hear cases wearing ordinary suits and without wigs and gowns, and with relatively informal procedures, presumably because it is only other lawyers who appear before them and not any ordinary members of the public who need to be impressed. (See Pannick, *Judges*, p. 145.)

5   Pannick, *Judges*, p. 142.

6 Judge Learned Hand, *The Spirit of Liberty* (Chicago, Ill.: University of Chicago Press, 1952), p. 47.

7 Again consider Dickens on the matter: 'The one great principle of English law is, to make business for itself. ... Viewed by this light it becomes a coherent scheme, and not the monstrous maze the laity are apt to think it.' (*Bleak House*, p. 603–4.)

8 Even here, the requirements of justice can be subdivided yet again. On the one hand, we say justice has been done only when the correct result is achieved. On the other hand, we say that justice has been done if the proper procedures have been followed (e.g. the accused had a fair trial and was properly represented etc.), even if the resulting outcome is incorrect (e.g. the jury concluded he was guilty when he was not). This latter sense, is sometimes referred to as 'natural justice' or 'due process'.

9 There is an excellent introduction in Philip Pettit, *Judging Justice: An Introduction to Contemporary Political Philosophy* (London: Routledge & Kegan Paul, 1980).

10 The best-known work of this type is John Rawls, *A Theory of Justice* (Oxford University Press, 1971). Though that is a long and complex book, one can get a good idea of Rawls's approach from reading carefully pp. 3–22.

11 See, e.g., Michael Walzer, *Spheres of Justice* (Oxford: Martin Robertson, 1980).

12 John Rawls put it this way at the beginning of his book: 'Justice is the first virtue of social institutions, as truth is of systems of thought. A theory however elegant and economical must be rejected or revised if it is untrue; likewise laws and institutions no matter how efficient and well-arranged must be reformed or abolished if they are unjust.' (*A Theory of Justice*, p. 3.)

13 This is part of what Marx is getting at in his rejection of any simple formula of 'equality' to describe workers' recompense under socialism: 'Right by its very nature can consist only in the application of an equal standard; but unequal individuals (and they would not be different individuals if they were not unequal) are measureable only by an equal standard in so far as they are brought under an equal point of view, are taken from one definite side only, for instance, in the present case, are regarded *only as workers* and nothing more is seen in them, everything else being ignored. Further, one worker is married, another not; one has more children than another, and so on and so forth.' (*Critique of the Gotha Programme* (1875; Moscow: Progress Publishers, 1960), p. 17.)

14 Bernard Williams puts it like this. Although it is true that, in order to be able to decide morally, a person must have internalized *something* that enables her to respond to new cases, 'it is not obvious that it must be a principle, in the sense of a summary and discursively stateable description that does not rely too much on vague references to degree ("too much", "balances out", "does not pay enough attention to...")'. (*Ethics and the Limits of Philosophy* (Cambridge, Mass.: Harvard University Press, 1985), p. 97.)

15 Luke 10: 29–37 (Revised Standard Version).
16 This conception of politics derives from Aristotle, *The Politics*, Book I, Ch. 2. Its modern exponents include Hannah Arendt, *The Human Condition* (Chicago, Ill.: University of Chicago Press, 1958), Chs. II and V, and Bernard Crick, *In Defence of Politics* (Harmondsworth: Penguin Books, 1963). I have developed this point a little further in my book *Nonsense Upon Stilts: Bentham, Burke and Marx on the Rights of Man* (London: Methuen, 1987), pp. 177–81.
17 See, for example, Alasdair Macintyre, *After Virtue* (London: Duckworth, 1981); Michael Sandel, *Liberalism and the Limits of Justice* (Cambridge, Mass.: Harvard University Press, 1982.)
18 For this criticism of the Leninist view, see Hugh Collins, *Marxism and Law* (Oxford: Clarendon Press, 1982), pp. 105–7.
19 Evgeny B. Pashukanis, *Law and Marxism: A General Theory*, edited by Chris Arthur (1929; London: Ink Links, 1978), p. 121.
20 There is an excellent introduction to these differences in J.H. Merryman, *The Civil Law Tradition* (Stanford, Calif.: Stanford University Press, 1969).
21 The image of the 'withering away' of the state and the law comes from Frederick Engels, *Anti-Duhring* (1878; London: Lawrence Wishart, 1975), p. 333: 'State interference in social relations becomes, in one domain after another, superfluous, and then withers away of itself; the government of persons is replaced by the administration of things, and by the conduct of processes of production. The state is not "abolished". *It withers away.*'
22 Marx made a similar point about theories of human rights: '...the so-called rights of man are nothing but ... the rights of egoistic man, man separated from other men and the community.' See Jeremy Waldron, *Nonsense Upon Stilts: Bentham, Burke and Marx on the Rights of Man* (London: Methuen, 1987), p. 145.
23 Adam Smith, *The Wealth of Nations*, ed. E. Cannan (1776; Chicago, Ill.: University of Chicago Press, 1976), Bk. I, Ch. 2, p. 18. There is an excellent general discussion of these themes in Michael Ignatieff, *The Needs of Strangers* (London: Chatto & Windus, 1984).
24 I have explored these ideas at greater length in Jeremy Waldron, 'When Justice Replaces Affection: the Need for Rights', *Harvard Journal of Law and Public Policy*, 11 (1988).

Bibliographical essay

This bibliography is intended only as a brief guide to the most useful recent work in the philosophy of law. It overlaps with, and should be used to supplement, the references given in the footnotes.

Introductions

There are a number of excellent introductions to jurisprudence. The most accessible is J.W. Harris, *Legal Philosophies* (London: Butterworths, 1980), with chapters covering all the main theories and topics in the modern philosophical discussion of law. It is also in itself an excellent source of further bibliographical information. David Lyons, *Ethics and the Rule of Law* (Cambridge University Press, 1984) is more discursively written and provides a valuable introduction to the way moral judgements are connected with legal judgements. Ronald Dworkin's collection *The Philosophy of Law* (Oxford University Press, 1977), in the 'Oxford Readings in Philosophy' series, has an excellent introduction to some of the main issues in contemporary jurisprudence.

H.L.A. Hart and modern positivism

The outstanding work of modern jurisprudence remains H.L.A. Hart, *The Concept of Law* (Oxford: Clarendon Press, 1961). Hart attempts to understand the concept of law as involving not only the idea of social rules, but also the idea that they are identified in each legal system by the use of a master-rule which he calls 'the rule of recognition'. The theory that Hart develops is the most sophisticated and accessible modern exposition of legal positivism – that is, the view that law can be identified descriptively as social fact, and that the concept of law is not in itself an evaluative one. Neil MacCormick's book, *H.L.A. Hart* (London: Edward Arnold, 1981) is an admirably clear introduction to this theory. Other major modern works of positivist jurisprudence are more technical: the most rewarding is Joseph Raz, *The Concept of a Legal System* (Oxford: Clarendon Press, 1980).

For other legal positivists and for discussions of some early versions of this approach, the essays by Hart in his collections, *Essays on Bentham: Jurisprudence and Political Theory* (Oxford: Clarendon Press, 1982) and *Essays in Jurisprudence and Philosophy* (Oxford: Clarendon Press, 1983) are recommended. Before the twentieth century, the most sophisticated positivist theory was undoubtedly that of Jeremy Bentham. Bentham's theory is comprehensively outlined in Gerald Postema, *Bentham and the Common Law Tradition* (Oxford: Clarendon Press, 1986). In particular, Postema does an excellent job of showing that legal positivism was itself partly a normative thesis: Bentham believed that the law *ought* to be such that it could be identified in a value-free way, and he criticized the common law of England for not living up to this prescription.

Natural Law

The contrary idea – that moral judgements do and should enter into the identification of something as law – has been taken up in a number of recent works. The best-known and most useful are Lon Fuller, *The Morality of Law* (New Haven, Conn.: Yale University Press, 1964) and John Finnis, *Natural Law and Natural Rights* (Oxford: Clarendon Press, 1980). Finnis's book presents a theory that attempts to meld ethics and jurisprudence into an intelligible whole. The controversy between these approaches is explored in an article by H.L.A. Hart, 'Positivism and the Separation of Law and Morals', reprinted both in Dworkin (ed.) *The Philosophy of Law* (Oxford University Press, 1977) and in Hart's 1983 collection, and in Lon Fuller's reply to the original version of that article, 'Positivism and Fidelity to Law – a Reply to Professor Hart', *Harvard Law Review*, 71 (1958), 630.

Judicial reasoning

Much of the most important work in modern jurisprudence has focused on legal reasoning and the judicial process.

The view that judges should be seen as articulating their own policy preferences rather than following the logic of legal doctrine was put forward by scholars in the 'Legal Realist' movement. There is a good overview in William Twining, *Karl Llewellyn and the Realist Movement* (London: Wiedenfeld & Nicholson, 1973), and Jerome Frank's book *Law and the Modern Mind* (New York: Anchor Books, 1963) remains the most provocative statement of the realist view.

Today that view is generally regarded as too extreme. Jurists stress the structures and principles that constrain legal reasoning: Neil MacCormick, *Legal Reasoning and Legal Theory* (Oxford: Clarendon Press, 1978) is the best introduction.

The revival of realism that some discern in the 'Critical Legal Studies' movement places more stress on the variety of principles implicit in legal reasoning and the tensions between them, than on the absence of such principles. Mark Kelman, *A Guide to Critical Legal Studies* (Cambridge, Mass.: Harvard University Press, 1987) outlines the way in which CLS thinkers perceive contradictions between individualist and communitarian themes in modern law.

Ronald Dworkin

The commanding work on legal reasoning is now undoubtedly Ronald Dworkin, *Law's Empire* (London: Fontana Books, 1986). Dworkin develops a powerful theory about judging both in common law and in statutory interpretation, and he connects it with a subtle theory of political legitimacy and obligation that requires the law to present itself to the citizen as a coherent whole. Legal interpretation, he argues, is an active process whereby one seeks to make the best that one can, in moral and political terms, of a body of legal material. It is not a matter of recovering the intentions of those who made the law; rather it is a matter of attributing to it purposes that make sense of it for us now.

Dworkin is undoubtedly taking sides in this theory against the positivist view that legal reasoning as such is non-evaluative, and that one only resorts to moral and political evaluation in 'hard cases' where the resources of legal reasoning run out. *Law's Empire* builds on Dworkin's earlier arguments in *Taking Rights Seriously* (London: Duckworth, 1977) to the effect that a legal system comprises not only the formulated rules which positivists emphasize but also moral principles which are implicit in common law adjudication.

Moral objectivity

The stress placed on moral evaluation in theories like Dworkin's raises questions about moral objectivity. Where do these evaluations come from and how are they justified?

The realist movement was associated with emotivism in ethics:

the view that moral evaluations were just expressions of emotion. Modern moral philosophers are still divided on the issue of whether values can be real and value-statements true. However, even those like J.L. Mackie, *Ethics: Inventing Right and Wrong* (Harmondsworth: Penguin Books, 1977) and R.M. Hare, *Moral Thinking: Its Levels, Method and Point* (Oxford: Clarendon Press, 1981) who remain sceptical about moral reality, still stress the possibility of moral argument.

Modern work in political philosophy like John Rawls, *A Theory of Justice* (Oxford University Press, 1971) and the accounts of human rights sampled, for instance, in Jeremy Waldron (ed.) *Theories of Rights* (Oxford University Press, 1984), tend to be developed as far as possible in a way that avoids metaphysical questions about ultimate justification. However, for a more robust defence of moral realism in a legal context, see Michael Moore, 'Moral Reality', *Wisconsin Law Review* [1982] 1061.

The rule of law

As well as these general controversies in moral philosophy, there is in jurisprudence a more narrowly focused discussion of the values and principles implicit in the idea of 'the rule of law'. Both F.A. Hayek, *The Constitution of Liberty* (London: Routledge & Kegan Paul, 1960) and Lon Fuller, *The Morality of Law* (New Haven, Conn.: Yale University Press, 1964) are committed to the view that certain ideas of universality, clarity, and prospectivity are part and parcel of the concept of law itself. In Hayek's work in particular, these ideas are linked to the value of individual liberty and are associated with some hostility towards the activist and welfare state.

There is an interesting debate about how comprehensive the values are which are associated with legality; the consensus seems to be that they provide necessary but not sufficient conditions for good government. There are excellent discussions in Chapter Eleven of Joseph Raz, *The Authority of Law* (Oxford: Clarendon Press, 1979) and in Chapter Ten of John Finnis, *Natural Law and Natural Rights* (Oxford: Clarendon Press, 1980).

Political obligation

All this discussion pushes eventually towards the question of the attitude we should take towards the law and the demands that it makes on us. Do we have an obligation to obey the law and support its procedures? Or is law nothing but the expression of class power?

The issue of legal obligation is dealt with in Joseph Raz, *The Authority of Law* (Oxford: Clarendon Press, 1979) and David Lyons, *Ethics and the Rule of Law* (Cambridge University Press, 1984). Both Ronald Dworkin, *Law's Empire* (London: Fontana Books, 1986), especially Chapter Six, and John Finnis, *Natural Law and Natural Rights* (Oxford: Clarendon Press, 1980) present their respective theories of law in a way that purports to explain how and why a legal system can command our obedience and respect. Finnis's view, however, has been challenged in a powerful and illuminating article by Leslie Green, 'Law, Co-ordination and the Common Good', *Oxford Journal of Legal Studies*, 3 (1983), p. 299.

A. John Simmonds, *Moral Principles and Political Obligation* (Princeton, N.J.: Princeton University Press, 1979) provides a general overview of the main philosophical arguments for political obligation. The challenge to legal authority is found in Robert Paul Wolff, *In Defence of Anarchism* (New York: Harper & Row, 1976) and there are excellent discussions in H.A. Bedau (ed.) *Civil Disobedience: Theory and Practice* (New York: Pegasus, 1969), Michael Walzer, *Obligations: Essays on Disobedience, War and Citizenship* (Cambridge, Mass.: Harvard University Press, 1970), and Ted Hondercih, *Violence for Equality* (Harmondsworth: Penguin Books, 1980).

Law and class

The view that law in itself commands little or no respect because of its class basis is a common theme in the Critical Legal Studies movement. Besides Mark Kelman, *A Guide to Critical Legal Studies* (Cambridge, Mass.: Harvard University Press, 1987), readers may also refer to Peter Fitzpatrick and Alan Hunt, *Critical Legal Studies* (Oxford: Basil Blackwell, 1987). Other discussions of the class thesis include Roberto Unger, *Law in Modern Society* (New York: Free Press, 1976), Zenon Bankowski and Geoff Mungham, *Images of Law* (London: Routledge & Kegan Paul, 1976) Bob Fine, *Democracy and the Rule of Law* (London: Pluto, 1980) and Timothy O'Hagan, *The End of Law* (Oxford: Basil Blackwell, 1984).

Index